Overcoming Trauma and Rejection with God's Love

Overcoming Trauma and Rejection with God's Love

NaTonya Scott

COPYRIGHT

Overcoming Trauma and Rejection with God's Love
©2024 by NaTonya Scott

All rights reserved. No part of this publication may be reproduced, distributed, or transmitted in any form or by any means, including photocopying, recording, or other electronic or mechanical methods, without the prior written permission of the publisher, except in the case of brief quotations embodied in critical reviews and certain other noncommercial uses permitted by copyright law. For more information, contact NaTonya Scott at natonya@lcacounseling.org
Published 2024

Printed in the United States of America
ISBN: E-book: 979-2-218-46944-3
ISBN: Paperback :979-8-218-95556-4
ISBN: Hard Cover: 979-8-218-58481-8

Unless otherwise noted, all scripture quotations are from the American Standard Version (ASV) of the Holy Bible. public domain.

THE HOLY BIBLE, NEW INTERNATIONAL VERSION
®, NIV® Copyright © 1973, 1978, 1984, 2011 by Biblica, Inc. ® Used by permission. All rights reserved worldwide.

Scripture quotations are from The ESV® Bible (The Holy Bible, English Standard Version®), © 2001 by Crossway, a publishing ministry of Good News Publishers. Used by permission. All rights reserved.

Scripture quotations marked KJV are from the King James Version of the Holy Bible, public domain.

DISCLAIMER

This book is inspired by actual people and events. Names, locations, and certain details have been altered to protect the privacy of individuals and to respect confidentiality. Any resemblance to individuals or events is purely coincidental. The contents of this book are the author's perspective. The author's use of literary license is intended to provide insight into the impact of unresolved childhood trauma. The author's goal is to illuminate the complex personal challenges, such as mental health, addiction, and dysfunctional relationships experienced by wounded adults.

The content is intended for informational purposes only and should not be viewed as advice of any kind, including but not limited to mental, physical, emotional, or spiritual health. It is not intended to diagnose, treat, cure, or prevent any medical or psychological condition. Readers are encouraged to consult with a qualified healthcare provider for any concerns related to their own health or well-being.

The author and contributors are not responsible for any damages resulting from the use of this book, including but not limited to direct, indirect, or consequential damages, or losses of any kind. This book is not a substitute for professional consultation with licensed healthcare providers.

Sensitive topics such as abuse, violence, physical and mental health, and trauma are addressed throughout the book. All readers should be aware this content may be disturbing. Readers who have had similar events may find the contents especially troubling. By using this book, you acknowledge and accept this disclaimer, confirming that you understand and agree to its terms.

Dedication

*With my deepest gratitude, I dedicate this book to my Heavenly Father for the abundant blessings
He has poured into my life.
His grace has not only shaped who I am but has also allowed me to be a blessing to others.
He will always remain my first love, and I am forever thankful for His unwavering presence, guidance, and love in every step of my journey.*

Table of Contents

Dedication. viii

Table of Contents IX

Preface. 10

Acknowledgments 13

Introduction. 15

Childhood. 19

Teen Years 49

Adulthood. 74

Emptying the Emotional Baggage 150

Restoration and Healing. 204

Being Set Apart 233

Church Hurt and the Search for True Faith. 288

The Battle Within 322

Turning Point 341

References 356

PREFACE

I hope the words on the pages of this book bring you relief, hope, and encouragement as you draw closer to God, the great Healer. Trust Him to fulfill His everlasting promises. He has never failed and will not start now. No matter how dark your moments may feel, dear friend, they are not your end. I encourage you to find the courage to rise, seek God, and release negative patterns, old ways of thinking, and every demeaning thought you have held about yourself. Despite any past failures, I assure you—you will rise again.

I firmly believe that true healing and transformation come from God through a relationship with His Son, Jesus Christ. I want to offer you hope and encouragement through the stories and experiences shared in this book. While the details may differ from your own, the journey of finding healing from rejection, abuse, abandonment, and generational trauma is one to which many can relate. I am confident that if healing and restoration are possible for one, they are possible for you, too.

That is why I am writing this letter to you—because I care deeply about your healing journey. You hold this book in your hands because I believe it is my purpose to use the gifts Jesus has given me to reach those who are hurting and to remind you that no matter what you have been through, there is always hope. I pray this book will be a companion for you—a reminder that healing is possible, and God's love is constant, even amid the hardest battles. You are never alone; there is always a way forward with Him.

Blessings to you as you walk this path of healing and restoration.

NaTonya Scott, LPC

Acknowledgments

To my children, Armund, Davesha, Griyana, JaFree, and Jeffrey III, I am immensely proud of each one of you. Your unique gifts, talents, and limitless potential fill my heart with joy. As you continue to grow, always trust God's promises. He has a wonderful plan for each of you, and by seeking His kingdom first, you will see how everything else will fall into place. Please know that I love you all deeply and unconditionally.

To the precious Namma babies. Daniel, Daiyanna, Ariyanna, and Delaysia, your joy, laughter, and love inspire me every day. I love you all deeply and unconditionally.

To my mother, Velma, affectionately known as "Squeak," thank you for your constant support throughout my life. Your strength and resilience have been an inspiration. I love you dearly and appreciate everything you have done for me.

Lastly, I want to express my sincere appreciation to all the professionals who contributed to the development of this book. Your expertise and guidance have been invaluable in shaping this work, and I am grateful for your contributions

Introduction

Imagine a life where every word spoken to you cuts like a blade—where those who should protect you are the ones who wound you the most. Have you ever been hurt by those you trusted or felt rejected by people who were supposed to love you? For many, this is not just a fleeting feeling. It is a daily reality. The cycle of trauma, shame, rejection, and abandonment can feel endless. Perhaps, like so many others, you have searched for healing in every corner of your broken world, only to sink deeper into loneliness and further away from the peace you desperately long for.

Do you ever feel like no matter how hard you try to keep everything under control, it is never enough? Does it feel as though you are constantly monitoring every move, hoping to prevent people from hurting you again—but somehow, the pain still finds its way in? Does fear rule your days, making it hard to truly love, trust, or even live? Do the memories of the past haunt you, threatening to steal your peace and sanity, even as you fight to hold it all together?

Have you ever wished that someone could genuinely connect with you and understand your pain without using your vulnerability against you? Do you long for someone to help you face the fears that keep you locked in the shadows of the past, where trauma and rejection seem to be the norm? Many people walk through life with a brave face, hiding the fact that their world is slowly crumbling.

Trauma is not a simple thing. It stems from a series of tragic events in a person's life—abuse, accidents, discrimination, betrayal, loss of a loved one—and it leaves deep scars that linger, often for a long time. It is easy to judge someone who's been traumatized because of the way they respond to these experiences, but if you look deeper, you will see there's more to it than meets the eye. It is essential to understand that everyone reacts differently to trauma.

For some, it is like being trapped in a labyrinth of the mind, where shadows of fear and doubt from the past and mistakes loom large, waiting to strike. It makes even the simplest tasks—like meeting new people, trusting others, or improving one's life—seem impossible. The memory of the past grips you with fear as if those tragic events are happening all over again. The world becomes a scary place as fear and self-doubt creep in, turning even the simplest decisions into daunting tasks.

It is scary, is it not? Many wonder if they can ever escape this darkness. And the truth is, it is not always easy, especially when you do not have the right support or coping mechanisms. Sometimes, when isolation fails, trauma victims turn to violence fueled by anger and resentment from their past. They look in the mirror and see a bruised, wounded person desperately seeking escape.

If this resonates with you, you are not alone. This book is for you—the wounded, the rejected, the abandoned. This story is one of deep pain but also one of hope, healing, and redemption. But what if healing was possible? What if there is a way to break free from the chains of your past?

Are you ready to take that step? Will you dare to believe that your story can be redeemed no matter how broken? This is a reminder that regardless of how shattered you feel, God is always ready to make you whole again.

He has sent His Son to walk alongside us as we travel the bumpy roads of our lives. Every painful moment is another chance to cling to the ultimate Comforter.

Come with me, and I will tell you the story of a young lady called Mara, a woman shattered and battered but finally navigated through the tragic events and overcame through the love of God. Though the names have been changed, the story is based on true events. Mara is a real person, saved by God's amazing grace and the atoning blood of His Son, Jesus Christ.

But Mara could be any woman; she could be any person. Maybe you have been Mara in your past; perhaps you still are. If you can relate to parts of Mara's story, just know you are not alone.

It is not just about Mara; I need you to journey with me in this story as we metaphorically tear away the tape of people-pleasing, rejection, abuse, fear, trauma, anger, insecurities, and low self-esteem that have clung to our identities. You will discover how Mara, through faith and trust in God, had a divine transformation.

Childhood
A Cry for Freedom

"God, I want to be free."

She had an appointment at the emergency room, but first, she had an appointment with the Great Physician. On June 29, 2015, Mara surrendered her life to Christ. That Sunday morning, she walked to the front of the church and prayed. She told God that she wanted to be free.

"If therefore the Son shall make you free, ye shall be free indeed" (John 8:36). She stood in front of the church with a heart full of desperation and hope. She whispered a fervent prayer, tears streaming down her cheeks. "God, I want to be free," she pleaded, her voice trembling with the weight of her pain.

Mara's life had been a series of battles. But, over the past year, she had spent countless nights in emergency rooms. Her legs had noticeable veins throbbing with unbearable pain. She had fallen out of bed, her body betraying her, leaving her feeling trapped and helpless. Each visit to the hospital was a reminder of the choices that had led her to this point—choices fueled by anger and a sense of abandonment.

She had once lived with a deep faith, but over time, her prayers seemed to go unanswered. Feeling forsaken by God, Mara sought answers and lived on her terms. But this path of self-reliance only led to more suffering. Deep down, she knew she was not living in a way that pleased the Lord, but the hurt was too overwhelming to see a way out.

As she stood in front of the church, memories flooded her mind. She recalled the nights spent crying out in pain, both physical and emotional, and the countless times she felt like giving up. Her trials broke her spirit and resentment hardened her heart. Yet, in that moment, a tiny spark of hope flickered within her.

Light in the Darkness

Several times during her childhood, Mara was a victim of sexual, emotional, and physical abuse. When she was nine, two family members took her innocence. At age twelve, a neighbor committed a similar violation with her, shattering any remnants of safety she had left. At thirteen, her brothers' friends began subjecting her to indecent acts, turning her home into a place of fear and shame. At fifteen, a community leader, someone she should have been able to trust, violated her again, leaving her feeling completely broken, devastated, and alone.

Sent to live with Aunt Sarah, Mara hoped for peace but found no refuge. Sarah's home was as unstable and unhealthy as her own, and Aunt Sarah's unresolved trauma consumed her.

Mara endured emotional and physical abuse at home. This generational cycle of pain, a dark legacy, passed from one woman to the next. Aunt Sarah, deeply scarred by her past, struggled to cope with her wounds. Unable to manage her pain in a healthy way, she often lashed out at Mara, creating a home filled with fear and instability.

Burdened with the responsibility of raising Mara while grappling with her inner pain, Aunt Sarah created an environment ruled by uncertainty. Instead of escaping the chaos, Mara found herself in yet another damaging situation, reinforcing her belief that she could never break free from the cycle of pain that had haunted her family for generations.

Mara longed for the love and safety every child deserves. Instead, she faced a world of hardship, enduring struggles no child should ever bear. This cycle of abuse Mara endured was a heavy burden, shaping Mara's early years and leaving scars that would take years of healing and faith to overcome.

This moment in Mara's life, hidden like a scar beneath the surface and buried deep within her soul, began when she was around nine years old. That marked the beginning of her trauma and loss of innocence. The pain of that moment etched itself into her very being, leaving wounds that went far beyond the physical. It was a violation that Mara could not comprehend at the time—a betrayal that would haunt her for years to come.

One night, Mara and her brother were sleeping on the couch at a relative's home. Mara's older brother, Kenneth, slept at one end and Mara at the other. Just as Mara had entered a deep sleep, she suddenly felt herself being lifted off the couch. Not realizing what was happening, Mara kept her eyes closed as if she were still asleep.

The big, strong arms carried her into a room and softly laid her on a bed. Mara could hear chatter, and she heard a voice say to "cover her face." At that moment, Mara felt the covers hit her face. It was not dark, for she could barely see a ray of light from the sides of her eyes. Mara lay motionless, still unsure of what was happening. She remained stiff and silent.

When Mara felt her underwear sliding down her legs, that was when fear crept in. Still in shock and scared, Mara heard the chatter of a female voice and a man talking in the background. And before little Mara could realize what was happening, someone defiled her. At first, it seemed like a bad dream. If it were, Mara could have screamed and awakened from the nightmare. But it was real; right there, she lay motionless until it was over.

Unfortunately, it was never really over—not in her mind. This was a harrowing experience for Mara that shaped much of the trauma that would affect her for the rest of her life. Mara's upbringing and traumas led to feelings of confusion and anger, emotions that often manifested in her lashing out in her childhood and as a teen and making poor decisions as an adult. The whole domino effect stemmed from this moment in her childhood.

These negative emotions stemmed deeply from her experiences of abuse, neglect, and rejection. The unresolved pain from her past influenced her behavior, causing her to impulsively and aggressively react in situations where she felt threatened or vulnerable.

She felt betrayed by those who were supposed to protect her, and her cries for help seemed to vanish into the void from an early age. As a teenager, Mara struggled with authority and often found herself in trouble at school and in her community. Her anger and confusion drove her to act out, seeking attention and validation in unhealthy ways.

The little girl inside her was always fighting, unknowingly trying to protect herself. Instead, people labeled Mara a bad child with problems and issues. No one could understand that she was depressed, fearful, and overstimulated. Her childhood trauma had cast a long shadow over her adolescence. Teachers, peers, and even family members failed to see the pain behind her rebellious behavior, misinterpreting her cries for help as mere defiance.

This misjudgment only deepened her isolation and reinforced the belief that she was undeserving of love and support. That belief was a manifestation of the deep-seated hurt she carried within her.

Imagine a child, fists clenched and eyes blazing, fighting with an intensity that belied her small stature. Each punch and kick were a cry for help that no one seemed to hear. Mara did not understand why she was so angry, only that it bubbled up inside her, erupting with the slightest provocation. She fought because it was the only way she knew to express the pain and confusion that had taken root deep within her.

Mara longed for a sense of connection and stability that seemed elusive in her tumultuous family life. The past is the foundation upon which the future is built.

As observers looking into Mara's past, it may often seem like we are viewing it through dark glasses. Perhaps it feels similar when you look back on your own life.

As an adult, Mara sought to find true love. She yearned to be heard. She desperately sought a man who would genuinely love and protect her. But the questions are, "Does such a man exist? Can anyone except God protect another human being?" Are you eager to know if she found a prince charming who would genuinely love her and help aid her healing? Keep reading to discover how Mara navigated her relationship life.

Family Dynamics

Family is significant to God. Since the beginning, when God made Adam and Eve to "Be fruitful and multiply, and replenish the earth, and subdue it;" (Genesis 1:28), He has been encouraging and blessing families. In the Ten Commandments, we are told everyone should "Honor your father and your mother, so your life may be long in the land the Lord your God gives you." (Exodus 20:12 NIV). Later, Jesus would teach about the importance of marriage: "What therefore God hath joined together, let not man put asunder" (Mark 10:9). God created the family so we could honor each other and cultivate a Christlike love. However, Mara rarely experienced this closeness while growing up.

Mara's childhood was not only traumatic with sexual abuse. Her aunt raised her because her biological mother had too much to deal with. Mara's Mom had her own childhood trauma that led to alcohol addiction and anger issues. Mara's Aunt Sarah, who Mara thought would do better, only worsened things. By now, you might be thinking, "Is this some sort of family circle or genetic dysfunctionality?" Well, only later in life would Mara find answers to this question.

As the only girl and the middle child, Mara felt caught between the challenges of her upbringing. Her father's incarceration meant Mara grew up without his guidance or presence, leaving a void she struggled to comprehend. Mara's home life offered no refuge.

Aunt Sarah, burdened by her pain and trauma, numbed herself with gambling and drinking to escape, making it difficult for the poor young Mara to connect with her.

Not only did Aunt Sarah struggle to connect emotionally, but she also had difficulty managing her own emotions. When Mara and her brothers got into trouble, her anger would explode into lashings, leaving Mara and her brothers caught in the crossfire. They got whoopings for simple things like drinking Kool-Aid when told not to.

Then there was the time pennies fell out of Mara's pants pockets and onto the floor. As Aunt Sarah entered the room, demanding to know who had scattered the coins, Mara's heart raced with dread. Fear enveloped her as she remained silent, paralyzed by the looming threat of punishment. But silence proved futile as Aunt Sarah's fury erupted into a storm of violence.

The air crackled with the sound of blows as Mara and her brother Kenneth endured the relentless onslaught, with Aunt Sarah taking periodic smoke breaks between rounds of beatings It felt like hours were passing; each strike an excruciating reminder of the price of "disobedience." In desperation to escape the torment, Mara begged her older brother, Kenneth, to take the blame.

The pain was overwhelming, and Mara feared she might not survive it. Finally, with a heavy heart, Kenneth agreed, shouldering the burden meant for her. As she listened to the sounds of his punishment, a flood of gratitude and guilt washed over her. Though spared, her brother's sacrifice haunted her, leaving her with a bitter mixture of relief and remorse.

Mara's fear of punishment was a heavy weight on her shoulders. Admitting she was wrong felt too dangerous—too risky. So, instead of confessing, Mara remained silent.

This was just one of many severe whoopings Mara and her brothers endured with hands, belts, and even closed fists. Every time Aunt Sarah got mad, tensions would escalate. Sometimes, Aunt Sarah would throw objects in Mara's way—either slammed onto the ground or hurled in her direction with terrifying force. She understood that Aunt Sarah's rage was driven by something deeper and more painful within her—a wound Mara could not fully grasp.

The echoes of those violent outbursts stayed with her. Every sharp word, every raised voice, and every unexpected movement triggered the same fear and anxiety she had felt as a child. The emotional scars lingered, shaping her relationships and the way she viewed herself. Though Mara tried to escape the past, the pain from those years was deeply woven into her being, affecting her long after the physical wounds had healed.

Yet, amid the chaos, a question lingered in Mara's mind. What was beneath Aunt Sarah's rage? Was it more than just spilled pennies that fueled her anger? Mara could not comprehend why Aunt Sarah was so enraged that day. Confusion and hurt welled inside her as Aunt Sarah's anger intensified without reason.

Mara was too young to understand this at the time. She only felt her own negative emotions. These things in Mara's childhood affected her later in life, just as the stuff in Aunt Sarah's past fed into her behavior. Is there such a thing as a generational curse? Psychologically speaking, perhaps there is.

Mara recognized the familiar pattern of inherited trauma from Aunt Sarah on her mother's side of the family. It was a relic of generations before her that she carried with her, shaping how she navigated her emotions and relationships. As she reflected on the past, Mara realized that understanding her aunt's pain was a journey fraught with uncertainty. Growing up, where anger was familiar, Mara struggled to navigate her emotions.

Mara's anger from her trauma often turned into defiance, leading her to challenge Aunt Sarah whenever she felt mistreated. Once, when asked to wash the dishes, Mara thought it was unjust since she was always responsible for the dishes. Standing there in frustration, she cried but refused to touch the dishes. Aunt Sarah, determined to assert control, told Mara she could stand there all night. And Mara did—she stood for hours, eventually dozing off until she fell asleep on the counter.

Their power struggles were constant. Whenever Mara pushed back, Aunt Sarah responded with harsher punishments to prove she was in control. One time, Aunt Sarah asked Mara not to play with her hair. Mara would continue to restyle her hair. Aunt Sarah told her to fetch the scissors, and Mara's heart sank.

In a panic, she ran up the stairs, tears streaming down her face at the thought of losing her hair. But this time, there was no escape. Aunt Sarah was not bluffing. Mara sat in a chair as her aunt cut away her hair, the locks falling to the ground like pieces of her breaking apart. Each snip echoed in the room, but to Mara, it felt like a sharp stab to her heart.

Her hair, one of the few things that made her feel beautiful, was now scattered around her feet. She crouched down, sobbing as she picked up the strands from the floor, each handful a painful reminder of what she had lost. Already struggling with low self-esteem, feeling small and insecure, this was the final blow. Now, her hair was gone, too.

When she looked in the mirror, the reflection staring back felt like a stranger. The girl who once hoped to find something beautiful in herself now stood with a raw vulnerability. This moment left Mara heartbroken, because of the hair she lost and the more profound belief she had lost even more of herself in the process.

This dynamic repeated itself many times, part of a generational trauma where mothers or female figures inflicted pain, called their daughters names, criticized them, or competed with them in unhealthy ways. Mara often questioned Aunt Sarah's harshness, sensing that the cruelty ran deeper than mere discipline. It was the continuation of a cycle of hurt passed down through generations. Mara would often recall witnessing Sarah's mother—Mara's grandmother—beating Sarah with a closed fist.

Twelve-year-old Mara stood there, terrified, watching as her grandmother unleashed her anger on Sarah. The memory of that moment haunted her. She understood the helplessness and fear her aunt endured. Mara now faced the same kind of pain. Even then, Mara sensed the heavy weight of unresolved trauma passed down like an unwanted heirloom.

Mara grappled with a profound sense of empathy for her aunt, tempered by the harsh reality of their shared trauma. Mara started to see her Aunt Sarah not just as a source of pain but also as someone burdened by her own unresolved trauma.

Now she understood that what she had witnessed was not an isolated act of cruelty—it was an unwanted, inherited legacy. The devastating patterns of behavior repeated in every generation, trapping them all in an unbroken cycle of suffering. This generational trauma had shaped Mara's life, and for years, she carried the weight of it. But deep within her, a quiet desire for something different began to grow. She longed to be the one to break free from the cycle, to finally end the legacy of pain and create a future where love and healing could flourish.

Would Mara be able to break free from the cycle of pain that had haunted her family for generations? Could she overcome the shadows of her past and create a future filled with love and healing? As Mara faces her inner struggles and the external battles of her life, would she find the strength to rewrite her story, or would the legacy of trauma continue to shape her destiny?

Shadows of Responsibility

Mara and her brothers often found themselves left alone, navigating a world without much adult guidance or supervision. Their Aunt Sarah, who was responsible for them, had a full-time job. In her free time, she frequently went out to gamble, drink, and socialize with friends, leaving the children to fend for themselves. Despite working all day, she rarely provided the nurturing presence they needed. In her absence, Mara's elder brother Kenneth had to step into a caretaker role far too early, ensuring that his siblings had food to eat and some semblance of stability.

With limited resources, Mara's brother would creatively cook and bake meals from the scraps left in the refrigerator. He became adept at making the most out of what little they had, turning meager supplies into something that could sustain them. His efforts provided a semblance of normalcy, though it was a heavy burden for someone so young. The strain of these responsibilities was evident in his eyes, which bore the weight of adulthood forced upon him too soon.

While Aunt Sarah was at work or out enjoying her life, Mara and her brothers often rebelled. They would venture outside, playing at neighbor's houses, seeking the attention and interaction they craved. With no adult supervision, they explored their boundaries and often crossed them, engaging in risky behavior.

In Aunt Sarah's absence, their home became a playground for mischief. They would sneak into her room, finding and exploring things they should not, like magazines and other adult items. The thrill of these discoveries was often mixed with a sense of foreboding, as they knew they were stepping into a world they were not yet ready for.

The lack of oversight led to even more severe actions. Mara and her brothers would invite friends over, often resulting in inappropriate and premature activities. The gravity of these experiences left deep imprints on their young minds, shaping their perceptions of responsibility and trust. What if you were told that Mara and her brother became parents in their teenage years? Would you believe that?

From the outside, they seemed like just another pair of siblings experiencing the challenges of growing up, dealing with the chaos of their family, and trying to find their place in the world. But what if those childhood struggles pushed them into adulthood far too soon? What if the weight of those experiences left them seeking love and validation in all the wrong places, leading them down a path they were unprepared for?

Their forced maturity and the need to take on adult roles early in life had lasting effects. Mara's brother, once a playful and carefree child, became withdrawn and serious-minded, the weight of his responsibilities etching lines of worry across his youthful face. Mara, too, felt the scars of their turbulent upbringing, her heart heavy with a mix of resentment and longing for the childhood she never had.

Reflections: Can You Relate?

As you read Mara's story, you might find echoes of your own experiences. Have you ever had to grow up too fast, taking on responsibilities that felt overwhelming? Did you find yourself stepping into roles meant for adults, all because those who should have cared for you were absent or preoccupied?

Think back to your childhood. Were there moments when you had to be the caretaker? Were you expected to ensure everything was in order? Did you have to cook meals, look after siblings, or manage the household while your parents were away or unable to provide the needed supervision?

Maybe, like Mara and her brothers, you sought refuge in friends, craving the missing attention and interaction missing in your life. Maybe your parents or guardians were absent when you needed their love and care most. How did that make you feel? Did you engage in risky behaviors driven by a need to break free from the weight of your responsibilities or the feeling of wanting to belong?

Consider the impact these experiences had on you. Did they leave you feeling resentful, burdened, or perhaps even lost? The absence of a nurturing presence during those formative years can leave deep emotional wounds, shaping how we view responsibility, trust, and ourselves.

Sharing these reflections is recognizing that many share these profound personal struggles. Perhaps it was not an aunt in your life—maybe it was your mother, father, grandparent, or another loved one with whom you did not connect emotionally or experienced trauma. You are not alone in your experiences; by acknowledging them, we take the first steps toward healing together.

Anger Becomes Aggression

Anger played a significant and destructive role in Mara's life. It was not merely an emotion she experienced but a pattern that shaped her behavior and relationships. Deeply rooted in the abuse and neglect of her childhood, Mara's anger often emerged as a response to the pain she endured during those formative years.

From a young age, Mara's anger functioned as a shield—a defense mechanism she used to protect herself from overwhelming emotions tied to her trauma. This aggression became her way of coping, a means of asserting control in a world where she often felt powerless. Rather than fostering connection or understanding, Mara's anger created barriers, pushing people away and making it difficult for her to form trusting, healthy relationships. Her outbursts, fueled by unresolved pain, frequently led to conflict and rejection, reinforcing her sense of isolation and perpetuating a cycle of emotional turmoil.

Proverbs 29:11 states, "Fools give full vent to their rage, but the wise bring calm in the end." This verse reflects the cycle Mara found herself trapped in. Her anger, instead of bringing resolution or peace, intensified her struggles, leaving her stuck in a loop of pain and frustration. Over time, her reliance on aggression to cope only deepened the emotional wounds she carried.

One pivotal memory from elementary school illustrates the depth of Mara's anger. One day, her teacher asked her to stop talking during class. Feeling singled out and angry, Mara ignored the request and continued speaking with her classmates. When the teacher sent her to the office, Mara stood up, flipped her desk, and stormed out of the classroom. This act of defiance was her way of shielding herself from feelings of vulnerability, but it ultimately left her feeling more isolated.

Mara's instinct to lash out or withdraw became her way of navigating a world that felt unsafe. These early behaviors, born out of survival, began to shape how she interacted with others and viewed herself. Without the tools to process her emotions or the ability to fully understand their impact, Mara carried the weight of her experiences alone, unable to see how they were already laying the foundation for her future struggles.

No Place to Call Home

Mara's life was molded by the ever-changing living situations she and her brothers faced, marked by instability and uncertainty that eventually led them into the foster care system during their early life. The first brush with foster care came when Mara was about eleven years old.

Her Aunt Sarah found herself homeless, with nowhere to go and no means to provide a stable home. In desperation, Mara and her brothers were placed into a foster home. Mara and her younger brother Anthony were placed in foster care together, leaving their older brother Kenneth to fend for himself. Mara's memories of this time are hazy, yet the feelings of fear and uncertainty are vividly etched in her mind.

The foster system, which was supposed to provide safety and nourishment, quickly became a source of deep resentment for Mara. She and her little brother were scarcely fed, and he often woke up in the middle of the night, crying from hunger. With a fierce determination to care for him, Mara would sneak into the kitchen, fill a cup with water, and hide pieces of a raw hot dog inside to feed him secretly in their room.

Mara's innate sense of justice burned brightly, fueling her desire to stand up for what was right. One morning, the foster mother served them cereal, but Mara could not stand the taste and asked for sugar. When the foster mother refused, Mara decided she would not eat.

The foster mother insisted, but Mara, feeling trapped and desperate to assert some control, slipped into her defense mechanisms. She knocked the bowl of cereal to the floor in defiance. The foster mother, enraged, commanded her to clean it up. Mara stood her ground, eyes blazing with silent rebellion, refusing to submit.

In that instant, she did not care about the consequences; what mattered was that she had stood up for herself and her brother. Yes, what she did was wrong, but it felt justified in the context of everything they had endured together. It was a minor act of rebellion, a way to reclaim some control in a life that often felt out of reach.

After the confrontation, Mara was put on punishment. She felt the weight of her defiance hang in the air, mixing with the sting of her foster mother's anger.

But that was not the end of Mara's woes. When she was twelve, Mara got into a fight with some cousins in her dad's family. Mara already felt displaced as she barely knew this side of the family because of her dad's incarceration. So, her grandmother called Aunt Sarah to come pick Mara up.

Aunt Sarah was furious because she did not want Mara to be an embarrassment. When she arrived to pick Mara up, Aunt Sarah's frustration came out the wrong way, and Mara got a whooping.

Mara had enough bruises and welts all over her body, and she was tired of it. So, she ran out of the house. The police found her in a dark alley at night, calling 911 on a pay phone. A police officer took her into custody and brought her to another foster home. She despised foster care, and this time, it was even worse. This time, she did not have her brother with her.

One day, Mara and her foster mother argued intensely, their words sharp and biting. In her frustration, Mara yelled back. Her enraged foster mother made Mara go to her room and shut the door, ordering her not to come out. Feeling rejected and isolated, Mara screamed and yelled, the walls of her small room amplifying her desperation.

The foster mother returned; her face was twisted with anger and threatened Mara with a weapon to get her to shut up. The threat silenced Mara but intensified the turmoil inside her, the silent screams in her head, and the burning anger in her heart. The following day, the caseworker arrived for a visit. Mara, feeling a mix of apprehension and desperation, spoke up about her experiences in the home.

Another foster home, where the situation was equally grim, became Mara's new placement. The foster siblings were involved in inappropriate behavior, even making water balloons out of contraceptives. The cycle of being transferred from one unhealthy foster home to another continued, and Mara questioned if staying at home with her aunt might be better. Desperate, Mara called her Aunt Sarah, begging and crying to come home.

However, the judge would not allow Mara to return to her aunt. Aunt Sarah had made it clear that she did not want Mara back in her home unless she was allowed to discipline her. She felt Mara was getting out of control, and if she couldn't "whoop" her to correct her behavior, there was no point in having her return. Mara pleaded with her aunt to agree not to whip her so she would not have to stay in the foster system. Eventually, her aunt, hearing the pain and desperation in Mara's voice, agreed.

This cycle of dysfunction became Mara's norm. Each new placement only reinforced the belief that no place was truly safe for her. The pain of being unwanted and unsafe haunted Mara, but it was these very trials that laid the groundwork for her journey toward healing. But how about her father? Has he always been an inmate? Moreover, how did he land himself in prison?

Absent Father

Her father's absence shaped Mara's early years, a figure largely unknown to her until she reached adulthood. Mental health challenges had clouded his life, diagnosed with schizophrenia, and marked by a tragic incident that led to his confinement in a psychiatric ward for stabbing someone. This left Mara with little more than fragmented stories and distant memories.

Throughout her childhood and into her twenties, Mara's father remained a detached and elusive figure. His presence in her life was confined to occasional visits to the psychiatric facility where he was held. It was not until Mara turned twenty-one that her father was released from the state hospital, presenting an opportunity for them to build a relationship.

Despite her hopes for connection, bridging the gap proved daunting. Their interactions were strained by years of separation and the weight of unresolved emotions. Mara tried to understand her father's struggles with mental illness and the impact it had on their family dynamics, but the distance between them seemed Unbearable.

As an adult, Mara tried to visit her father and mend their fractured bond. Each meeting was a mix of longing and hesitation, navigating the complexities of their shared history and the challenges of forging a new relationship. Her father's release was a chance for reconciliation, yet it also underscored the profound effects of his absence during her formative years.

Mara often felt a deep ache in her heart whenever she thought about her father. Family members' taunts echoed in her mind like a cruel refrain. "You're just like your daddy!" they would sneer, their laughter ringing in her ears.

To them, it was a harmless joke, but for Mara, it felt like a dagger. Every time she heard those words, she heard rejection.

Mara saw in her father's struggles the very traits she feared would define her.

She did not want to be like him; she wanted to be loved by him. The thought of becoming like him—lost and unlovable—was a haunting shadow that followed her.

As Mara navigated her own journey with mental health, she couldn't help but feel the weight of his legacy. She often grappled with feelings of inadequacy, wondering if the scars of his struggles would mark her life as well. There were days when the darkness felt too heavy, and she feared she might follow in his footsteps.

The lack of a father figure left Mara feeling vulnerable. She craved someone to affirm her worth, to teach her how to navigate relationships, and to show her the beauty of a father-daughter bond. Instead, she felt adrift, struggling to understand her value in a world that often seemed harsh and unforgiving.

Years before, her father had shared something that shook her to her core: he had another daughter, born when he was just fourteen years old. This sister and Mara had different mothers. Mara's father and the mother of his daughter were too young and had to give her up for adoption.

He had always wondered about this daughter, hoping to find her someday. He gave Mara the name he remembered. As he spoke, Mara felt the weight of this revelation, mirrored her own journey of longing for connection and understanding.

Mara also realized she needed to forgive him—not for his sake, but for her own. She chose to let go of the resentment that had built up over the years. In understanding that he had fought battles she could only herself to love, forgiveness, she found a sense of peace.

him from a distance, acknowledging his struggles without letting them consume her.

One day, she received a call that her father was in the hospital. Without hesitation, Mara rushed to his side. There, she witnessed the frailty of the man who had caused her so much pain. Sitting beside him, she softly said, "Daddy, can you hear me?" The steady hum of the breathing machine filled the room, and she noticed the slightest movement of his eyelid—a flicker of recognition that brought tears to her eyes.

In that moment, Mara felt a rush of emotions—anger, sadness, but also a profound sense of compassion. She realized that despite the years of hurt, she could still offer him love.

It was a brutal reality to face—a man who was her biological father yet felt like a stranger. And now, despite their distant relationship, Mara had to take charge of his affairs and plan his memorial. Have you ever felt the weight of losing someone who shares your blood but not your life? The confusion and the mix of grief and detachment are a pain that tugs at the heart in ways words can barely express.

Mara confronted an even greater struggle: the heartfelt pleas from her father's brothers. Mara's uncles urged her to make decisions about her father's medical care, decisions she was not ready to make. Despite their impassioned appeals to let him go, Mara could not make that final call. Conflicted and overwhelmed, she turned to prayer, seeking clarity and peace amid her turmoil.

Days later, a ray of unexpected relief pierced through the grief-stricken haze. Hospital staff discovered a document outlining her father's wishes against resuscitation. Mara felt a profound gratitude, thanking the Lord God that she did not have to make that heart-wrenching decision herself. She knew deep down the choice would be incredibly difficult for her, and she was relieved that her father's wishes were clear, sparing her from a decision she could hardly bear.

As Mara stood by her father's side in his last days, the weight of their fractured relationship and the unspoken words hung heavy in the air. During this emotional whirlwind, Mara leaned heavily on her faith, praying earnestly for guidance and strength. He eventually passed away in 2015. The news of his passing flooded Mara's heart with a mix of sorrow, regret, and a profound sense of duty.

Though financially unprepared for the costs of her father's cremation and memorial, Mara experienced the quiet yet powerful presence of her Savior, who was with her every step of the way. In His infinite grace, the Lord made a way for Mara, even when she could not see one. Hospital staff and others around her stepped in, offering help, expecting nothing in return. Remarkably, Mara did not have to pay a single penny—every need was met through the generosity and kindness of others.

The memorial service became a moment of reckoning for Mara and a testament to how the Lord provides, even in the most challenging times. It was as if He was reminding her, "I am with you, even here, even now." Have you ever felt that divine hand guiding you when everything seemed impossible? It was a moment of profound faith for Mara, where she could see God's love in the compassion of those around her.

Driving home alone after the memorial, the weight of the day pressed heavily upon Mara. Tears streamed down her face as she traversed a highway filled with memories, emotions, and unanswered questions. In that solitary moment of vulnerability, Mara found strength, not in closure, but in the enduring faith that guided her through the tumultuous journey of saying goodbye.

The Roots of Rivalry: Unveiling the Past

Mara and her two brothers, Kenneth, the older brother, and Anthony, the younger, were like any other siblings. There were moments of laughter and mischief, followed by bickering and bouts of sibling rivalry. Her older brother, always quick-witted, loved to taunt her with jokes and call her names. "Hey, ugly," he would tease, grinning as he poked at her sensitivity. Mara would always try to come up with a comeback, but it never seemed to land the way she wanted.

Her younger brother, on the other hand, was the baby of the family, often escaping the scrutiny the older two endured. Mara and her older brother occasionally teamed up to tease him, making him the target of their playful jabs.

But there were moments when the balance of their dynamic tipped, and one sibling bore the brunt of the others' jokes or perceived favoritism. For Mara, one moment stood out vividly.

One day, Mara was so excited to have this new blue toy water gun. Mara's heart thudded in her chest as she clutched the shiny blue water gun, her fingers gripping its plastic curves with the desperation of someone holding onto far more than a toy. Her younger brother stood a few feet away, his wide, pleading eyes fixed on her.

"I just want to play with it for a little while," he whined, his tone innocent but insistent.

Mara narrowed her eyes, the words spilling out before she could stop them. "No. It is mine. Go play with your own stuff."

From around the corner, Aunt Sarah's voice sliced through the tension like a whip. "Mara, let him play with it. He is just a little boy."

Mara's stomach twisted. She had heard those words too many times before, and every time, they cut deeper. He is just a little boy. It did not matter that the water gun was hers. Her feelings never seemed to count when it came to her younger brother.

"Mara," Aunt Sarah snapped, her tone brooking no argument. "Do not be so selfish. Give it to him."

Tears stung Mara's eyes as she handed over the water gun, her fingers lingering for a moment longer than necessary. She watched as her brother's face lit up with triumph, the way his small hands gripped the toy that had once been hers. He darted outside, his laughter echoing through the air as Mara turned away, fists clenched at her sides.

Her chest heaved with a mix of anger and humiliation as she stormed up to her room, slamming the door behind her. The sound was loud and satisfying, but it did nothing to quiet the storm inside her.

Why does no one ever care what I feel?

Sitting on the edge of her bed, she swung her legs back and forth, hot tears spilling down her cheeks. Her brother's laughter floated through the open window, each burst a sharp reminder of her defeat.

A few minutes later, the door creaked open. Mara did not bother to look up. She recognized the hesitant footsteps, the faint creak of the floorboards beneath her brother's small frame.

"You can have it back," he said softly, placing the water gun on the bed beside her.

Mara did not reach for it. She did not even glance at it. "I do not want it anymore," she muttered, her voice hollow. "I do not want anything."

Her brother frowned, his small face scrunching in confusion. "What do you mean?"

The words tumbled out before she could stop them, raw and jagged. "Maybe I will just hurt myself. Maybe then someone will finally listen to me."

The younger brother tried telling Mara not to say those things, then he turned out of the room and told Aunt Sarah. Moments later, Aunt Sarah appeared in the doorway, her face calm and indifferent.

Mara's heart sank. She had expected concern, maybe even fear. Aunt Sarah told Mara's little brother she was just vying for attention and did not come to check on her. Maybe she was looking for some type of attention.

Mara's world shattered in that moment. She had said it to be heard, to make someone—anyone—understand how much she was hurting. But her aunt's response confirmed what she had feared all along: her feelings did not matter.

Sibling Dynamics

Sibling dynamics can be complex when one child receives more attention than the others. This often happens for various reasons, such as behavioral challenges, emotional struggles, or a greater need for support. When a family's attention is focused on one child, it can leave other siblings feeling neglected, leading to emotional tension and strained relationships.

In some families, the youngest child receives the most attention. Parents often show extra care for the youngest, but this can cause resentment among older siblings. Older siblings may feel overshadowed, leading to feelings of jealousy or isolation. They might question their own value, believing their needs are less important. This imbalance can create competition for attention and affection, ultimately leading to resentment.

Sometimes, a sibling requires more attention due to behavioral issues or emotional difficulties. Their actions, such as acting out or seeking attention, may be signs of unmet needs. While these behaviors often signal a desire for help, they may be misunderstood by others as disruptive or demanding. This misunderstanding can leave the child feeling unseen and unworthy of love unless they exhibit certain behaviors.

For siblings who do not display such behaviors, witnessing this dynamic can be painful. They may feel overlooked because their needs are less visible. Quiet, reserved siblings often feel their emotional needs are secondary, leading to feelings of neglect and resentment. These unmet needs can cause emotional withdrawal and internalized feelings of being unimportant.

In some cases, one sibling assumes the role of the "caretaker." Typically, this child takes on responsibilities within the family, striving to maintain peace. This role may cause them to prioritize others' needs above their own, often resulting in emotional burnout. The caretaker sibling might feel trapped in a cycle of perfectionism, attempting to meet expectations without receiving emotional support. Over time, they may develop resentment for being burdened with the weight of responsibility.

For Mara, the imbalance in attention created strain in her relationships with her siblings. As a child who needed emotional support, her behavior may have been viewed as disruptive or attention-seeking. However, it was a plea for validation, affection, and recognition. When these needs were unmet, she felt misunderstood and resorted to acting out. Her siblings, on the other hand, may have felt overshadowed and disconnected from their roles within the family. Kenneth's teasing might have been a way to mask his own emotional hurt, while Anthony, the youngest sibling, may have felt the family's attention shifted toward Mara's needs.

In families where one child requires more attention—the emotional impact can be long-lasting. Children who feel overlooked may internalize a sense of inadequacy, believing their needs don't matter. On the other hand, children who receive heightened attention might experience guilt or feel pressured to meet high expectations. They may grow up feeling responsible for others, often at the expense of their own well-being.

Sibling Dynamics and Emotional Imprints are more than just childhood squabbles or memories of who got the bigger piece of cake. These roles—the caretaker, the overlooked child, the "problem child"—leave emotional imprints that follow us into adulthood.

Perhaps you were the one who always had to be "good" to avoid conflict. Or maybe you felt like the "forgotten" sibling, invisible unless you achieved something noteworthy. Others may relate to being the "responsible one," the unofficial peacekeeper burdened with the emotional weight of family harmony. These roles do not just stay in the past—they become internal scripts that play out in your friendships, romantic relationships, and even your career.

But recognizing these roles is the first step toward healing. Which role did you play in your family, and how does it still show up in your life today? Reflection is a powerful tool for change. It is not about blaming your family but about understanding the story you have been living. The good news is that stories can be rewritten.

As you think about your own experiences, remember this: You are not defined by the role you played as a child. You have the power to step outside those roles and create a new narrative for yourself. The caretaker can learn to set boundaries. The "forgotten" child can learn to make themselves seen. The "problem child" can realize they were never the problem to begin with.

Take a moment to ask yourself: What story am I still living from my childhood? Your healing journey does not start with perfection—it starts with awareness. And if you are reading this, you have already begun.

Before You Were Born

Mara's family was not into church or God; she did not grow up in a religious household where you have family devotions and prayers. She never knew what it felt like sitting at your parent's feet and listening to them tell you about Jesus. This is where many children learn about Jesus and the importance of Bible study. But Mara was not fortunate enough to have all these.

When she was little, something happened that she did not understand. A church van started coming into the neighborhood to pick kids up. When the other kids said they were going to church, Mara, confused but curious, asked her mother if she could go with her friends.

She never understood or knew what a church was or what went on there. But her curiosity to know where her friends always went intrigued her. On the other hand, her mother agreed, perhaps seeing an opportunity for a break.

Mara sat quietly in the corner of the church, her heart beating faster as she felt the warmth of the women gathered around her. They had welcomed her with open arms, their voices gentle and their prayers filled with love. The familiar sound of the congregation's songs echoed through the room, but it was the words of the women who surrounded her that pierced through her thoughts.

"Do you accept Jesus into your life?" one of the women asked, her eyes kind and inviting. Mara, unsure of what the question fully meant but feeling a deep sense of belonging, nodded slowly. "Yes," she said, her voice soft but certain.

That one word, spoken in a moment of uncertainty, marked the beginning of a new chapter in Mara's life—one that would unfold with both challenge and grace.

She was not sure exactly what she was saying yes to, but the warmth of the community around her made it feel like the right choice. The words of the women, so filled with conviction, somehow made Mara believe that in this moment, something significant was happening.

Mara's most desperate prayers came during terrifying car rides with her Aunt Sarah, who often drove while drinking. Despite the danger, Mara never wanted to leave her side. They would swerve around corners, sometimes coming perilously close to lakes, and Mara would pray fervently the entire time: "Lord, please get me and Aunt Sarah home safe." Each time, God answered her prayers, and they made it home safely. This shows how much God loved Mara. Even though she did not fully grasp the significance or impact of her prayers, God still answered them. All these experiences unconsciously shaped Mara's growing sense of spiritual awareness.

Amid the chaos and uncertainty of her upbringing, Mara found comfort in believing God had known her and watched over her even before she was born. This realization, drawn from passages like Jeremiah 1:5 ESV, "Before I formed you in the womb I knew you, and before you were born, I consecrated you. I appointed you a prophet to the nations."

All this made her realize that her life had a purpose, and she was not alone in her struggles. But the question was, "What was that divine purpose?" Could God not unveil it already? Why did she have to suffer so much before the revelation of that purpose? These were questions that raced through her mind daily.

These experiences, though sporadic, planted seeds of faith that would continue to grow and sustain her. Though Mara was not fully aware, God was working in the background, training her spiritual life for the journey ahead. Mara maintained a conviction that God would answer her calls in moments of need. She found comfort in prayer, believing in divine intervention when she reached out to Him.

Reflection: Are You Aware God Created You for a Purpose?

Maybe, in one way or the other, you are going through a situation like Mara's. It is okay if many questions are racing through your mind. But amid all these, always remember the words of Jeremiah 1:5.

> *Before I formed thee in the belly I knew thee, and before thou camest forth out of the womb I sanctified thee; I have appointed thee a prophet unto the nations."*

In that scripture, the same way God spoke to Jeremiah, He is speaking to you today.

Teen Years

Hasty Temper Exalts Folly

A man of wrath stirs up strife, and one given to anger causes much transgression. Proverbs 29:22

This is the Bible's warning about anger, its consequences, and the need to avoid it. The rage and abuse that colored Mara's childhood continued to paint a dark picture of her years as a teenager. By the time she was in high school, Mara was cursing at her teachers when she got angry, and she kept fighting with her peers. If any of her peers at school got in her way, Mara would fight them—girls and boys. She fought all the time, in and out of school, sometimes taking part in fights with three to four girls on each side. She would pick up weapons and anything within her reach. Be it staplers or chairs, as long as she could lay her hands on any of them, she would lose her composure and have to be taken out of class and suspended from school.

Her anger was so bad that sometimes Mara went into a full-blown rage and blacked out. She wouldn't stop fighting and they had to physically pull her away from other students. In her freshman year, Mara was involved in a huge fight consisting of her and three friends against four other girls. It was not Mara's fight, but she wanted to prove her loyalty, so she jumped in to help. As a result, the police arrested her and took her to juvenile detention.

This constant violent behavior led many teachers to want her out of school. However, she was a very gifted young lady who performed in many talent shows and high school performances, leaving many with mixed emotions about her behavior and undeniable capabilities. The two seemed to be a mismatch.

Finally, Mara's favorite principal, who always had her back in the past, had to sit her down to inform her of the need to continue in another school for kids with behavior challenges. So, the principal expelled Mara and sent her to an alternative school. But to everyone's surprise, the fights and chaos did not stop. If anything, she fought her inner chaos even more after that. This was a course for alarm. It was nearly impossible for people to relate to her, especially people her age, because of fear of a misunderstanding and subsequent fights.

One fateful day, Mara walked home through the project apartment complex where some friends lived. Out of nowhere, she saw a group of girls standing around watching her, and Mara could tell that they meant trouble. But the Mara everyone knew was never one to back down. She put down her one-year-old son and stepped up to fight three girls at once.

She was about seventeen years old and about 100 pounds at five feet and six inches, but Mara stood her ground. Outnumbered, she pulled out a knife.

Mara ended up stabbing one of the girls. She had acted in self-defense, but that didn't make it any less terrifying. Shaken and afraid of what might happen—both to the girl and to herself—Mara prayed with all her heart that the girl would be okay, and that she wouldn't face serious trouble for what had happened.

Thankfully, the young woman recovered after a few stitches. Mara was overwhelmed with relief and deeply grateful to the Lord—not just for the girl's healing, but for giving her another chance.

By now, you might be wondering how and when Mara became a mother. We'll come back to that shortly.

Mara's anger did not come out of nowhere. From the outside, it seemed like she was always ready for a fight, always on edge, no matter who it was. But beneath the surface, a world of hurt and buried pain lay hidden. From a young age, Mara had learned that life was about surviving, and to survive, she had to be strong—strong enough to never let anyone see her vulnerable, and she let no one close enough to hurt her.

The first time she felt truly powerless was a moment she wouldn't forget. She was just a child, and someone she should have been able to trust betrayed her in the most devastating way. She did not have the words for what happened, did not know how to explain the sense of shame or confusion she felt. So, she locked that pain inside, burying it deeper and deeper, hoping it would disappear if she ignored it.

But it did not disappear. As she grew older, she found that the buried hurt turned into something else—anger. It bubbled up when she felt rejected, thought people were judging her, or feared someone might hurt her again. Her anger had become automatic, a shield she could not put down, even if she wanted to. For her, losing control was terrifying, but strangely, it felt like the only way she could release the emotions she did not know how to handle. Mara's anger was her way of saying, "I won't let anyone hurt me again."

Mara's journey shows that behind anger, there is often a world of unspoken pain. Hurt people often think anger is their only protection, but anger also isolates them from the love and understanding they need.

An Unprepared Journey into Motherhood

At age fifteen, Mara became pregnant before her sophomore year in high school. One would think carrying a baby would force her to calm down and behave better. Mara still fought all the time, even while she was pregnant. Her reckless behavior worried those around her, especially Aunt Sarah, who tried to intervene.

Tension between Mara and Aunt Sarah continued to build at home. Eventually, Mara was sent to live in a maternity home for pregnant women, where she was expected to learn how to care for herself and prepare for motherhood. The hope was that the structured environment would give Mara the guidance she needed.

Mara's fiery temper proved difficult to manage, even in the maternity home. Despite efforts to help her, her behavior remained challenging. Mara's ninth month of pregnancy ended with her release from the maternity home and return to Aunt Sarah's, primarily due to her anger problems.

Mara delivered her first child when she was sixteen years old. The day her water broke, Mara had to ask Aunt Sarah repeatedly to take her to the hospital.

"The baby's coming!" Mara said.

"Go back to bed," Aunt Sarah replied. "You just peed yourself." But soon enough, it was apparent that Mara's water had broken, and Aunt Sarah finally brought her to have her first baby delivered.

Mara lay in the hospital at age sixteen, feeling a profound sense of isolation. Although Aunt Sarah's physical presence was there, it seemed her attention was solely fixated on the impending arrival of Mara's firstborn, leaving Mara feeling neglected. Aunt Sarah's actions seemed to ignore Mara's needs and well-being, focusing instead on the baby.

Aunt Sarah had been drinking the night before, and despite her best efforts, her intoxication became apparent. Even though Mara could see that Aunt Sarah had made some effort to be present and supportive, she still felt the sting of neglect.

Seeing the strain this caused, Mara's grandmother urged Aunt Sarah to leave, hoping to alleviate the tension. Yet Aunt Sarah continued to prioritize her interest in the baby over Mara's comfort. The ongoing friction between her grandmother and Aunt Sarah was a constant, uncomfortable backdrop to Mara's upbringing, adding to the emotional weight she carried.

Mara lay on the hospital bed, her thoughts racing as she awaited the arrival of her first child. She had an epidural, which helped ease the intense pain she had never experienced before. In those quiet moments before her son was born, Mara couldn't help but wonder what kind of mother she would be. Questions swirled in her mind as she thought about her past and the challenges she had faced, hoping she could give her child a life free from those same pains.

Moments later, her first child came into the world, Fizzle. Holding him close, a flood of emotions—joy, fear, and an intense determination to protect him—overwhelmed Mara. As she gazed down at her newborn, she felt the weight of her past mingling with the hope of a new beginning, filling her with both resolve and tension.

Her fears of inadequacy and the possibility of repeating the cycle of pain she experienced overshadowed the joy of bringing a new world. Would she be able to provide the love and stability she never had? Would she inadvertently hurt her child the way others had hurt her?

The fear of failure loomed large in Mara's mind. She worried that her unresolved trauma could affect her parenting, leading to moments of doubt where she questioned her ability to connect with her son. Her experiences made it difficult for her to trust herself fully, and she often wrestled with feelings of unworthiness.

In spite of her fears, Fizzle became a source of hope and motivation, inspiring her to strive for a better future. Yet, at that moment, it appeared God had other plans to support her on this journey. How did He do this? Through the gift of genuine friendships.

I know it is tough to believe that someone genuinely cared for Mara. What if I told you she had genuine friends who indeed cared for her? Beloved, God has designated a few people to love, care, and support you in genuine friendships. We were not designed to walk or do life alone.

Friendships: The Ties That Bind

Mara's reputation at school was a mix of contradictions. People knew Mara for her fiery temper and quick fists, often getting into fights that puzzled others. Despite her tough exterior, Mara's friends loved her. They saw past her aggressive outbursts to the caring heart that lay beneath. Mara's humor and deep sense of loyalty made her someone they cherished. Her close-knit group Sweetie, Heaven, and Calina often spent nights at each other's houses, taking pictures and creating memories that would last a lifetime.

Among Mara's friends, each had their own reasons to fight, preferring Heaven and Sweetie never had avoided conflicts altogether, while

Calina had her share of scuffles but always managed to steer clear of Mara's battles.

Even with their differences, they never turned their backs on Mara. They understood that her fighting was a defense mechanism, a way to protect herself from a world that had often been unkind. Their friendship was unwavering.

Mara was the only one among them with a child. While this set her apart in some ways, it never alienated her from her friends. They embraced Mara's son, including him in their outings and making him feel like part of the group. Their bond was strong, forged through years of shared experiences and a deep mutual respect.

Humor was one thing they all enjoyed, often finding fun in karaoke nights and watching Sweetie's older brother and his friends dance and perform just to entertain them.

Life took them in different directions as they grew older, but their friendship remained constant. They would sometimes lose contact, only to reconnect at birthdays and celebrations. Even after twenty-five years, they still shared a special bond.

One of Mara's dearest friends was Rhondy, a girl who came from a very different world. Rhondy grew up in the middle-class southern part of town and was the baby of her family. Mara was raised in the projects where she was always in trouble and fighting. Rhondy dressed nicely with her hair perfectly styled and her clothes and shoes always on point. On the other hand, Mara often wore old clothes and jeans, her hair in an afro that others would mockingly compare to Woodstock.

Mara was not one to focus on taking care of herself, but one day, Rhondy extended a hand of friendship that would ultimately change her life. She invited Mara to her home, a place so different from Mara's that it left her in awe. They skipped school together, catching the bus to her house, where Rhondy ordered pizza for Mara and led her to her room. Rhondy let Mara try on her clothes and shoes, combed her hair, and applied makeup. When Mara looked in the mirror, she could hardly believe her eyes. For the first time, she saw herself as pretty.

Rhondy gave Mara a new wardrobe that day, and from that moment on, Mara took more pride in her appearance. She started dressing up, wanting her hair done, and embracing the idea of looking pretty. Mara had always thought she was too thin, but seeing how Rhondy was beautiful and slim helped her accept herself. Their bond grew stronger, and they became best friends, a friendship that would endure for decades.

"Two are better than one, because they have a good reward for their labor. For if they fall, the one will lift up his fellow: but woe to him that is alone when he falleth, and hath not another to lift him up" Ecclesiastes 4:9-10. This scripture emphasizes the importance of unity and support, showing that we are meant to lift each other up in times of hardship, not tear each other down. When we walk in love and compassion, we become the helping hand God intended us to be.

Beloved, this verse is not just about romantic partnerships but about having a true support system—people who can lift us up when life gets tough. Without these genuine relationships, it is harder to rise and thrive. As Proverbs 27:17 says, "Iron sharpeneth iron; so a man sharpeneth the countenance of his friend."

I encourage you to take a moment now, bow your heart, and pray that the Lord will bring genuine, soul-lifting friends into your life. When you have just a few of these people, your journey to wholeness and healing will be fast-tracked. It does not matter how broken your past or present may be; these friends will lift you up and love you for who you are. They are not transactional or seeking relationships with benefits; instead, they show God's unconditional love.

These kinds of friends exist and reflect the true nature of God's love for us. May you find those who will walk beside you, helping you grow and heal. God can direct them your way.

But even in the safety of newfound friendship, Mara carried wounds far deeper than anyone could see. The love she found as a teen mom was healing—but it came after a relationship that nearly destroyed her. Before she ever held her first child in her arms, Mara endured a kind of pain no one should ever face.

Condemnation Instead of Compassion

Her boyfriend at the time, Mark, made it clear from the beginning—he did not want to be a father. They were young, and the idea of parenthood felt overwhelming. But his refusal ran deeper than fear; it was rooted in his own broken past. Still, when Mara discovered she was pregnant, she chose to keep the baby. That decision marked a turning point. The tension between them exploded into violence. One night, after the baby was born, Mark showed up drunk and furious. He beat her—hitting her with a broom, knocking her down, and stomping on her face.

It was cruelty beyond anything Mara had known. But heartbreakingly, it was not the end. Sometime later, Mara became pregnant again. This time, Mark gave her no choice. He forced her to go to an abortion clinic. Too afraid to face more violence, Mara complied.

She was only seventeen. Pulling into that clinic was one of the most painful moments of her life. Already overwhelmed, Mara was met by a wall of religious protesters yelling slurs and holding signs that read, *"Baby killer!"* and *"Mommy, do not kill me!"*

Their words pierced deeper than they knew. They did not see the bruises, the fear in her eyes, or the hopelessness in her heart. If they had, perhaps their anger would have softened into compassion. Inside, Mara was already breaking. The shame and guilt she felt were only amplified by their condemnation. She did not need more punishment—she needed mercy. She needed refuge.

But instead of finding healing, Mara found rejection—especially from those who claimed to follow a God of love.

The church, meant to be a sanctuary, often becomes another source of pain. For Mara, the voices of condemnation that day did not draw her closer to God—they pushed her further away. Not because she did not believe in Him, but because the people who claimed to speak for Him made Him feel unreachable.

Mara did not need to be shamed.
She needed to be seen.
She needed to be loved.
She needed to be reminded that God's grace is big enough even for this.

This is the reality for so many: instead of meeting grace in their darkest moments, they are met with judgment.

The Weight of Judgment

Mara faced harsh criticism and condemnation after her abortion. The Bible tells us God is love, and His Word calls us not to judge or condemn others but to reflect His grace and kindness. The individuals Mara encountered could have been part of the solution to her struggle, leading her toward healing and hope in Christ. His desire is for us to love and support one another, even in our sin, just as "He who converteth a sinner from the error of his way shall save a soul from death, and shall cover a multitude of sins" James 5:20.

The greatest commandments, according to Jesus, center on love. When asked which commandment was the greatest, He responded, "Thou shalt love the Lord thy God with all thy heart, and with all thy soul, and with all thy mind. This is the great and first commandment. And a second like unto it is this, Thou shalt love thy neighbor as thyself" Matthew 22:37-39.

Mara would have welcomed one of these individuals to reflect Jesus's love in several practical ways when she came to the abortion clinic. They could have stayed by her side, offering comfort through their presence rather than just words, reflecting the love that "is not easily angered" and "keeps no record of wrongs."

Instead of judging Mara, they could have extended grace, showing her that true love does not dishonor or disrespect, even in hard conversations. One person might have volunteered to help Mara find resources, offering support that went beyond the immediate moment—helping her understand her options with patience and kindness. Another could have invited her to share a meal, reminding her that her worth is not tied to her decisions, but to the deep, unwavering love God has for her.

Simply being present and listening without judgment could have shown Mara unconditional acceptance, a reflection of the way Christ loves us all. Jesus provided a powerful example in the parable of the sheep and the goats, saying, "For I was hungry, and ye gave me no meat: I was thirsty, and ye gave me no drink: I was a stranger, and ye took me not in: naked, and ye clothed me not: sick, and in prison, and ye visited me not" Matthew 25:42-43. When we overlook those in need, fail to show kindness, or judge without compassion, we stray from God's command to love others.

It is not acceptable to call others sinners, play God, or judge who is worthy of heaven. The Bible says, "Judge not, that ye be not judged. For with what judgment ye judge, ye shall be judged: and with what measure ye mete, it shall be measured to you again" Matthew 7:1-2.

This verse emphasizes that when we judge others, we invite the same level of judgment upon ourselves, showing why it is crucial to show compassion—it keeps us from being judged harshly.

The Lord Himself said He did not come to condemn but to save the world. On Judgment Day, many will come before the Lord, saying, "Lord, Lord, did we not prophesy by thy name, and by thy name cast out demons, and by thy name do many mighty works?" Yet, Jesus will respond, "I never knew you: depart from me, ye that work iniquity" Matthew 7:22-23. This shows us that entry into heaven is not based on religious acts or good deeds, but on truly knowing Christ and living out His love.

As 1 Corinthians 13:4-7 (emphasis added) says: "Love suffereth long, and is kind; love envieth not; love vaunteth not itself, is not puffed up, doth not behave itself unseemly, seeketh not its own, is not provoked, taketh not account of evil; rejoiceth not in *unrighteousness*, but rejoiceth with the truth; beareth all things, believeth all things, hopeth all things, endureth all things."

Mara was at one of the lowest points in her life and wanted someone to show her this Christlike love. Even in her most vulnerable moment, she needed to know that she was worthy of compassion, hope, and a love that never fails and always perseveres. This experience was pivotal for how she would respond to others in the future.

Reflection: What She Never Knew

Mara was not just scared—she was uninformed. No one had ever explained to her what sex was truly meant to be. She did not understand that God's design for intimacy came with both beauty and boundaries. When she and Mark became physically involved, they did not plan for a child. They did not use protection, and they never talked about consequences. They simply did not know. At the time, no one had told her that her body carried something sacred.

Looking back, Mara realizes that if she had known then what she knows now, she might have made different choices. She now understands that abortion wasn't a solution—it could not undo what had already been created. It was not meant to be used as a form of birth control. God forms every life with purpose and intention. God's Word is not a list of rules meant to restrict—it is a blueprint meant to protect. The world may tell us that life is disposable or that sex is just physical, without consequence.

But Mara has come to understand the truth: life is sacred, even before birth, and intimacy is a gift meant to reflect God's heart, not bring harm. As Psalm 139:13-16 says, "For you created my inmost being; you knit me together in my mother's womb... Your eyes saw my unformed body." And Hebrews

13:4 reminds us, "Marriage should be honored by all, and the marriage bed kept pure."

The Lord does not condemn her. Instead, He walks with her—offering truth, grace, and restoration. That is what He's done in her life. He met her in her pain, not with shame, but with compassion. And through His Word, He began to guide her—giving her principles that would protect her from walking through that same pain again, especially the kind of pain brought by people who did not love her well or didn't value her deeply.

God's love is strong enough to meet us where we are, and wise enough to lead us somewhere better. Mara has found freedom in that truth. As Romans 8:1 declares, "There is now no condemnation for those who are in Christ Jesus." And Isaiah 30:21 gently reminds us, "Whether you turn to the right or to the left, your ears will hear a voice behind you, saying, 'This is the way; walk in it.'"

Embraced by Unshakable Love

Have you ever felt like Mara—judged, condemned, maybe even by those who were supposed to care for you with love and compassion? That pain cuts so deep it can make you feel you will never be enough, like you do not deserve the kindness or acceptance you so desperately need. But there is One who sees all of you—the flaws, the past, the fears—and still loves you unconditionally, just as you are. Know this: the harshness you may have faced is not from God. His love is the gentlest embrace, an unbreakable promise that no one, nothing, can take from you.

Maybe you have doubted that love, wondered if your mistakes have somehow disqualified you from His grace. But Romans 8:1 gently whispers the truth: "There is therefore now no condemnation to them that are in Christ Jesus." That means God sees beyond every misstep and regret. His love is not held back because of your past; it is poured out over you right here, right now. God does not see you through the lens of your worst moments—He sees you as His precious child, fully and perfectly loved.

Imagine that kind of love. A love so vast and consuming that it pursues you in your darkest hour. A love that weeps with you in your pain and stands firm beside you through every storm. It is not a love that comes and goes based on how "good" you are; it is a love that stays. He sacrificed everything so that you could know this profound love, a love that exceeds all human understanding.

Romans 8:38-39 powerfully declares: "For I am persuaded, that neither death, nor life, nor angels, nor principalities, nor things present, nor things to come, nor powers, nor height, nor depth, nor any other creature, shall be able to separate us from the love of God, which is in Christ Jesus our Lord." Hear this in the deepest part of you—no amount of guilt, no mountain of shame, not even the harshest judgment could separate you from His love. God's love reaches you at the heart of who you are, where no one else can see, where no one else knows. There is no place you can hide that His love will not find you.

This love, so pure and fierce, asks nothing in return but your trust. It waits for you like a light in the dark, offering healing, acceptance, and peace. Can you let yourself feel it? Can you rest in it, knowing that nothing you have been through, no words of judgment from anyone, could ever take this love away?

As you open your heart to this truth, may you feel God's love surrounding you, breaking through every hurt and filling the empty places. His love is your safe place. It is here for you now, as you are—because you are His, and that alone is enough.

Generational Trauma

Devastated and broken at the trajectory of her life, Mara, at nineteen, had a crucial conversation with her Aunt Sarah.

Aunt Sarah had wanted to know why Mara never wanted to talk about a particular relative on the phone when she called. The person she referred to was the same relative who was responsible for the sexual abuse Mara endured ten years earlier. For a long time, Mara would not talk about it.

Mara finally shared with Aunt Sarah what had happened to her when she was young. The sadness on Aunt Sarah's face was intense. She looked at Mara.

"Wow," Aunt Sarah said, "I never thought they would do this to you, too." Then, Aunt Sarah told Mara that when she was a child, the same thing had happened to her by the same relative. Yes, you read that right: the same relative sexually assaulted Mara and her aunt.

As Mara and Aunt Sarah sat together, the sad moment weighed heavily on them, yet it also marked a pivotal realization. Mara recognized that the cycle of generational trauma needed to be broken. She was determined to end it, but this commitment came with its challenges in parenthood.

Generational trauma is often a silent presence within families, lingering from one generation to the next. It can begin with those before us, or even generations ago, carrying the scars of difficult pasts—stories of neglect, trauma, and abuse that were never openly discussed or addressed. This silence allows pain to fester beneath the surface, unseen but deeply felt, perpetuating a cycle that continues through time.

Children are raised in homes where emotions are often hidden behind closed doors. Unspoken vulnerabilities stifle the feelings that need nurturing. Tragically, the pain does not always come from strangers. It can emerge from the very people who are supposed to protect and love. Cousins, uncles, aunts, grandparents, siblings, neighbors, community people, and even parents—those who should be a source of warmth and safety—sometimes cause deep, lasting wounds.

Imagine the confusion and heartache of a child who reaches out for comfort only to be met with coldness or, worse, abuse. The people they trust most betray that trust, leaving scars that may never fully heal. "It takes a village" now feels like a betrayal. Instead of being a haven, the village has become a source of pain for many.

This can be a traumatic experience that leaves the child no choice but to seek ways to fill that void. It becomes difficult for such a child to embrace or reciprocate love. Have you ever felt this type of betrayal from someone you trusted in your life or community? It is a pain that is hard to describe, a hurt that cuts deep and leaves you questioning everything. But you are not alone.

These long-term effects linger, shaping how these children view themselves and the world around them. The wounds of their past dictate their future, making it hard for them to trust, love, or even believe in their own worth. They learn early to hide their pain, sometimes labeled as "tattletales" or silenced altogether, grappling with why their protectors did not shield them from harm.

This cycle of trauma perpetuates through generations, staining what should be a supportive community with hidden anguish. Innocent childhood games become unwitting stages for acting out these unresolved hurts, echoing the unspoken traumas of their elders. Children innocently play house and make-believe games, unknowingly re-enacting the cycles of abuse they witnessed.

Family secrets persist, breeding a legacy of hurt that children may attempt to cope with through promiscuity, drug and alcohol abuse, sexual addiction, pornography, domestic abuse, or other destructive behaviors.

Perhaps you did not face Mara's exact hardships, but you might have felt the sting of emotional neglect and rejection. Maybe one or both parents failed to connect with you emotionally, leaving you feeling ignored and abandoned, just like Mara, while hiding your true self behind facades of composure. But beneath the surface, resentment simmered.

Each generation bore the scars of their predecessors. But can this cycle be stopped? If yes, how? How can this traumatic chain be broken? No matter the efforts put in, it takes someone with the right spirit, that is, the Holy Spirit, to prayerfully and intentionally stand against this generational cycle, which is what Mara later did. But how did she go about it? Keep reading.

Cycles of Love and Loss

Let us revisit Mara's love life. Mara's journey to finding love was anything but simple, especially after the heartbreak and trauma she had endured with Mark. When she finally managed to free herself from that toxic relationship, she believed she was headed toward healing. However, what awaited her was another chaotic relationship, one that felt like her past. It appears she was caught in a never-ending cycle, repeating the same painful patterns, unsure of how to break free.

Her next relationship was with Tim. Their connection was intense, but it was marked by constant power struggles. They were both tough and stubborn, often engaging in battles to see who could exert more control. Beneath the surface, though, they were both hurting. Their arguments reflected the pain they were carrying, rather than their true feelings for each other. Tim was always drawn to trouble, and that was how Mara met him—at the alternative school. Despite their efforts to maintain a long-distance relationship when Tim had to leave town, it quickly became clear that Tim was not able to stay faithful.

A few years after her relationship with Tim ended, Mara found herself in a new chapter of her life. She moved to another state, hoping to escape the chaos and pain that had followed her. She thought a change in scenery might bring the peace she desperately needed. However, as she soon realized, moving away did little to heal the deep wounds in her heart. Unresolved trauma does not stay behind—it travels with you.

It was during this period of searching for a fresh start that Mara met Sam, a charming young man with a troubled past of his own. Like Mara, Sam carried his own emotional baggage, rooted in a childhood where his parents were absent or unhealthy presences in his life. The two of them spent long hours together, and Sam, who lived with his uncle, often stayed at Mara's place. Despite their connection, Sam's unhealed trauma frequently surfaced through angry outbursts and unpredictable behavior.

Sam's troubled past ran deeper than just emotional wounds. He sold and used drugs, dragging Mara into a dangerous world she had never fully known before. Despite her initial resistance, Mara eventually joined him in smoking marijuana, though she never liked the feeling it gave her. It left her feeling out of control, disconnected from herself. After a few attempts, she knew this was not the escape she was looking for. Sam's unresolved trauma from not having his parents in his life in a healthy way most times manifested in angry outbursts and erratic behavior.

One night, while Mara spent the night in Sam's uncle's house, she was jolted awake by the sound of a gunshot. Her heart raced as Sam jumped up to investigate. Only to discover that an associate of Sam's uncle had shot someone, claiming the person had robbed him. Mara, trying to suppress her screams, was told to keep quiet and leave immediately.

The scene was surreal, like a nightmare. It was raining and thundering, and as Mara prepared to leave, a flash of lightning illuminated a lifeless body. She screamed but was quickly silenced and told to hurry. With tears in her eyes and terror in her heart, she stepped over the body, seven months pregnant, and ran to her car. That night, sleep eluded her as she wondered what she had gotten herself into.

The next day, the culprit was arrested, and Mara vowed never to return to Sam's uncle's house. Her relationship with Sam was tumultuous, filled with fights and jealousy. This was not the new life she had envisioned. Unfortunately, in a twist of events, Sam's life was cut short, a tragic end she had foreseen in a dream.

Mara had a recurring feeling that something was off, especially since she had a dream months before that hinted at this tragic outcome. When she shared it with Sam, he dismissed her concerns and continued living his lifestyle.

Mara had a feeling in her heart, as she had sensed something was wrong. They had just had a fight, and she had chosen to stay home, missing him deeply. She wanted to visit his uncle's house but hesitated, as her clothes had just been washed and hung to dry.

Then, the knock came at five o'clock in the morning. Mara jumped up, her heart pounding. She heard someone calling her name, and as the reality sank in, she began screaming, "No! No!" Sam's family urged her to open the door, but she did not want to hear the news.

When she finally opened the door, she stood back, unable to comprehend what they were saying. "No, no, it can't be true!" she shouted, struggling to accept the reality of their words. Despite her disbelief, Mara knew she had to go see Sam for herself. She went with his family to confirm the truth, but the traumatic realization shattered her world. It was never the same for Mara after that day; it took her a long time to process the loss and the pain that came with it.

Mara had never experienced anything like this before, and it was a challenging moment for her. Despite knowing that her relationship with Sam was unhealthy, the loss still ran deep. Mara did not know how to cope with the pain of losing someone she loved. To move on, she considered leaving the state to live with a friend. She hoped to start anew and give her life to God, seeking healing and guidance in the process.

A Sisterhood Forged in Faith

After Sam's passing, Mara found herself in one of the darkest times of her life. Grief threatened to swallow her whole, but through it all, one person remained steadfast by her side—Baps. The bond between Mara and Baps was more than friendship; it was a sisterhood that had withstood the test of time. They had so much in common, and their lives were intertwined, making them almost inseparable.

A FRIEND LOVETH AT ALL TIMES; AND A BROTHER IS BORN FOR ADVERSITY.

PROVERBS 17:17

Their children grew up together. Mara and Baps did everything together, from sharing their deepest thoughts to supporting each other through their toughest trials.

Their journey was not just one of shared experiences, but also shared faith. Mara and Baps got baptized at the same time. This spiritual connection deepened their bond as they navigated their paths toward healing and growth side-by-side.

Baps and her children always held a special place in Mara's heart. The memories of their long-standing relationship, the things they shared, and the commonalities that brought them together created an unshakable foundation. Even after they went on their own journeys in their late twenties, the impact of their friendship remained. Mara cherished the memories they created, the laughter they shared, and the spiritual journeys they embarked on together.

One thing they always had in common was the special name "Niques." Though they used it differently, the significance of that name was undeniable. It was a bond that tied them together in a way that nothing else could—an unforgettable connection.

HE THAT MAKETH MANY FRIENDS DOETH IT TO HIS OWN DESTRUCTION; BUT THERE IS A FRIEND THAT STICKETH CLOSER THAN A BROTHER. PROVERBS 18

Not Forsaken

Mara often found herself lost in thoughts of her father's absence, a void that shaped her childhood in ways she could not fully grasp at the time. His emotional absence left her with an unspoken longing, a desire for the kind of affection she saw other girls receive from their fathers, but which was never extended to her. Psalm 27:10: "Though my father and mother forsake me, the Lord will receive me."

Without this critical influence, Mara struggled to understand what a healthy relationship should look like. She had no model for how a man was supposed to treat her or what it meant to be loved unconditionally. These questions lingered unanswered in her mind, often leaving her confused and unsure. As she moved through her teenage years and into adulthood, Mara realized that her relationships with men were built on these fragile, incomplete ideas. She had no blueprint for emotional intimacy, and the models she encountered were often far from healthy.

Her relationships with men reflected the deep emptiness left by her father's absence. Time and time again, she found herself in partnerships with men who were emotionally unavailable or even outright dismissive of her needs. Their criticism stung, echoing the unresolved pain of her childhood. Every harsh word, every dismissal of her feelings, reminded her of her father's emotional neglect. In these relationships, Mara found herself trying to prove her worth, unconsciously seeking the approval she had never gotten from her father. Yet, these men could not provide the love she so desperately needed, and the cycle of emotional deprivation deepened.

To shield herself from further heartbreak, Mara built walls around her heart. These walls were thick and high, designed to keep others at a distance. She convinced herself that she did not need anyone—that if she could remain emotionally self-sufficient, she would never be let down. She buried her vulnerability deep inside, convinced that showing any weakness would leave her open to rejection. In this self-imposed isolation, she believed she could protect herself from the pain of abandonment that she feared most.

But while her emotional walls kept others out, they also trapped her in a cycle of loneliness and emotional exhaustion. Beneath the strength she showed to the world, Mara struggled with an overwhelming sense of inadequacy. The perfectionism that had quietly crept into her life became a constant companion, urging her to be flawless in everything she did. If she could just get everything right—if she could prove to herself and others that she was worthy—then maybe, just maybe, she could fill the empty space her father's absence had left behind. But no matter how hard she tried, no matter how many times she pushed herself to be better, the void remained.

This fear of abandonment and of not being enough shaped her interactions, her choices, and even her relationships. She threw herself into every relationship, every task, with an intense desire to prove her worth. Yet the more she gave of herself, the more exhausted she became, and the more unfulfilled she felt.

Her emotional self-sacrifice became a pattern that defined her life. She gave, and gave, and gave—but in return, she often felt unseen and unloved. She could not understand why the harder she worked to be perfect, the more distant people seemed. It was not love that she was seeking—it was validation, approval, and reassurance that she was not invisible, that she was worthy of being loved. But in her attempts to meet these demands, she only distanced herself further from the love she sought.

Mara was still trapped in the patterns of her past, still searching for love in all the wrong places.

Reflection

Have you ever found yourself in relationships that echoed the pain of your childhood? The feeling of being unseen or unheard? You try to prove your worth, only to feel like you never quite measure up. Maybe these triggers remind you of younger versions of yourself — that child who longed for love, attention, or affirmation but never fully received it.

No matter how much time passed, certain triggers transported her back to that younger version of herself, still longing for the comfort and validation she did not receive.

Your worth is not defined by who abandoned you; it is defined by who holds you up when you feel like you are falling. The love you seek may not have come from your earthly father, but it flows freely from your heavenly Father, who sees you, knows you, and loves you unconditionally.

Psalm 27:10: "Though my father and mother forsake me, the Lord will receive me."

Adulthood

The Power of Our Words

It is funny how powerful the tongue is and how we can manifest things into our lives without realizing what we are doing? The Bible clarifies this, saying life and death are in the power of the tongue, and those who love its fruits will eat it. So, the choice is ours.

One day, in her late twenties, Mara sat in a training class for a new job. The atmosphere was casual, and during a break, she found herself chatting with a few fellow trainees during a break, engaging in the kind of light small talk that usually passes without much thought. They joked about future dreams and shared a few personal stories, unaware that these conversations were weaving themselves into the fabric of something greater.

"I am going to marry one of two guys," Mara said. "Either Mike or Lou."

"What is Mike's last name?" asked another woman in the class.

"Why do you want to know?" Mara asked back, with a playful smirk, her tone lighthearted and teasing. The group chuckled, not sensing the depth beneath her casual remark.

"I know someone named Mike," the other woman said. When Mara told her Mike's last name, she smiled. "That is my cousin!" The two women became very close from that moment on.

Mara met Lou in 2002 when she was in her late twenties.

At the time, she was visiting T, a close friend whom she considered a sister, at her workplace. As she exited the elevator, Mara made eye contact with a guy who just about took her breath away. He was tall, dark, and handsome with braids to the back.

"Who is that?" Mara wondered in her head, but it must have been obvious that she was admiring him.

"That is Lou," T told her with a knowing smile as she pointed him out. Mara, still reeling from the intense moment of eye contact, looked back at T, who was clearly aware of Mara's interest.

T wasted no time and introduced Mara to Lou. They exchanged numbers, and it wasn't long before they began to talk more frequently. The connection between them seemed to grow quickly. But this man did not take long to show his true colors.

It seemed Lou wanted the benefits of a long-term relationship without the commitment of one. Mara learned from T that Lou was messing around with other girls at the office. This angered Mara, reminding her of all the betrayals in her life. So, she called to let Lou have it. Lou and Mara began arguing, and she pressed him to explain why he had not been honest with her. Lou replied, "We're not in a relationship," implying he felt free to lie and cheat. This response hurt Mara deeply, igniting feelings of betrayal and anger. In her frustration and driven by a mix of hurt and a desire for retaliation, she threatened to damage Lou's car. Unfortunately, she did not expect the response that followed.

"I'll slice the tires on your car!" Mara even threatened.

"Go ahead," Lou replied. "I'll dump Tweet Thang in the river!" Tweet Thang was the nickname for Mara's car; it even said so across the windshield since she was such a big fan of Tweety Bird.

Believing Lou would make good on his threats, Mara left his car alone. He had called later that day to apologize, but Mara knew his apology was not genuine and was not ready to forgive him. She would not talk to or see him for another thirteen years.

Discernment

Mara seemed to have unknowingly spoken the relationships with Lou and Mike into her life. Knowing the power of the tongue, we must ask: how can we use it responsibly for good? What if we could manifest and speak faith to our situations? This is very possible, after all.

Instead of dwelling on doubt and fear, imagine if we replaced negative talk with positivity. What would happen if thanked God in advance for His promises to manifest in our lives in His perfect timing? We do not want to manifest the wrong things in our lives, so we must be intentional about our words.

"Ask, and it shall be given you; seek, and ye shall find; knock, and it shall be opened unto you" Matthew 7:7. And how can you ask if not with your words?

No doubt, though, you have heard the old saying: "Be careful what you wish for." The Bible contains numerous passages that warn about the consequences of not taming one's tongue. Does the same thing not happen to us sometimes?

"For out of the abundance of the heart the mouth speaketh" Matthew 12:34. Sometimes, we literally speak our hearts' desires into existence. Rarely will you hear anyone talk about anything different from what is in their hearts.

God answers prayer, but oftentimes you do not like the answer—especially if you do not ask for the right things. The answer to prayer is sometimes "no." But even if it is "yes," it will come in God's time and be done His way. His way is far beyond what we can imagine and often different from what we desire. "Thy kingdom is an everlasting kingdom, And thy dominion endureth throughout all generations." Psalm 145:13.

When we seek things in life, we must use discernment. Discernment comes from the indwelling Holy Spirit. The more you allow the Spirit to flow through you, the more you can tell right from wrong and make better decisions in life, including what to pray for. That is why the Holy Spirit is our guide. He helps us make decisions, even on the most trivial things.

We read in Philippians 1:9-10: "And this I pray, that your love may abound yet more and more in knowledge and all discernment; so that ye may approve the things that are excellent; that ye may be sincere and void of offence unto the day of Christ."

Sometimes, you might feel empty, like you long for something but do not know what it is you need. These are the times you should pray for discernment. Ask the Lord to show you the way at the crossroads, and He will tell you which path to take.

Acknowledge Him in All Thy Ways

Shortly after breaking up with Lou, Mara met Mike. Mike was in the lives of Mara and her children, bringing a spark of hope and the promise of a fresh start. Mike was undeniably charming, and his eyes twinkled with a kindness to which Mara was drawn.

She felt maybe Mike was the one she had been waiting for all her life. However, beneath that charm, Mike was struggling with issues of substance use. Early on, Mara recognized that Mike had an addiction issue. She had discovered marijuana and confronted him about it. At first, Mara tried to brush it off as a minor issue. She thought maybe it was just a phase or something she could overlook. But as time went on, the situation seemed more complicated. Despite these challenges, he strongly desired to marry Mara and become a part of her family's journey. This new relationship, full of potential and peril, set the stage for another chapter in Mara's complex, yet resilient, life.

Mara felt the Lord had given her many signals about Mike and his struggles with addiction. However, she had fallen in love with his potential, and it was hard to ignore the warning signs.

Mike's behavior became increasingly erratic, and he was often secretive about his activities. Mara began to suspect that there was more to his situation than just marijuana. She saw how his mood swings and denial about the seriousness of his problem were affecting their relationship.

Mike met Mara's confrontation with defensiveness and evasion. Though he downplayed the issue. She knew that sometimes marijuana use could be a gateway to more severe problems. She had heard about people who started with one substance and ended up struggling with harder drugs.

Then came the day when Mara's worst fears were confirmed—she found out that Mike had been using harder drugs. His unpredictable behavior, unexplained disappearances, and increasing emotional distance all pointed to something more than casual marijuana use. The discovery shook her as it became clear Mike's addiction was far more severe than she initially thought. The once minor issue had spiraled into a serious and dangerous battle with substances that went beyond what she was prepared to handle.

Several times during the relationship, she had to pack up her kids and flee to shelters for battered women. These shelters became her only refuge, a place where she and her children could find temporary safety from the relentless cycle of abuse. Each time she left, it was a desperate attempt to protect her family yet fear and trauma always seemed to follow her.

The decision to seek shelter was never easy. Mara and the children often left with only the clothes on their backs, her heart pounding with fear and uncertainty. The shelters offered a glimpse of life without fear, where she and her children could finally heal and find peace. This was what she had to fight for. Mara's journey revealed the immense pain and suffering endured in abusive relationships and the extraordinary courage needed to break free. Yet, she couldn't help but wonder: how could she continue living like this?

The memories of hurriedly gathering her children and escaping in the dead of night haunted Mara, each incident a painful reminder of the life she was so desperate to leave behind. Every promise of change, every fleeting moment of peace, seemed to draw her back, only to be shattered by another episode of violence and abuse. Mike's manipulation and threats, combined with Mara's fear of abandonment and rejection, kept her trapped in the toxic relationship.

The relationship was riddled with lies, betrayal, and drug use. Despite her strong faith, she felt as though her prayers went unanswered, leaving her trapped in a cycle of enabling behavior. Fear of her safety and the well-being of her children kept her bound to Mike, even as his actions continued to harm them all.

Moments of clarity and opportunity had appeared, yet she always returned to Mike, driven by her deep-seated trauma, fear of abandonment, and rejection.

This emotional baggage kept her locked in a state of codependency, where her self-worth became entangled with Mike's approval and behavior. She believed that by staying, she could somehow fix him or keep the family intact, but this only deepened the dysfunction.

In her effort to manage Mike's addiction and volatile behavior, Mara inadvertently became an enabler. She often excused his actions, took responsibility for his mistakes, and kept the peace to avoid conflict. By doing so, she shielded Mike from the full consequences of his choices, allowing the cycle of abuse and drug use to continue unchecked.

Mara's enabling was rooted in her own unresolved wounds. Yet, each time she ignored the opportunities God presented for freedom, she unknowingly prolonged her suffering and allowed the unhealthy patterns to persist. Her prayers had not gone unanswered. Blinded by her trauma and fear, she simply had not been able to accept the deliverance when it came.

Mara and Mike's relationship deteriorated further as he began cheating on her. One time, Mike disappeared for weeks, a pattern he followed periodically. When he finally called Mara from an unfamiliar number, she called back, and a lady answered. Mara, desperate for answers, asked, "Is Mike there? He called from this number." The lady replied, "I did not know he was in a relationship with you. My friends and I took turns sleeping with him all night."

Mara's heart dropped as she waited to speak to Mike, her mind swirling with desperate hope for some explanation to ease her torment. Mara heard Mike in the background as he approached the phone. Overhearing him say dismissively, "This is my baby's mama." She felt a pang of betrayal cut deeper than anything she had experienced. Mike got on the phone and, with a chilling coldness, told her, "Don't call here no more," before hanging up.

The words echoed in Mara's mind, each a dagger to her already fragile heart. The realization that Mike had been unfaithful and had spent the night with other women shattered her. Her world spun as the full weight of his betrayal crashed down on her. The physical and emotional pain she felt was overwhelming, almost paralyzing.

Tears streamed down her face as she stood there, unable to move with her heart breaking into pieces. The man she had loved and trusted had not only betrayed her but did so with a callous disregard for her feelings. Each moment of infidelity, each lie, and each disappearance now had a new, more painful context. The depth of his addiction and the extent of his betrayal became painfully clear.

In the following weeks, Mara replayed that phone call in her mind, haunted by the casual cruelty in Mike's voice and the laughter she had heard in the background. She grappled with the intense pain of infidelity, feeling as though a part of her had been torn away. Despite trying hard to rid herself of the thought, it kept ringing in her mind and would go away. The reality of his betrayal was a heavy burden that she struggled to carry as she navigated the shattered remnants of their relationship.

This painful chapter in Mara's life highlights the risks of trusting the wrong people and the hurt from betrayal. Her experience shows how crucial it is to find comfort and strength in God instead of relying on imperfect humans. Psalm 34:18

reassures us, "The Lord is close to the brokenhearted and saves those who are crushed in spirit."

Mike's addiction led him to a life in and out of jail. His habit was so severe that he would steal Mara's belongings, even gifts given to her by family members, and pawn them for drug money. Despite these betrayals, Mara remained entangled in the toxic relationship, hoping for a change that never came.

When Mike was home and not in jail, his behavior was nothing short of a nightmare for Mara. He was extremely emotionally and verbally abusive, cheating on her and subjecting her to relentless verbal, emotional, and physical torment. Verbal and emotional abuse can cause deep wounds and lingering pain, leaving scars that are not visible but are profoundly damaging.

Mara's relationship with Mike was bombarded with cruel, cursed words that chipped away at her self-worth and sense of safety. She endured the humiliation of being spat on in the face, a degrading act that left her feeling worthless and dehumanized.

The abuse did not stop there. On several occasions, Mike tore up her car and shattered her windows. His violent outbursts completely eroded the sense of safety and stability she once craved.

Adding to her torment, Mike twisted the Bible against her, manipulating its words to paint himself as righteous and Mara as the sinner. He weaponized her faith, using it to control and demean her further. "You are a red flag," he would sneer. "No man will ever want you because of your past relationships and all your kids." These words cut deep, attacking the core of her self-worth and fueling her insecurities.

He would tell her she could not find another relationship again, manipulating her beliefs to keep her trapped in the cycle of abuse. This relentless abuse eroded her confidence and left her feeling isolated and unworthy of love. Mara did not want to believe Mike's cruel accusations but hearing them over and over made them hard to ignore.

The constant barrage of abuse and manipulation wore her down. This made her wonder if Mike truly loved her or was just bent on ruining her life and making her miserable. Deep down, she knew she deserved better, yet the repeated assaults on her self-esteem made her doubt her worth and her ability to find happiness elsewhere. This doubt perhaps explained why she kept letting him come back, even after his repeated infidelities and relentless abuse.

Mara often found herself questioning her sanity within her relationship. Whenever she voiced her needs—whether it was asking for more time, help with the kids, or emotional support—Mike's reaction left her feeling like she was the problem. This pattern of emotional manipulation was subtle at first but grew more apparent as time passed. Each time Mara gathered the courage to speak up, Mike's response was a calculated mix of guilt, blame, and deflection. If she requested time for herself or help with the children, he twisted the situation to make her feel selfish or demanding.

When Mara's patience ran thin and she contemplated leaving, the manipulation escalated. Mike's tone shifted to desperation. He made declarations like, "If you leave me, I will have nothing left," or worse, he threatened self-harm. These threats planted seeds of fear and responsibility in Mara's heart, making her feel as if she alone held the key to his survival. The weight of it all was crushing.

When Mara tried to assert her independence, she faced a whirlwind of emotional tactics designed to keep her tethered. Every time she took a step toward freedom, an invisible force pulled her back—sometimes with guilt, sometimes with anger, and often with subtle manipulation.

Her internal battle became relentless. It was exhausting, like walking on eggshells—where every word she spoke had to be measured carefully, every glance calculated, and every action tiptoed around, lest she trigger a sudden outburst or disappointment. She never knew when a simple question or a small request might ignite a storm, leaving her scrambling to pick up the shattered pieces of peace.

It was constant tension, as if the ground beneath her was fragile and unpredictable. One misstep could send everything crashing down, so she learned to hold her breath and tread lightly, hiding her true feelings behind a mask of calm.

This was Mara's daily reality: a tightrope walk between wanting to live authentically and fearing the consequences of doing so.

Have you ever felt like you are constantly to blame in your relationships? Do you find yourself questioning your own feelings, wondering, "Am I being too sensitive?" or "Am I just overreacting?" These are common experiences for people who are dealing with gaslighting and manipulation. The sad reality is that many people do not even realize it is happening until the damage has already been done.

Gaslighting and manipulation can leave you feeling confused, isolated, and powerless. For so long, she questioned herself, wondering if her reality was worth acknowledging. She convinced herself that staying silent was easier—that her voice did not matter. But what if she had known the truth? What if

Mara had understood, deep down, that her emotions deserved space and that her experiences were real, no matter who tried to dismiss or diminish them?

The ongoing pain and suffering she endured were overwhelming, a heavy burden she struggled to bear alone. This was never easy for her, but she did not know what else to do other than carry her burdens. The destructive cycle of abuse and the insidious ways it can trap even the strongest of spirits are indescribable.

When Mara got her associate's degree, the day that should have been filled with pride and joy turned into a nightmare. Mike chased her through the hotel, trying to fight her, cursing and yelling. Trembling and desperate to avoid his wrath, Mara was forced to hide by the front desk in a bathroom, hoping to make it to her graduation ceremony unscathed. One would wonder what kind of couple they were.

He was never happy about her accomplishments, always trying to tarnish her special moments. He never congratulated her, instead ensuring that what should have been joyous occasions were marred by his anger and jealousy. Was he insecure or unhappy that he could not measure up to her achievements?

Mike promised not to act up when she earned her bachelor's degree, and he kept his word during the ceremony. But on the drive home, his true nature resurfaced. He began throwing CDs Mara was listening to out the window, making it hard for her to concentrate on driving. He yelled and cursed at her in front of their children, shattering any semblance of peace.

Deep down, Mara knew this was the moment she had to escape. She prayed to the Lord for guidance and strength. She was done. She had fallen out of love with Mike and wanted to leave, but she did not want to do it in a way that would be hard on the kids. She sought the Lord's guidance in planning her exit, determined to create a better life for herself and her children.

The weight of the abuse and the constant turmoil had become unbearable. Mara's resolve hardened as she prayed, asking for courage and wisdom to break free from the toxic relationship.

The emotional and psychological toll of the abuse had not only affected her but also left deep scars on her children. She never wanted them to have the ugly childhood she experienced. As she planned her escape, she clung to her faith, finding solace in Psalm 46:1: "God is our refuge and strength, A very present help in trouble."

Months later, the tension in the house reached a breaking point once again. Mike was yelling and cursing, trying to come at her. Fear surged through Mara as she grabbed her keys and ran to the car. The kids were still inside, and her heart pounded with urgency.

Mara had been preparing for this moment in secret. She had given her children a cell phone for emergencies, saved $5,000 in the bank, and discreetly searched for housing. She had not yet found a place despite attending a few house viewings. But now, the urgency of the situation demanded immediate action.

She quickly got into her car, and drove a short distance away. With her heart racing, she called her children on the cell phone she had provided them.

"Kids!" She called out urgently over the phone. "Get ready to run halfway down the street when I give you the signal!"

Her voice trembled with both fear and determination as she watched Mike closely. The kids were on the phone with her, their whispers urgent and full of anticipation. Mara sat parked at the bottom of the street, her eyes fixed on the patio where Mike usually stepped out.

He had not taken a smoke break yet, and she knew she had to act quickly before he caught on to her plan.

Suddenly, Mara saw her opening. Mike finally took a smoke break, giving her the chance she needed. Without hesitation, Mara drove back to the front of the house, knowing her children were ready and waiting.

"Kids!" she suddenly shouted as she pulled up in front of the house. "Come out to the front door! Bring the bags!"

The children, already prepared for this moment, dashed out with their bags and jumped into the car. Mara's hands shook as she gripped the steering wheel, adrenaline coursing through her veins. In that critical moment, she knew she had to act swiftly.

Ignoring Mike's shouts and curses echoing behind her, Mara pressed the gas pedal and sped off, leaving their turbulent past behind in a cloud of dust. She did not look back, driving toward a future of safety and hope.

In that moment, she felt the presence of the Lord guiding her, finally giving her the strength to break free. And she indeed broke free. Oftentimes, what it takes to break free from whatever is limiting us is fierce courage and bravery to step out of our comfort zone into the unknown future while we trust God for direction. This action requires facing our fears and doubts head-on and taking bold actions while trusting God to guide us.

This will not always be easy, especially as we must not have it all figured out. With God in our boat, we can be sure we will sail safely to the other side. Trusting God for direction gives us the courage to take the first step, then the next, even when we are unsure of where we are headed.

For those still struggling, refuge and support are available. The National Domestic Violence Hotline can be reached at 1-800-799-7233 or via text by texting START to 88788.

God did not intend for us to be joined together with unhealed individuals to hurt each other. His divine plan for marriage involves bringing together two people who have allowed Him to heal their wounds and guide their union.

The Bible tells us in Mark 10:9 , "What therefore God hath joined together, let not man put asunder." This verse emphasizes the sanctity and permanence of marriages that God ordained.

When we seek relationships with the ultimate goal of marriage under God's guidance, we can experience His true and transformative love. This love is free from manipulation, unhealthy communication, infidelity, and anger. Instead, it offers a foundation of mutual respect, genuine connection, and spiritual unity.

As it says in 1 Peter 3:3-4, "Let your beauty not come from outward adornment, such as braided hair or the wearing of gold jewelry or fine clothes. Instead, let it be the inner beauty of a gentle and quiet spirit, which is of great worth in God's sight."

This reminds us that true beauty and worth don't come from what we wear or how we look, but from having a heart that seeks to honor God.

When Mara placed her hope in Mike's change, she was unknowingly trusting in him more than in God. The Bible warns us in Jeremiah 17:5: "Cursed is the one who trusts in human beings, who relies on their own strength and whose heart turns away from the Lord."

In Exodus 20:3, God commands, "You shall have no other gods before me." By putting her trust in Mike, Mara was placing him in a position that only God should hold, and this led to her ongoing struggle and pain.

Let us not dishonor the sanctity of relationships or marriage through lust or misplaced desires. Instead, we should seek God's grace to heal and unite hearts in His perfect timing.

In marriage or any relationship, remember: it is not the responsibility of one person to fulfill all your emotional or spiritual needs alone. God must be the foundation for both. Ecclesiastes 4:12 states: *"And if one prevail against him, two shall withstand him; and a threefold cord is not quickly broken."*

God is that third cord. Without Him, even the strongest bond will eventually fray.

True peace and contentment come from a relationship with Christ, the source of perfect love. When we allow Him to fill us, we are able to love and be loved in a way that brings life and glorifies Him.

Some can fall in love with the potential we see in others, ignoring t Mara eventually realized that fulfillment doesn't come from another person—it comes from God. When we seek Him first, He meets our needs in ways no human ever could. he warning signs that God presents to us.

Psalm 118:8, advises, "It is better to take refuge in the Lord than to put confidence in man." Mara's repeated returns to an abusive situation illustrate the struggle some face when they prioritize human relationships over their relationship with God.

Mara had to learn the critical importance of acknowledging God in all her ways, especially when making life-altering decisions, such as choosing relationships.

When Mara pursued her own desires without seeking God's guidance, she ended up in unhealthy and abusive relationships. This led to pain and heartache, which could have been avoided if she had sought God's will instead of relying solely on her own understanding.

Mara's story reminds us that disregarding God's signs and following our own desires can lead to heartache and turmoil. Psalm 37:4 encourages us with the truth that when we delight in the Lord, He aligns our desires with His will.

The verse says, "Delight thyself also in the Lord; and He will give thee the desires of thy heart." This assures us that when we place our trust in God, He not only knows our deepest longings but also provides for them in ways that lead to abundant life.

Let us place our full trust in Him, knowing He will lead us to the desires that align with His perfect will.

TRUST IN THE LORD WITH ALL THINE HEART; AND LEAN NOT UNTO THINE OWN UNDERSTANDING.
IN ALL THY WAYS ACKNOWLEDGE HIM, AND HE SHALL DIRECT THY PATHS.

PROVERBS 3:5-6 KJV

Effects of Codependency and Enabling

After Mara left Mike, she continued to meet him, giving him money to cover his hotel stays and buying him food, despite the years of separation. Mara felt guilty for not doing more. She was convinced that, somehow, it was her responsibility to keep him afloat. She could not shake the belief that withholding her help would make her heartless, even though deep down, she knew her continued support was only enabling his behavior.

This pattern became a source of inner conflict for Mara. She knew she was not helping Mike heal or change, but her fear of what would happen if she stopped kept her locked in this cycle.

Mara's struggle was not only with Mike but with herself. She had to confront the painful reality that by continuing to "help," she was only prolonging his suffering—and her own.

The journey of healing would require Mara to confront her own patterns of codependency and enabling.

Each time Mara intervened to keep the peace or protect their family, she sent the message that his actions did not have real consequences. He never had to face the full weight of his choices, and so he had no real motivation to change.

As a result, he remained in denial about the seriousness of his actions, knowing that Mara would always step in to fix things or soften the blow. This created a toxic dynamic that allowed his behavior to worsen over time.

The effect of Mara's enabling was not just on Mike either. It spilled over into their children, who witnessed the dysfunction and learned unhealthy patterns of love, boundaries, and conflict resolution. The very behavior she hoped to shield them from became part of their reality, as they saw their mother sacrifice herself emotionally for someone who continued to harm them all.

Mara had to understand that real love sometimes means stepping back and allowing someone to face the consequences of their actions, trusting that God could manage what she could not. Only then could true healing begin for both.

Mara had to surrender Mike to the Lord—she was not responsible for his salvation, and she had to realize that only the Lord could save him. Mara needed to release control and stop living in fear of what might happen to Mike or what he might do, trusting that as long as he had Mara to depend on, he might continue down his path. But by letting go and trusting God, she could find peace.

Reflection:

Can you relate to staying with someone who you know is not only hurting you but also themselves? Have you found yourself in a relationship where, despite the pain and chaos, you keep going back or letting them back in—only to watch the same hurtful patterns play out again? You've carried the weight of loving someone battling addiction, dishonesty, or betrayal, holding on to hope that things will change—only to find yourself trapped in a cycle of enabling their behavior.

It is difficult to be torn between the desire to help and the fear of abandonment or rejection. You might have prayed for change, fought to hold things together, or even sacrificed your own well-being for the sake of the relationship. Yet, no matter how much you give, the same destructive behaviors continue to hurt you and the people you care about.

Were there moments when you recognized opportunities for change but could not take them—held back by fear, guilt, or the hope that things might somehow improve? How do you cope when love binds you to someone who repeatedly causes pain, making the cycle feel impossible to escape?

If you have ever experienced this kind of struggle, you are not alone. Many people find themselves in this challenging place, caught between love and the desire for healing. While the journey is difficult, there is hope for growth and transformation for everyone involved.

With the strength found in Christ, you can break free from the cycle of enabling and dependency. Through faith and support, you can begin to heal and find a path toward healthier relationships and genuine change.

Remember, it is never too late to seek help, embrace accountability, and trust in the Lord's plan for your life.

When we acknowledge God in all our ways, we submit our decisions to Him, allowing Him to guide us toward healthy and life-giving relationships.

> *TRUST IN THE LORD WITH ALL THINE HEART; AND LEAN NOT UNTO THINE OWN UNDERSTANDING.*
> *IN ALL THY WAYS ACKNOWLEDGE HIM, AND HE SHALL DIRECT THY PATHS.*
>
> *PROVERBS 3:5-6 KJV*

The Devasting Effects of Trauma

Trauma is a deeply distressing or disturbing experience that overwhelms an individual's ability to cope. It can result from events or situations that are shocking, harmful, or life-threatening. Trauma affects people emotionally, mentally, and sometimes physically, and it can have long-lasting effects on how a person feels, thinks, and behaves.

For years, Mara navigated life as though she was swimming against a powerful current, struggling against unseen forces of functional depression, anxiety, and post-traumatic stress disorder (PTSD). Her days were marked by a constant battle with fear and an obsessive need for control, leading her to feel overwhelmed and unable to find peace in her circumstances. The unpredictability and chaos of her childhood had left her craving a sense of order and control, but the effort to maintain this control often left her exhausted and isolated.

As a single parent, she had a lot of worries concerning her life and those of her children. She was afraid she would not be able to provide for her children. Somehow, she feared she would fail them as a mother, and they would no longer love her.

She was afraid they would experience what she had gone through. She feared what the future held for her and her children. Everything triggered her and brought panic to her.

Panic attacks were common for Mara, a haunting reminder of the traumatic childhood and relationships that had plagued her life.

The suffocating fear and overwhelming sense of doom were not new sensations but resurfacing old demons triggered by memories she could never fully escape.

The emotional and psychological turmoil she faced as a child never truly faded; instead, it lingered in the shadows of her mind, waiting to resurface in moments of vulnerability.

The panic attacks were more than just episodes of intense fear; they were the echoes of her past, the unresolved pain and fear that had become a part of her.

Every time one hit, it was as if she was back in those moments of terror and helplessness, reliving the traumas that had shaped her life. The sensation of losing control, overwhelmed by a fear she could not name, was unbearable, yet all too familiar.

One night, after yet another tense phone call with Mike accusing Mara of keeping the kids away from him, Mara suddenly awoke.

Once again, the conversation had been an unhealthy interaction, triggering her deeply. Her chest tightened as if an invisible weight were pressing down on her. Gasping for air, she struggled to breathe, each inhale a desperate attempt to claw her way out of a suffocating fog.

Her heart pounded in her ears, drowning out all other sounds. For a moment, she thought she might be dying. Her mind raced with fear and confusion.

The panic attack seized her with a ferocity that left her trembling. Her entire body was caught in the throes of a terror she could not name. It felt like being trapped in a dark, endless tunnel, with no light at the end. She sat up in bed, clutching her chest, trying to ground herself, but the room seemed to blur around her.

Her thoughts spun in a chaotic whirl, making it impossible to think clearly. The walls of her bedroom, once familiar and safe, now felt like they were closing in on her.

As the minutes ticked by, Mara's breathing gradually steadied, though the aftershocks of fear continued to rattle her. Finally, when she could not hold it in any longer, Mara would let out a loud, belching scream. Her children, though startled at first, became used to these outbursts, never really questioning them. It happened many times, especially after a disturbing interaction or increased stress, worry, and fear.

The panic attacks would come out of nowhere, like a wave crashing over her. The fear and anxiety she kept bottled up would erupt, and the only way she could find release was through a sudden, loud outburst.

When you are in a situation that echoes a deep fear or unresolved issue from a traumatic experience, it can manifest unexpectedly, pulling you back into that moment of terror or pain, even if the present situation is not the same.

For Mara, the stress of interacting with Mike, who often manipulated, verbally abused, and accused her, frequently yelling, cursing, and criticizing her, tapped into old wounds from her past.

These encounters brought back memories of other times when she felt powerless, trapped, and afraid. It is a reminder that trauma can linger beneath the surface, influencing reactions and emotions in ways that are not always easy to understand or control.

Depression, which had first crept into her life unnoticed, was now an ever-present companion. It was not just sadness; it was a pervasive heaviness that clung to her, making even the simplest tasks seem daunting. Days blended into one another, and the thought of facing the world felt like an overwhelming challenge. Staring at the ceiling from her bed, Mara often felt trapped, unable to escape the oppressive weight of her own mind.

Sometimes, Mara would experience suicidal ideations, further intensifying the battle within her mental and emotional well-being. For Mara, these moments often occurred late at night when the world was quiet, and her mind had no distractions. She might find herself thinking, "Maybe everyone would be better off without me," or "I just want the pain to stop." At first, she had dismissed her feelings as mere exhaustion or stress. But over time, the darkness grew stronger, its grip tightening around her, pulling her deeper into its depths. She tried to hide her struggles and push through, but the effort left her feeling increasingly isolated.

These thoughts would often feel intrusive and persistent, making it difficult for her to find peace. Recognizing these thoughts as signs of crisis, however, is an essential step toward seeking help and support. If you have these thoughts, reach out and talk to someone today. There is a national suicide prevention number, 988, that you can text or call 24/7 to receive support from trained counselors who are ready to listen and help.

It was a daily battle and relentless struggle to keep the darkness at bay. There were days when the fog lifted, allowing her to see the world in brighter hues. Yet, there were also days when the darkness returned with a vengeance, dragging her back into its shadowy embrace.

Mara knew she was not alone in this struggle. Many people suffer in silence, their pain invisible and often undiagnosed. Depression could go unnoticed for years, making its victims feel as though they were losing their grip on reality.

Mara would cook all the food for Thanksgiving and Christmas, going above and beyond to please everyone. She took pride in preparing meals for others because she liked seeing them happy.

Mara often felt overwhelmed by the presence of so many people. Even while she was busy cooking, Mara struggled with an intense need to retreat from social interactions. After the meal, while everyone enjoyed each other's company, Mara would retreat to her bed, seeking solitude.

She never experienced the joy she hoped for during the holidays and often felt sad and disengaged. With limited family around and mostly just her kids with her and a few family members, she spent much of the time alone in her efforts to make the holidays special, but it never seemed to bring her the happiness she desired.

Mara's experience during the holidays highlights the deep sadness and lack of motivation that often accompanies depression. While others might look forward to festive gatherings and joyful moments, for Mara, the holidays became a time of emotional exhaustion and isolation. Even with her best efforts to make the season special for her children and the few family members around, it often felt like an impossible task.

Depression can sap one's ability to feel motivated, even for things that once brought happiness. Tasks like showering, getting dressed, or cleaning the house can feel like monumental efforts. It wasn't that Mara didn't want to care for herself or her home—she did. But the weight of depression made even the smallest tasks feel impossible.

For many people struggling with depression, this lack of motivation is not a sign of laziness or failure, but rather a symptom of the mental and emotional burdens they carry. Depression can make it difficult to find the energy or desire to engage in things that typically bring joy.

Like Mara, you might go out of your way to please everyone around you, believing that by giving them whatever they want, you will earn their love. Despite your efforts, you may still feel unfulfilled and joyless.

You have felt a sudden wave of sadness, with no clear reason behind it. You may often find yourself lost in thought, replaying painful memories over and over, as if reliving the hurt can somehow change what happened.

Do you ever notice that you are constantly overthinking and feeling anxious about everything? It is like there is always something on your mind—a persistent fear that never leaves.

That relentless worry is often a response to trauma, making it hard to trust others, even when you try to convince yourself otherwise.

You have seen how your pain spills over onto those around you, causing stress and tension. You have noticed yourself snapping at your children, restricting their freedom out of fear, or being overprotective to the point of smothering them.

When you speak, do you sometimes hear the voice of your mother, father, or another person who hurt you? Does that realization fill you with self-loathing?

Have you noticed your children or others around you acting in ways that remind you of your abuser? Does it trigger a reaction in you that feels beyond your control?

Have you ever experienced intrusive thoughts that seem to come out of nowhere, taking over your mind? These thoughts are involuntary thoughts that will pop out of nowhere and stay in your mind. They come when you do not want to have such thoughts, and you cannot shake them off. They take over your mind and become distressing. These thoughts can make you uncomfortable and disturbed, even though they do not reflect reality or your true intentions.

Do you find yourself battling feelings of guilt, inadequacy, and worthlessness, fearing that you are not good enough to handle life's demands? Each day, do you wake up bracing for the worst, convinced that disaster is just around the corner? You have told yourself that you are simply preparing for disappointment, but you might be reacting from a place of deep pain.

The headaches, uneasiness, stomach pains, and heart palpitations you experience when you are reminded of the past are not just random—they are your body's way of telling you something is unresolved. These symptoms are more than just physical discomfort; they are echoes of trauma that should not be ignored. Until you address and heal from these past wounds, they will continue to influence your future, leading to unnecessary stress and difficulty finding rest, regardless of the many blessings and good things God has provided.

If any of this resonates with you, know that you are not alone. These experiences are common among those who have faced trauma and understanding them is the first step toward healing. Recognizing these patterns can help you break free from the cycle and begin to heal the wounds that still affect your life today.

Your silent struggles and heartfelt desires for a lasting solution have not gone unnoticed. God has guided you to this book for a reason, and it is here to help you embark on a journey toward healing from trauma.

As you begin this journey, remember that healing is a continuous process of growth and self-discovery. Pretending everything is fine while hiding your struggles won't lead to true restoration. The Lord offers a path to genuine healing, reminding us through His Word that we are deeply loved, valued, and never alone.

It's okay if trusting others feels impossible right now—especially after experiencing so much betrayal, disappointment, or harm. Opening up can feel terrifying when the world has taught you to guard your heart. But healing doesn't happen all at once.

>Take one small step at a time.
>Allow the process to unfold with grace.
>Let hope walk with you, even if it's quiet at first.

You don't need to have it all figured out. You just need the courage to begin again—and the faith that you won't always be where you are now.

While prayer is a powerful tool for believers, it is also important to seek professional help if you are experiencing symptoms of trauma, anxiety, depression, or PTSD. Therapy and counseling are valuable resources that God can use to bring healing. Mental health professionals are trained to provide guidance and support, and their work can be a means through which God offers wisdom and care. Just as we seek medical help for physical ailments, it is equally important to seek support for mental and emotional health.

Amid her darkest moments, Mara turned to her faith as a source of strength. She sought comfort in Bible verses, finding comfort in passages like The **LORD** is nigh unto them that are of a broken heart; and saveth such as be of a contrite spirit." — Psalm 34:18.

Through prayer and meditation on the Word of God, Mara began to experience a sense of peace and renewal. The journey to healing was gradual, but with each step, she felt the weight of her suffering lift, replaced by the light of Christ's love. In her quiet moments, she would often repeat Scripture aloud, holding tightly to God's promises.

"My grace is sufficient for thee: for my strength is made perfect in weakness." — **2 Corinthians 12:9.**

Mara clung to those words, believing that even in her lowest moments, God's strength would sustain her. She also cried out for the kind of peace only God could give.

"And the peace of God, which passeth all understanding, shall keep your hearts and minds through Christ Jesus." — Philippians 4:7. KJV.

These verses became her anchor, helping her release fear and receive the comfort only the Lord could provide—not the world's temporary peace, but the lasting peace of Christ.

The Struggle to Move Forward

After Mara's relationship with Mike ended, the aftermath of trauma and abuse was debilitating. Navigating life as a parent and attempting to move forward after years of trauma left her in constant fear. She would wake up in the middle of the night, plagued with deep anxiety and terror, fearing that Mike would come for her.

In these moments of overwhelming fear, she would pack up her kids and sleep in parking lots, opting for places like QuikTrip, McDonald's, and Home Depot where cameras provided a semblance of safety. She outfitted her house with cameras inside and out, but Mara trusted no one by this time.

Mike showed up at her door a few times, trying to get in. Mara would call the police, and Mike would be escorted off the premises. He would tell Mara she was not allowed to be with anyone else and would speak against the promises God had made to her. Mike's relentless pursuit and threats made her question whether his words could stop the promises of God.

But can a mere mortal's words stop God's promises? Of course not! She felt overwhelmed by his continuous harassment, afraid for her life as he showed up at her jobs and other places she frequented. At this point, she knew her life was in danger, and she needed to act fast before it was too late.

Despite getting restraining orders multiple times, Mike would be released the next day, undeterred. The fear of leaving an abusive situation is overwhelming. Mara's heart raced every time she heard a noise at night, and she lived in constant fear of Mike's return. This fear was not just emotional; it was physical and palpable. It affected her sleep, her ability to function daily, and her sense of security.

The thought of Mike's retaliation if she left kept her trapped. It is a fear many abused women know too well, and it is a fear that society often underestimates. People frequently say, "If the relationship is abusive, why not walk away?" Yes, that is the best thing to do, but most times, the fear of the aftermath of that decision is what keeps many stuck in abusive relationships like it was with Mara. But the onlookers never get to understand it.

The emotional toll of domestic abuse is profound. Mara felt a tangled mix of terror, guilt, and confusion. She had once loved Mike, the thought of leaving him for good brought a strange sense of loss—despite knowing deep down it was the right decision.

It's hard to explain to anyone who hasn't lived it: the fear of not being able to manage alone, the lack of income, no family support, and the shame or fear that stops you from involving loved ones. Mara feared for her children's safety and her own life. Every decision she made was weighed against the possible consequences. She lived in constant calculation, where survival meant anticipating danger at every turn.

Domestic abuse is a grave issue, and some support systems often fall short of providing the protection needed for women trying to leave abusive situations.

For Mara, the only one who consistently promised to protect her was her Lord and Savior. Mara would constantly lean on Psalm 91 and other comforting verses from the Psalms, reminding herself of God's promises of protection and strength. These scriptures became her anchor, especially in moments of fear or uncertainty.

> HE THAT DWELLETH IN THE SECRET PLACE OF THE MOST HIGH SHALL ABIDE UNDER THE SHADOW OF THE ALMIGHTY. I WILL SAY OF THE LORD, HE IS MY REFUGE AND MY FORTRESS: MY GOD; IN HIM WILL I TRUST.
>
> PSALM 91:1-2 KJV

This passage, along with others, helped Mara feel shielded by God's presence, reminding her that she did not have to face her struggles alone. Each time she repeated these promises, her heart filled with a renewed sense of courage and peace. Mara's trust in God's protection became a foundation for her boundaries, resilience, and healing, empowering her to make choices that honored her well-being and reflected her faith in God's enduring care.

In Mara's journey, she finally reached a point where she felt compelled to set a firm boundary with Mike. After his last threatening call, Mara made it clear that if he continued to cross this line, she would no longer communicate with him. True to her word, when he disregarded her boundary and resorted to manipulation, Mara cut off all contact. She left the door open only for their children to reach him if needed but otherwise stopped all communication, maintaining a firm stance.

For Mara, this was not only an act of self-protection but a step toward breaking the cycle of codependency that had held her back. Setting and following through on this boundary allowed her to reclaim her peace and distance herself from the chaos he brought into her life.

It also reinforced the lesson for her children: boundaries are essential for self-respect and well-being. Mara encouraged her children to set their own boundaries if they ever felt threatened or disrespected, knowing that boundaries become more powerful when consistently upheld.

When Mara heard Mike raising his voice or acting disrespectfully on the phone, she intervened immediately, taking the phone if necessary and firmly stating, "This is Mike's choice, but respect is required."

Over time, her children saw that enforcing boundaries was not just about setting them but about consistently following through. She finally moved, stopped giving Mike her new address and phone numbers and ceased telling him where she worked. She cut off all contact with him. This was an essential step to moving forward and attempting to heal.

Setting boundaries is a vital step in exercising wise stewardship over the heart and fostering respect, healing, and inner peace. As Proverbs 4:23 KJV. instructs, **"Keep thy heart with all diligence; for out of it are the issues of life."** In other words, we are called to guard our hearts carefully. By courageously drawing the line with Mike and standing firm,

Mara reclaimed her God-given voice, modeled healthy boundaries for her children, and began to break free from cycles of manipulation and codependency—trusting God to be her ultimate protector throughout the process.

Setting and upholding boundaries takes strength, especially when it means walking away from familiar but unhealthy patterns. However, as Mara's experience shows, every step we take toward enforcing boundaries brings us closer to healthier, more respectful relationships. By choosing respect for yourself, you pave the way for a life rooted in self-worth, resilience, and emotional freedom.

And yet, in all the confusion, she taught her children not to harbor hatred toward Mike. She helped them understand that addiction is a disease. This helped restructure the children's minds, so they did not look at Mike with disdain. It might be difficult, but it is for the children's good.

Through years of studying addiction, trauma, and their long-term effects, Mara gained profound insights into how childhood experiences and family dynamics shape a person's behavior and relationships.

With this deeper understanding, she came to forgive Mike—not because what happened was excusable, but because she recognized how their shared trauma and the dysfunction, they both grew up in had kept their relationship from ever being truly healthy or divinely ordained by God.

Mara struggled with relinquishing control, anger, fear of rejection, and vulnerability and prioritized her children's well-being over the relationship. Mike, too, struggled with his own trauma and how to handle his emotions, often turning to drugs to numb his pain, which further exacerbated their issues.

However, through the power of prayer and God's healing, Mike has experienced transformation. He has found freedom from his past struggles with addictions and is now working to rebuild his relationships. Just like Mara's, Mike's life is a testimony to how the healing power of God can work in our lives. He found true redemption and grace—a quiet testament to the power of faith and the transformation that unfolds when a soul yields to God's will.

THAT YE PUT AWAY, AS CONCERNING YOUR FORMER MANNER OF LIFE, THE OLD MAN, THAT WAXETH CORRUPT AFTER THE LUSTS OF DECEIT; AND THAT YE BE RENEWED IN THE SPIRIT OF YOUR MIND, AND PUT ON THE NEW MAN, THAT AFTER GOD HATH BEEN CREATED IN RIGHTEOUSNESS AND HOLINESS OF TRUTH.
EPHESIANS 4:22-24

What was Mara supposed to do with all this pain and feelings of being lost, rejected, unloved, and afraid? Old doubts crept back in, and with them, an urge to retreat into her familiar comfort zone—seeking out the same kinds of relationships she had always known, even if they did not bring her true happiness.

Remember not the Former Things

In the aftermath of her breakup with Mike. The scars of her past ran deep, rooted in relationships that only seemed to amplify her sense of rejection, loss, and loneliness. One year after the breakup, Mara reconnected with good old Lou through Facebook. He said he was recently divorced, so they hooked back up. It was a rebound relationship for both.

In her vulnerable state, it felt comforting to return to something familiar, but it raised a deeper question: Was this truly God's will, or was she returning to what He had already called her away from?

The compliments, the warm attention, the sense of being wanted—these felt like a balm to her aching heart. But even as Mara felt herself slipping back into old patterns, part of her wondered if she was just returning to a place that might feel familiar but would ultimately keep her trapped.

Once, they spent an entire day together. It was all good until Mara said it was time for her to go.

"No," Lou said, "stay longer."

"I cannot," Mara told him. "I must get home to my kids. I have work and school." Lou was not trying to hear it.

"I need you here with me," he said, but instead of sounding like he cared, his voice strained with anger. Lou's response turned from pleading to a demand. Mara went home, and from that day on, Lou became a bit more distant, and his calls came less frequently. The affection seemed conditional, and Mara felt the familiar sting of someone pulling away.

Mara needed to know if Lou's love was true. Desperate for love, Mara turned elsewhere for answers.

And flashed on her phone with a tempting offer: "Want to know how he feels about you? Call now." She was curious, and before she knew it, she was dialing a psychic.

The psychic's words were comforting, telling Mara exactly what she wanted to hear: "He cares about you. He is just busy." Mara latched onto this message, filling the silence with promises the psychic made—promises Lou never kept. Seeking psychics became an addiction and lifeline to the fantasy to which she was clinging to. Each call chipped away at her doubt, even as the truth was in plain sight: Lou was drifting away.

Mara's coworker, V, saw what was happening and tried to warn her. "Stop listening to those psychics," V told her. "They are just out to make money by leading you into dark places." But Mara was not ready to listen. She was hurt and angry, particularly with God, who she felt was ignoring her pain. The idea of Bible studies and prayer groups seemed pointless, a reminder of a God she felt had been silent too long.

V had invited Mara to join a Bible study group several times, but each time, Mara declined.

But was God truly silent, or had Mara been ignoring the signs He had been sending? Often, God answers our prayers in ways we do not expect, and when His answers do not align with our desires, it is easy to overlook them.

Lou remained distant despite what the psychics said. Were they betraying her? Was Lou truly rejecting her again? Mara prayed to God for a husband, and she could have sworn He said He would bring her one. But was he even listening now? She had so many questions and so few answers.

One day, Mara's oldest daughter told her she had seen Lou at the mall and hugged up on another girl. But Mara did not want to believe it. "Her daughter is just making it up," she thought. Mara knew that none of her kids liked Lou because of how he treated her, so she believed it was not true. What a way to console herself! Eventually, Mara confronted him, and Lou said it was not true.

A few weeks later, Lou posted a picture on Facebook with the caption, "My first love." It was a picture of a female, but it was not Mara. The younger woman in her twenties was the lady Mara's daughter had mentioned to her and Mara had dismissed. Lou soon deleted the photo, but Mara had already seen it, and the damage had been done. She was hurt and filled with regrets, wishing she had listened to her daughter earlier rather than convinced herself that Lou loved her.

Mara called Lou multiple times, but he did not answer until the next day. That is when he told her that the person she saw in the picture was his new girl.

The truth finally came out: Lou was still a player. He lied to Mara and strung her along while he messed around with another woman. On June 28, 2015, the relationship ended. Lou had left Mara for another younger woman, breaking her heart into pieces.

Mara's journey reveals how unresolved pain, and unhealed trauma can twist our sense of self-worth, often leading us to seek comfort in places that ultimately leave us feeling even more empty. She was reaching for healing in her own way, but instead, it led to deeper entanglements and a widening distance from the love she so deeply needed.

Another powerful reminder comes from Isaiah 43:18-19, which says, "Remember ye not the former things, neither consider the things of old. Behold, I will do a new thing; now it shall spring forth; shall ye not know it? I will even make a way in the wilderness, and rivers in the desert."

God calls His children not to dwell on the past but to trust in the new things He wants to do in their lives. By revisiting a relationship marked by instability and brokenness, Mara risked stepping out of alignment with the fresh path God was preparing for her.

Mara's reconnection with Lou highlights a deeper truth: recognizing God's will requires prayerful discernment, quiet trust, and surrendered hearts. In times of emotional strain or inner conflict, it's easy to reach for what feels familiar or immediately comforting. But it is in moments like this—when we are weary, uncertain, or aching—that we must stay grounded in God's truth.

The enemy, Satan, is always watching for these cracks in our armor. As Scripture warns: *"Be sober-minded; be watchful. Your adversary the devil prowls around like a roaring lion, seeking someone to devour"* 1 Peter 5:8 ESV.

He rarely shows up with obvious destruction. Instead, he whispers lies into our vulnerable places, twisting our insecurities into chains. What feels like a way out may actually lead us further from God's presence.

Mara's journey is a reminder that discernment does not come from impulse or emotion but from seeking God first. Not every opportunity is a divine invitation. The real battle often takes place in the quiet of our hearts—where faith is tested and decisions are made.

Crying Out in the Wilderness

Mara felt defeated and rejected once again. Lou had chosen this younger female over her, adding another layer to her fears of rejection and abandonment. That was it for Mara. She let out a loud, heart-wrenching scream of pain, screaming "Noooo!" as The anguish in her voice echoed through the room.

She lay on the floor, balled up like a fetus, crying her eyes out. "Lord, why? Why would You let him hurt me like this if You love me?" she cried out, her voice breaking. The pain in her heart was unbearable, and the questions swirled in her mind. She had trusted God and sought His comfort, but now, all she felt was the sting of betrayal.

Satan wasted no time poking at Mara in her time of vulnerability. He egged on the lies of her unworthiness, making her emotional pain match the physical discomfort she felt at the same time. "You are not worthy of marriage; you are a red flag." This is what Satan said. "God does not keep His word" is what the liar spoke to her.

Mara felt defeated and wanted to take her life. This was just the latest in a long line of many rejections and physical, verbal, and sexual abuse throughout her life. At that moment, Mara felt nobody loved her, not even God.

"God, you promised me a husband who would love me like You do! I have no reason to stay on this earth. My life is nothing. I am in debt; my bills are overwhelming. I am alone. I have no help with these kids."

Mara's voice grew louder, filled with anger and desperation. "Is this all you want for me, to be hurt over and over again? How could you possibly love me, Lord? How? I have been doing this on my own all my life, and all the fathers get to leave and do whatever they want while I stay here in misery, trying to figure out what to do next.

I am tired of being a mother and father. I am tired of doing this on my own. I'm tired of being rejected, hated, misused, abused. I am just tired. Is this the life you ordained for me? What about the purpose and fulfillment you promised? Where did all that go? Or am I truly unworthy? Why am I here? I do not want it anymore!"

Mara screamed and cried in so much pain she could not move. She lay there for hours, feeling numb. She heard a still, small voice say, "Mara, I do have a husband for you. I love you, and I keep my promises. Get up, Mara. I will never leave you nor forsake you. I am going to do what I promised. You're my diamond in the rough. I am going to clean you up for your spouse."

The words penetrated her heart, bringing a flicker of hope amid the overwhelming despair. The intensity of her emotions began to shift as she lay there, contemplating the promise and love she heard in that still, small voice.

The Lord came to save and fight for Mara in her despair, keeping His promise that He would never leave or forsake her. He wants to fight for you as well.

Then, as Mara got up, she received an email. She read it this time; it was from a prophet, not a psychic. The message said, "A double-minded man is unstable in all his ways." This helped Mara understand why she should not seek love from someone unstable.

Have you ever sought love or validation from people who were unstable or unreliable? How did it affect you? Consider how James 1:8 describes a double-minded person—someone unstable in all their ways.

Reflect on how seeking true, stable love and support from God can change your experience of pain and betrayal and how grounding yourself in His faithfulness can provide stability and reassurance that unreliable sources cannot.

Guidepost: Do not be Deceived

Have you ever felt like Mara? Have you been angry with God and, feeling abandoned because your life is not going as the way you planned? Maybe, like her, you have withdrawn from Him, hurt and confused, thinking He let you down. It is a painful trap that many fall into.

But the truth is, distancing ourselves from God only leads us further into a cycle of hurt and despair, leaving us vulnerable to the enemy's lies. Satan's plan is to "steal, and kill, and destroy" John 10:10, and he deceives us by making us believe that God is the one who is failing us.

It is easy to blame God for the consequences of choices we made on our own, but it is important to recognize that God was never the cause of the pain we face—He was not a part of those destructive decisions. Satan thrives when we take matters into our own hands and later blame God for the aftermath.

He is the father of lies John 8:44, and his goal is to separate you from the love and grace of God. But God's love is constant, and His arms are open, waiting for you to come home.

Romans 8:38-39 reassures us, "For I am persuaded, that neither death, nor life, nor angels, nor principalities, nor things present, nor things to come, nor powers, nor height, nor depth, nor any other creature, shall be able to separate us from the love of God, which is in Christ Jesus our Lord." When we place our expectations on others to fulfill the love that only God can provide, we set ourselves up for disappointment.

No person, however well-intentioned, can perfectly fill the deepest needs of our heart. Only God, in His boundless love and wisdom, can offer the unchanging love, peace, and comfort we seek. As humans, we all have flaws and limitations, and when we look to others to be what only God can, we are left feeling unfulfilled and let down.

Ultimately, Psalm 62:5 encourages us: "Yes, my soul, find rest in God; my hope comes from Him." Our expectations, our hope, and our search for true love can only be fully met in the One who is perfect and eternal. In Him alone, we find rest and love that satisfies our deepest longings.

Trusting God Trusting God in the Wilderness

Mara had been walking through her own wilderness, a season marked by doubt and uncertainty. At times, she questioned whether the Lord's promises would ever come to pass. Yet, even in her darkest moments, she held on to the truth she had learned: God's Word does not fail, and His promises remain steadfast, even when life feels unbearable.

In the quiet of the wilderness, Mara often felt the weight of uncertainty pressing in. Life was silent, the path unseen, and yet the Word of God remained alive and active. She remembered how Jesus spoke in parables to reveal truths about the Kingdom of God.

One parable echoed in her mind: the Parable of the Sower. The sower went out to scatter seed, and the seeds fell on different kinds of soil—some on the path where they were eaten by birds, some on rocky ground where they sprang up quickly but withered, some among thorns where they were choked, and some on good soil where they produced a harvest Matthew 13:3-9, 18-23.

The wilderness was like the soil; each heart responds differently to God's Word. Some hear it but allow distractions or fear to choke it. Some hear it but quickly falter when hardship comes. Some hear it but never let it root deeply. Others experience the Word and allow it to grow, even amid struggle, even when the path is quiet and the outcome unseen.

Mara's days were often marked by silence and waiting, moments that felt like rocky ground or thorns. Yet Scripture reminded her that the Lord's Word is living and active, able to take root and grow in ways unseen: "So is the kingdom of God, as if a man should cast seed into the ground" Mark 4:26-29. The work of God happens quietly, in hidden places, over time.

As believers, it is important to understand that nothing we face in life is a surprise to the Lord. He sees every struggle, every test, and every moment of hardship. Consider Matthew 4:1: "Then was Jesus led up of the Spirit into the wilderness to be tempted of the devil." Even Jesus Christ, God's own Son, entered a season of wilderness by the Spirit's leading. It may seem unimaginable that our Savior would endure such trials, but He did so for a greater purpose and glory.

When believers walk through their own wilderness seasons, they may wonder if the Lord has forgotten them or question why God would allow them to face such difficulties. The truth is that these experiences are not detours from God's plan; they are often part of His refining work. Just as Jesus faced temptation and hardship in the wilderness, we also encounter moments designed to strengthen our faith and deepen our reliance on the Lord.

What enabled Jesus to withstand Satan's temptations was not simply His knowledge of Scripture, but His unwavering faith in the power and authority of God's Word.

Consider the life of Job. He experienced tremendous loss, pain, and confusion, and he grew weary under the weight of his trials. In his despair, he questioned God, pouring out his anguish and asking, "Why dost thou hide thy face, and holdest me for thine enemy?" Job 13:24. Yet, despite his questioning, Job's faith endured. He declared in Job 13:15, "Though he slay me, yet will I trust in him." This combination of honest emotion and steadfast trust demonstrates that God can bear our doubts and pain while urging us to remain firm in faith.

Even Jesus expressed deep anguish, crying out from the cross, "My God, my God, why hast thou forsaken me?" Matthew 27:46. Jesus understands our feelings of abandonment because He experienced them firsthand. These moments show us that walking through trials will not always be pleasant or easy, but faith is about trusting in who God is and what He has promised, even when the path is difficult. As 2 Corinthians 5:7 reminds us, "For we walk by faith, not by sight."

He is with us through every storm, every wrong turn, and every painful step. These painful seasons serve a purpose beyond our present understanding. In this process, the Lord removes impurities, shaping us into vessels that reflect His holiness and glory. Though difficult, these trials mature our faith and teach us to depend on God rather than ourselves.

In seasons of hardship, remember that Jesus Himself walked through the wilderness. The Bible recounts many others who endured trials and experienced the Lord's guidance and deliverance. Embrace these truths and hold on to God's promises. The wilderness may be lonely and challenging, yet the Word of God continues to work quietly, shaping hearts and preparing them for the harvest to come.

Letting Go of Idols

One day, Mara heard a still, small voice saying, "Seek my kingdom first, and all these things will be added unto you. I will give you the desires of your heart. I will give you the life you want—free from debt, sickness, poor credit, and worldly men—and give you a man after God's own heart who will love you like me."

Between Bible study, fellowship with other Christians, and intimate conversations with God, Mara began to change in profound ways. God had to prepare her heart for the plans He had for her.

"My grace is sufficient for thee: for my power is made perfect in weakness." 2 Corinthians 12:9. Mara clung to these words. As a new believer, she quoted this verse often. She still felt weak in spirit, but the Word gave her strength and guidance. Another comforting promise reminded her of God's care: *"Cast all your anxiety on him because he cares for you."* 1Peter 5:7.

J, a fellow believer, gave Mara advice for growing in faith. She told her to begin by asking God to speak and then open the Bible. Whatever page she landed on was what God wanted to speak to her about.

Sitting in her prayer closet, Mara followed this practice. Time and again, she found verses about idols and the worship of Baal in the Old Testament. She was puzzled. How were ancient idols relevant to her life?

"Why do I keep landing on verses about idols?" Mara asked J one day. "What is God saying to me?"

J replied, "What idols do you have in your life?" Mara was confused. She thought, *I don't bow before any idols.*

J explained, "Modern-day idols can be anything you place in your heart above God." She listed possibilities: marriage, children, money, material things, status, work, influence, fame, comfort, physical appearance.

As J went down the list, Mara recognized a few things. She had pictures of her wedding and of Lou in her prayer closet. She had been praying for him to change and come back to her, holding him as if he were an idol.

But that is not how it works. When you ask for something, you must accept that God may have different plans. Only He knows what is truly best. It was not God's will to bring Lou back.

Mara changed her prayers: "Lord, let thy will be done." God worked on her heart to remove her idols and selfish desires. Instead of asking for Lou to return, she prayed for his salvation—that even if he never came back to her, he might find the peace of God that she now had.

What idols do you have in your life? Even if you do not worship graven images, anything you place above God becomes an idol. Money, careers, relationships, and desires can all take precedence over Him.

"Put to death therefore what is earthly in you: sexual immorality, impurity, passion, evil desire, and covetousness, which is idolatry." Colossians 3:5.

Take a moment to reflect. What occupies the innermost part of your heart? Is it a person, a goal, a habit, or a desire that distracts you from God? Anything that directs your choices, focus, or devotion more than God has become an idol.

Jesus said the greatest commandment is to love the Lord your God with all your heart, soul, and mind. Notice the word *all*. Your love for God cannot be partial or half-hearted.

God is jealous for you, His chosen one. He longs for your devotion. When you prioritize someone or something above Him, it diminishes your relationship with Him and hinders your growth.

Idols can appear even in good things. Work, relationships, or ambitions can become idols if they take God's place in your heart. The Bible warns that when you approach God with idols in your heart, your prayers are influenced by those idols:

"Therefore speak unto them, and say unto them, Thus saith the Lord God; Every man of the house of Israel that setteth up his idols in his heart, and putteth the stumbling block of his iniquity before his face, and cometh to the prophet; I the Lord will answer him that cometh according to the multitude of his idols." Ezekiel 14:4.

Mara's story illustrates this. Early on, she voiced desires to marry Lou or Mike. Her words reflected what was already rooted in her heart. Lou, though kind, was unstable and often broke promises. Mike struggled with addiction and abuse. Mara's need for love and security had become an idol, shaping her prayers and choices.

God detests idol worship. The first commandment says, "You shall have no other gods before me." Prioritizing your walk with God ensures that your love for others is grounded in Him. Abraham loved Isaac but placed God first, demonstrating healthy relationships built on devotion to God.

An old saying goes: "If you love something, let it go; if it comes back, it is yours." Let us amend that: *If God brings it back, it is yours; if it is not pleasing to Him, it is not good for you.* Letting go is a sign of strength, not weakness.

"My little children, guard yourselves from idols." 1 John 5:21. The Bible will not ask more than you can do. Freedom from idols comes from loving God with your whole heart.

Prayer is key. "The supplication of a righteous man is availing much." James 5:16. Pray for God to cleanse your heart from idols. This is a personal conversation with Him—bringing each idol before Him and submitting fully to His Lordship.

From Suffering to Salvation

Mara was trying to break the habit of seeking psychics and instead trusting God more. But she still struggled to stop completely, sneaking back to it from time to time. "Why do I keep doing this?" she wondered.

Deep down, she knew the psychics were not giving her real

answers. They were only telling her what she wanted to hear. Their words felt shallow and empty, providing only fleeting comfort. And when she hung up the phone, the aching in her heart returned even stronger. Yet, she kept their numbers, hoping each time would be different. But it never was.

It reminded her of stories in the Bible, where people cried out to false gods but received no response. No matter how desperately or loudly they called or cried, or how long they waited, nothing ever happened. As the Bible says in 1 Kings 18:26.

"And they took the bullock which was given them, and they dressed it, and called on the name of Baal from morning even until noon, saying, O Baal, hear us. But there was no voice, nor any that answered."

Her story did not begin with those phone calls.

Years earlier, Mara had quietly scrolled through horoscopes and astrology charts, searching for insight into a relationship that mattered deeply to her. Was she really compatible with the guy she liked? Were their stars aligned? She wanted clarity—a simple "yes" to calm her restless heart. What began as harmless curiosity soon turned into an unspoken ritual. Instead of bringing her uncertainty to God in prayer, Mara turned to algorithms and trends. She traded God's voice for constellations, and her spiritual authority for false signs.

One tarot reading had especially shaken her. The cards claimed a family curse would block her chances at love. That moment planted fear in her heart—and it became clear that the enemy's goal was to trap Mara in fear and hopelessness.

She did not know it at the time, but these practices—horoscopes, astrology, tarot—were not just spiritual detours. They were rooted in paganism, leading her to seek answers from creation rather than the Creator. And with each act, doors were opened in the spirit that she could not see.

Scripture is clear about these things:

"There shall not be found among you any one that maketh his son or his daughter to pass through the fire, or that useth divination, or an observer of times, or an enchanter, or a witch, Or a charmer, or a consulter with familiar spirits, or a wizard, or a necromancer. For all that do these things are an abomination unto the Lord: and because of these abominations the Lord thy God doth drive them out from before thee."

Deuteronomy 18:10-12.

Mara did not realize the danger. But God, in His mercy, does not leave His people to perish for lack of understanding.

"My people are destroyed for lack of knowledge; because you have rejected knowledge, I also reject you from being a priest to me." Hosea 4:6.

God's desire is not to condemn, but to lead His people into truth—truth that frees and restores.

"Then you will know the truth, and the truth will set you free." John 8:32.

"Have nothing to do with the fruitless deeds of darkness, but rather expose them." Ephesians 5:11.

Unlike the silence of false gods, God's Word is alive—filled with authority and eternal power. It does not change. It does not waver. And it does not depend on our approval to be true. As it is written in Isaiah 45:5-6:

I am the Lord, and there is none else, there is no God beside me. I girded thee, though thou hast not known me, that they may know from the rising of the sun, and from the west, that there is none beside me. I am the Lord, and there is none else.

This is not the voice of a distant deity but the declaration of the one true God—the Creator of heaven and earth. His power is not hidden in secret rituals or dependent on human effort.

He alone strengthens, upholds, and reveals Himself so that all the world may know: there is none beside Him.

In a world filled with noise, opinions, and spiritual counterfeits, it is easy to lose sight of who truly holds the power. People chase after what feels good, what seems mystical, or what promises control—yet all of these paths lead to confusion, bondage, and spiritual dryness. Practices rooted in the occult or self-worship lure many with promises of peace or power, but they leave the soul empty, vulnerable, and far from God.

Even when we do not acknowledge Him—even when we walk in ignorance or rebellion—He girds us. He covers us. He waits patiently for the moment our hearts will turn toward Him. God's mercy is not weakness. His boundaries are not punishment. They are invitations—into safety, into truth, into life.

Mara's stronghold with the psychic was rooted in her deep need for validation and control. Uncertainty and unresolved pain from her past led her to place her trust in external sources who claimed to have special knowledge and power. She desperately craved answers, particularly during chaotic times, and was satisfied with counterfeit versions of the answers only God could provide. Even as her friends and conscience warned her, Mara felt trapped in a cycle she could not escape.

As Mara continued to dabble in these dark places, she noticed a growing sense of unease and a weight on her spirit, but it was not until the pain became unbearable that she realized the toll these practices were taking on her body and mind. She had unknowingly invited destructive forces into her life, and now they were manifesting in ways she could not ignore. What begins as curiosity can quickly grow into a spiritual entanglement.

It was spiritual—and it was real. The further she drifted from

God's covering, the heavier the weight became. At first, it was subtle: restless nights, a tight feeling in her chest, anxious thoughts she brushed off.

But soon, the spiral began—emotionally, spiritually, physically. Then came the symptoms—persistent fatigue and unexplained pain. The doctors could not explain the root. But Mara knew. Deep in her spirit, she understood she had given the enemy access.

Sharp pains coursed through her body, and deep veins surged up her legs, causing an overwhelming sense of dread. As the pain worsened, she could not help but wonder if this was it—if this was the moment she was finally about to die.

She was so scared that on the way to the hospital, she stopped at the church. She went up to the altar around the pulpit and asked for prayers. Yes, she realized that only God could genuinely help heal her. She trusted that He works through the hands of skilled doctors, whose efforts and compassion are invaluable. But she also knew that, in the end, the outcome rests with Him—because God has the final say. And whatever He says stands!

"God," Mara prayed, "Please heal my body. I want to live and be here for my kids."

Her story echoes the cry of David in Psalm 38:

"There is no soundness in my flesh because of thine anger; neither is there any rest in my bones because of my sin."

David knew the agony of separation from God, not only emotionally and spiritually, but physically.

"My wounds stink and are corrupt because of my foolishness... I am feeble and sore broken."

When we step outside God's protection, we become vulnerable to the consequences of rebellion. But the moment we turn back, the Father runs to meet us.

The question is not whether God will forgive—it is whether we will fully return.

And when she left the church, she heard a familiar whisper in her ear.

"You are healed."

That was an assurance and a confirmation of God's finished work in her life.

At the emergency room, they hooked Mara up to an electrocardiogram and ran all kinds of tests on her. As she waited for the results, she kept herself in prayer.

Healing begins with repentance. With that understanding, she felt the deep urge to repent.

"Lord, I turn away from my wicked ways. I am sorry for seeking answers in places that were never meant for me. Please forgive me. Heal my body, my mind, and my soul. Lord, I will not go back to those psychics. I will do better."

As she prayed, she remembered the promise in 2 Chronicles 7:14:

"If my people, who are called by my name, will humble themselves and pray and seek my face and turn from their wicked ways, then I will hear from heaven, and I will forgive their sin and will heal their land."

That was the turning point for Mara—a moment of repentance, a moment of surrender. God heard her prayer, and in His mercy, He brought healing. Not just physical healing, but spiritual restoration. She knew that as she turned away from the darkness, God would bring her the peace and healing she had been searching for all along.

"Thank You, Jesus!" Mara yelled out.

That day, Mara learned firsthand that the Lord never forsakes us. In our brokenness, He remains faithful. Even when we walk away from Him, He never walks away from us.

"I will in no wise fail thee, neither will I in any wise forsake thee."
— Hebrews 13:5

Hope for the Prodigal Heart

Mara believed she was too far gone. But Jesus had His arms open wide, ready to receive her. Through Him, she was welcomed back into the loving presence of God the Father. The Father and all of heaven rejoiced at her return, just as Jesus taught in the parable of the prodigal son, where the father says,

"For this my son was dead, and is alive again; he was lost, and is found." — Luke 15:24.

This parable reveals the heart of God the Father. Luke 15:10 tells us,

"There is joy in the presence of the angels of God over one sinner that repenteth."

No one is beyond the reach of God's love. No mistake, no distance, can separate us from His grace and forgiveness.

Like Mara, you may carry the weight of your past or feel overwhelmed by your current struggles. But through Jesus, there is grace and salvation available to you. We don't move from suffering into healing by our own strength—but through His help and mercy. It is never too late to turn back to Him.

As you continue this journey, remember: guilt and shame are not your destination.

Never Succumb to Guilt and Shame

Have you ever felt ashamed of something you did, something you were involved in, or something you were subjected to? As ambassadors of Christ, it is believed we are no longer strangers to guilt and shame because even our Savior, Jesus Christ, was subjected to shame by the same people He came to save. His disciples also experienced it, and the Christians followed suit after them.

These emotions are like thieves who steal our peace, joy, and stability, sometimes even attempting to erode our identity. This was precisely what Mara constantly faced in her relationships. But do you know you do not have to continue living with that guilt and shame?

You can break free and walk in the freedom and light of God's love. As Apostle Paul reminds us in Romans 8:1-2, *"There is therefore now no condemnation to them which are in Christ Jesus. For the law of the Spirit of life in Christ Jesus hath made me free from the law of sin and death."*

No matter how complex this scripture might seem, one truth stands clear: under the umbrella of God's love, we are no longer condemned or held captive by our past mistakes. That is why, whoever God sets free is truly free. You have what it takes to release guilt and shame—don't let those heavy emotions take root in your heart any longer.

Now is the time to come out of your own "Egypt"—to leave behind the bondage of the past and step into the abundant life God has prepared for you.

Coming out of Egypt

"By a strong hand the Lord brought us out of Egypt, from the house of slavery" Exodus 13:14.

The book of Exodus includes the story of how God delivered the Israelites from Egypt. They were enslaved by the Egyptians and separated from their homeland by the Red Sea and a vast wilderness.

But God sent Moses to liberate them. And even though His people murmured and complained along the way, God still brought them home. He caused them to wander in the wilderness for a while because of their disobedience, but he kept His promise and brought them to the Promised Land.

What are you in bondage to? Whatever has enslaved your mind and left you wandering in the wilderness, you can overcome it through the Savior. Mara was trapped in her past; that is why no matter how hard she tried; all her efforts yielded no positive results until she turned to God.

We may live for decades wondering why things do not seem to be how God promised them. But until we play our part, we will not see any change. Although God had the power to turn Mara's life around from the onset, He wanted her to realize that she needed Him.

That is how God works! He will never forcefully make us relinquish control. Instead, He allows us to face the consequences of doing things our way until we are ready to surrender. Mara felt trapped for as long as she could remember. No matter how hard she tried, nothing seemed to change. Her past clung to her like a shadow—old mistakes, regrets, and fears she couldn't shake. Every day felt like wandering through a wilderness, searching for freedom that seemed just out of reach.

For years, she tried to take control. She pushed herself, tried to fix what was broken, and hoped things would turn out differently. But the harder she fought, the heavier life felt. It wasn't until Mara stopped relying solely on herself that she began to feel even a small measure of relief. She realized that surrender didn't mean giving up—it meant acknowledging that some things were bigger than she was.

Looking back, Mara understood how much holding on to the past had kept her stuck. Regrets, "what-ifs," and familiar pain had been anchors, keeping her from moving forward. Slowly, as she loosened her grip, the path ahead became clearer. Philippians 3:13-14 became a quiet truth she held close: "But one thing I do, forgetting those things which are behind, and reaching forth unto those things which are before, I press toward the mark for the prize of the high calling of God in Christ Jesus." Moving forward wasn't about perfection; it was about trust—in herself, in God, and in the life waiting beyond her old patterns.

Even as she began to feel freedom in one part of her life, Mara realized that her heart still had challenges. Love, trust, and relationships were complicated in ways she hadn't expected. Some connections were genuine, some were not. Some lessons came through disappointment, heartbreak, or betrayal—but each one shaped her, taught her boundaries, and helped her grow stronger.

Mara's "Egypt" wasn't just a place of struggle. It was a story of survival, growth, and courage. She didn't have all the answers, and the road ahead was still uncertain—but she was moving forward, ready to face whatever came next, remembering that "Woe to them that go down to Egypt for help...but they look not unto the Holy One of Israel, neither seek the Lord" Isaiah 31:1. What she had learned in leaving her Egypt—the patience, the surrender, the courage to move forward—would be the very foundation she needed to step into this next season. Mara understood that growth wasn't always comfortable, and the fire could be painful, but she also knew that what survived the heat would be unshakable. And so, she stepped forward, ready to be refined through the fire.

Refined Through the Fire

When Mara first gave her life to Christ, she imagined it would be easy. She thought that once she surrendered and invited the Lord into her heart, all her problems would disappear. But soon she realized salvation was just the beginning — God was starting a refining work in her, like a diamond being purified by fire.

"I will bring that group through the fire and make them pure. They will call on my name, and I will answer them." — Zechariah 13:9.

At first, Mara didn't understand why life seemed harder after saying yes to Jesus. But the Lord was breaking off old layers — fear, pride, habits, and thought patterns that couldn't stay in the new life He was giving her.

She began reading her Bible daily, and though some verses made her uncomfortable, she soon realized that conviction was not condemnation — it was healing. Some days it felt like the Bible was telling her how bad she was, but she learned it was God's way of lovingly correcting and guiding her..

"For whom the Lord loveth he correcteth; even as a father the son in whom he delighteth." — Hebrews 12:6.

At first, Mara noticed the subtle ways the world tugged at her: the music she loved, the movies she watched, and the conversations she once thought harmless. Old friends invited her to places that no longer felt right, but saying yes to Christ meant saying no to things that could dim her spirit. Even social media became a battlefield. Pictures she once posted — ones that earned hundreds of likes — no longer received the same attention. Mara had to learn to be okay with that, understanding that her worth was no longer measured by the world's approval, but by God's love.

"Guard your heart above all else, for it determines the course of your life." — Proverbs 4:23.

"The eye is the lamp of the body. If your eyes are healthy, your whole body will be full of light." — Matthew 6:22.

"Let your beauty not come from outward adornment, but from the inner self, the unfading beauty of a gentle and quiet spirit." — 1 Peter 3:3-4.

Mara began to see that the world often calls evil good and good evil. What seemed like rules or restrictions were actually boundaries God set to protect her light. Saying yes to Him did not make life perfect — it made it real, alive, and truly free in His Spirit, who works in us to cleanse, guide, and make us holy.

Through prayer, she learned to say, "Holy Spirit, cleanse me. Make me holy." She held onto God's Word:

"Be ye holy; for I am holy." — 1 Peter 1:16.

Slowly, her ashes turned into beauty. She remembered what the Lord had whispered at the start of her journey:

"You are My diamond in the rough."

Every challenge, every moment of letting go, was shaping her into something radiant.

"He will sit as a refiner and purifier of silver." — Malachi 3:3.

"When you walk through the fire, you shall not be burned; the flames shall not consume you." — Isaiah 43:2.

One day, Mara paused while reading the story of Lazarus:

"Then Jesus called in a loud voice, 'Lazarus, come out!' The dead man came out, his hands and feet wrapped with strips of linen, and a cloth around his face." — John 11:43-44.

Her heart whispered, "This is for me too." Just as Lazarus stepped out of the grave clothes, the Lord was calling her to step out of the fears, regrets, old habits, and worldly pressures that had bound her — to fully embrace the new identity He had given her. Her spiritual grave clothes were being removed, layer by layer, as God polished His diamond in the rough.

Mara began to realize the depth of God's promise in Isaiah: "When you pass through the waters, I will be with you; and through the rivers, they shall not overwhelm you; when you walk through fire you shall not be burned, and the flame shall not consume you."

She had walked through waters of fear, through rivers of adversity and loss, and through fires of testing. At times, she questioned God's presence in her pain. But now she saw that He had been with her all along — sustaining her, shaping her, and refining her faith in the middle of every trial.

The very fires she once feared had not destroyed her; they had revealed who she truly was in Him. Each hardship became a holy place — proof that God's Word was not just spoken to her, but lived with her.

Guidepost for the Reader

Have you struggled to follow the Lord consistently? Do you find yourself getting frustrated when it feels like you are failing, falling behind, or even feeling alone on this journey? Do others notice changes in you that make you feel isolated? Always remember: as you walk this path, His grace is sufficient. Growth and refinement are a process. The beauty of the diamond — the person God is shaping you to be — is on the other side. Keep reading His Word, leaning on Him in prayer, and trusting that each step, even the difficult ones, is preparing you for His best.

Mara and the Counterfeit Love

Mara often wondered how to tell if love was real or counterfeit. Time and time again, she found herself in relationships that felt right at first but left her questioning in the end.

Each time, she prayed, "Lord, what are You trying to teach me? Is this the one? Does he love me? When will the right one come?"

And the Lord answered her gently:

"Mara, when the right one comes, he will love you like I do. Do I leave you confused? Do I fail to provide for you? Do I not listen to you, care for you, and meet your needs? The man I send will reflect My love—not just in words, but in action."

He continued:

"If someone only gives you a feeling of love, but no fruit behind it, be careful. Ask yourself this: does he love Me more than he loves you? A man who submits to the King, who loves Me first, will know how to love you rightly. Without My love in his heart, he cannot truly love you at all."

Mara realized she had been asking the wrong questions. Instead of asking, "Lord, is he the one?" she began to pray, "Lord, does he love You first, above all else? Does he seek you in everything he does?"

She began to see clearly that love without God at the center could never last. How could anyone understand real love without first knowing the love of God?

Learning from Past Relationships

In past relationships, Mara had shifted her focus from God to the man—letting fear, insecurity, and the need for approval guide her. But God used those counterfeit loves to reveal what was hidden in her heart: her idols, her wounds, and the ways she had placed man above her Maker.

When those men left, ignored her, or misread her, Mara realized something profound: God had never left her. He had been there the whole time—comforting her, wiping her tears, and holding her close.

Mara finally understood: the truest love is not found in being chosen by man, but in knowing she was already chosen by God. That love—faithful, enduring, and true—was the love she had been searching for all along.

Reflective Question: Have you ever sought love in the wrong places because you didn't fully trust God's timing?

Healing Before Love

Healing allows you to approach relationships from a place of strength, self-worth, and clarity. It gives you the ability to choose people who are truly right for you, not just convenient or familiar. Leaning on God's wisdom and allowing Him to shape your heart empowers you to build relationships that honor Him and reflect His love.

We often rush into relationships without waiting for God to heal our hearts first. When we do, we carry baggage, insecurities, and unaddressed wounds that can harm the relationship's foundation. We may seek validation, cling to unhealthy dynamics, or attempt to "fix" ourselves or our partner.

Only when we allow God to restore our hearts can we fully contribute to a healthy, fulfilling relationship. His healing gives us the clarity to choose wisely and the strength to love genuinely.

Reflective Question: What areas of your heart still need healing before you can fully love and trust another person?

Trusting God's Timing

Learning patience is often difficult. Abraham's story offers a powerful example. God promised Abraham a son, and he believed. Yet after years of waiting, Sarah grew impatient and tried to "help" God by having a child with Hagar. This decision led to Ishmael's birth but also brought jealousy, conflict, and emotional pain that could have been avoided.

Like Sarah, we sometimes take matters into our own hands when God's timing seems slow. But scripture reminds us to trust Him:

Psalm 27:14: "Wait for the Lord; be strong and take heart and wait for the Lord."

Romans 12:12: "Be joyful in hope, patient in affliction, faithful in prayer."

Philippians 4:6: "Do not be anxious about anything, but in every situation, by prayer and petition, with thanksgiving, present your requests to God."

Patience is not passive. It is trusting that God sees the bigger picture and is working all things together for your good.

Reflective Question Are you willing to wait for God's timing, even when it feels difficult or uncertain?

God's Restoration

God is the God who restores. Even in seasons of suffering, He is at work, bringing beauty out of brokenness and purpose out of pain. What feels like the end may be the beginning of something new.

He does not discard us when we falter. Instead, He gently redirects us, drawing us back to His heart. His grace covers the gaps we cannot fill. When we surrender, He aligns our steps with His perfect will, turning detours into testimonies.

Romans 8:37 reminds us: "In all these things we are more than conquerors through Him who loved us."

No struggle is wasted. Like Job, who endured much but ultimately gained more, your season of restoration is already unfolding. Stand firm—what God has spoken over your life will come to pass.

In the next season, many will be drawn to what sounds good rather than what is God. Stay rooted. Stay discerning. Be ready—not just to receive restoration, but to walk in wisdom, guarding your heart and your hearing.

Guidepost: Discerning Voices vs. Itching Ears

Mara was in a vulnerable season of waiting. Her heart longed for clarity—especially concerning her future husband. The silence felt heavy, and hope came in flickers. Desperate for direction, she began turning to spiritual voices online—those who claimed to speak for God.

Many of them offered encouraging words:
"Your husband is coming."
"You are next in line."
"He is waiting on you to prepare."

Their messages were soothing, like a balm to her anxious heart. Unlike the obvious counterfeit sources she had already rejected—psychics, tarot readings, astrology—these voices used Scripture, prayer language, and divine-sounding insight. That made them feel safer. More trustworthy. Maybe even right.

Mara convinced herself: If I am not turning to the occult, surely God understands if I seek His prophets instead—especially when it comes to something He promised me.

It was not that Mara did not hear from God—she did. She had walked closely with Him for years, tuning her heart to His voice in quiet moments. She had trusted Him, waited patiently, lived righteously. She had remained celibate, guarding her heart and body, even when it was hard.

But weariness was settling in—a heavy weight pressing down until her heart felt sick with longing and anxiety. The heat of waiting felt like a fever, draining her strength. The passing days brought another ache—the ache of getting older, of time slipping through her fingers. Each birthday was a quiet reminder that the promise had not yet come.

> Hope deferred maketh the heart sick:
> but when the desire cometh, it is a tree of life.
> —Proverbs 13:12.

Her prayers had shifted from faith to urgent questions:

Lord, when? Am I close? I have waited so long. I have been faithful. I have done it Your way... Have I not?

The questions did not come from rebellion—they came from deep exhaustion, the kind of tired that settles into your bones after years of hoping.

And in the stillness, the enemy whispered:
What if God forgot?
What if you are not chosen?
What if you missed your moment?
What if it is too late?
Is the promise still coming at all?

Confusion grew as Mara found herself bombarded with mixed signs and messages online—some urging her to prepare this way, others demanding she change something else. One prophet said, "You have to fast before he comes." Another insisted, "Pray without ceasing for your breakthrough." Yet another promised, "In two weeks, a miracle is coming."

The pressure mounted like walls pressing inward. The enemy was attacking Mara's fears relentlessly, whispering, One more thing. One more test. One more preparation. You are not ready yet.

When fear and doubt crept in, online prophetic voices felt like light in the darkness. They spoke the words she longed to hear—confirming what she hoped God had said. And maybe... just maybe... they would tell her when.

But deep inside, a quiet warning stirred—a whisper from scripture reminding her:
"For false messiahs and false prophets will appear and perform great signs and wonders to deceive, if possible, even the elect." Matthew 24:24.

At first, these messages felt like divine signs. But as time passed, Mara noticed something unsettling: the words always echoed her desires, never challenged her, and never pointed her toward deeper surrender.

Instead of growing closer to God, she began depending on outside voices to direct her path. Over time, the Holy Spirit began to gently convict her. Her heart was not truly seeking God's will—it was chasing confirmation of what she already wanted. Her pursuit of guidance had become a spiritual shortcut—not unlike consulting a psychic. The language sounded biblical, but the motive behind it was rooted in fear and control.

This is the warning Scripture gives in 2 Timothy 4:3-4:
"For the time is coming when people will not put up with sound teaching. Instead, to suit their own desires, they will gather around them a great number of teachers to say what their itching ears want to hear."

That phrase—"itching ears"—describes the part of us that only wants to hear what makes us feel good. It can be dangerously deceptive, especially when clothed in spiritual language. Mara realized she was not trusting God with her future. She was trying to gather answers that matched her own timeline.

Deception, she realized, did not always come in loud, obvious ways. Sometimes it sounded like hope. Sometimes it came wrapped in scripture, prayer language, and promises. It was a subtle snare, especially for those who longed deeply for answers.

> THEN CERTAIN OF THE SCRIBES AND OF THE PHARISEES ANSWERED, SAYING, MASTER, WE WOULD SEE A SIGN FROM THEE. BUT HE ANSWERED AND SAID UNTO THEM, AN EVIL AND ADULTEROUS GENERATION SEEKETH AFTER A SIGN; AND THERE SHALL NO SIGN BE GIVEN TO IT, BUT THE SIGN OF THE PROPHET JONAS:
> — MATTHEW 12:38–39 KJV

Mara had been seeking confirmation more than communion. And now, she knew: she needed to return to God's voice—no matter how long the waiting—before she was led astray.

It was in that moment of spiritual fog that Mara made a bold choice—she shut it all down. All of it.

No more prophetic binge-watching.
No more scrolling for signs.
No more chasing comfort through voices that catered to her emotions.

She fasted. She prayed. She asked God to strip away the noise and speak to her through His Word. And in that quiet space, something shifted. Her prayers changed from "When will he come?" to "Lord, change me. Shape me. Have Your way in me."

Instead of needing constant reassurance, Mara found confidence in God's presence. She no longer needed to be told what she wanted to hear—she wanted to hear what God was actually saying, even if it meant letting go of her timeline, her dreams, or her plans.

God's timing is perfect.
His voice is enough.
The Author of time doesn't miss divine appointments.
And He never forgets His promises.

I am the Lord; in its time I will hasten it.
— Isaiah 60:22.

As Mara was walking closely with the Lord—He was gently peeling back the layers of pain and brokenness, transforming her from the inside out. This is what happens when you enter into a true relationship with Jesus: healing begins, and real change takes root.
God the Father, in His perfect love and sovereignty, was at work in her life—guiding the plan of restoration. Jesus, His Son, who gave Himself as the sacrifice for her sins and offers new life, was renewing her heart and mind. And the Holy Spirit, God's presence living within her, had become her constant counselor—speaking truth, guiding her steps, and showing her what needed to be surrendered.

Together, the Father, Son, and Holy Spirit were reshaping Mara's identity and teaching her how to trust again.

But Mara's journey wasn't over. Though she had made great progress, healing wasn't only personal—it was generational. As a mother, she had to face the painful truth that the scars of her past had not stayed with her alone. They had silently touched her children's lives, marking them in ways she hadn't fully recognized—until now.

Iniquity Upon the Children

The concept of generational curses is often discussed in light of biblical teachings. To understand this, it is helpful to examine scriptures that address the inheritance of sin and consequences through family lines.

In Exodus 20:5, God states, "I the Lord thy God am a jealous God, visiting the iniquity of the fathers upon the children unto the third and fourth generation of them that hate me." Here, God is addressing the Israelites who turned to false idols, suggesting that the consequences of certain sins can impact future generations. This principle underscores the spiritual influence that one generation can have on the next.

However, the Bible also emphasizes personal accountability for sin in Ezekiel 18:20, it says, "The soul that sinneth, it shall die. The son shall not bear the iniquity of the father, neither shall the father bear the iniquity of the son." This verse clarifies that each person is judged for their own actions, not those of their ancestors. Although patterns of sin, dysfunction, or trauma may recur through family lines, individuals are not bound to their forefathers' choices.

The New Testament reassures believers that through Jesus Christ, there is freedom from spiritual bondage and any inherited cycles of sin. Galatians 3:13-14 declares, "Christ hath redeemed us from the curse of the law, being made a curse for us … that the blessing of Abraham might come on the Gentiles through Jesus Christ." Through Christ's sacrifice, believers have the power to break free from destructive patterns and embrace a new legacy of hope and renewal.

Despite M ara's efforts to change, she realized that without divine help, breaking free from these patterns was impossible. As Psalm 127:1 reminds us, "Except the Lord build the house, they labour in vain that build it." Mara came to understand that only through God's intervention could she truly break the cycles that had bound her family for so long.

Mara had five children: Fizzle, Lady, Blue, Aqua, and JJ. Each one was unique, with their own strengths and quirks that brought a special sparkle to her life. They painted her world with vibrant colors she could never have imagined. Despite their distinct personalities and talents, Mara's love for each of them was unwavering and profound.

As a teenager thrust into adulthood, and later an adult raising children by herself, Mara struggled to form the emotional connection with her children that she so deeply intended.

The abuse she endured during adolescence and early relationships had left her unequipped to give what she had never known herself. Being a single mother, Mara felt the weight of society's expectations and was held to a higher standard for being both a nurturer and a father figure.

This was much easier said than done. No matter how hard we try, most times, we cannot deny the fact that each parent has a unique role to play in a child's upbringing. If one is missing and the other tries filling that gap, it often proves difficult. But that does not mean to stop trying. It might not be easy, but God's guidance will take you one step ahead.

Navigating parenting with anxiety and fear was a constant battle for Mara. Anger often bubbled to the surface when she felt overwhelmed, and perfectionism loomed over her like an unyielding shadow. She wanted to be the perfect mother, but the weight of her expectations was often suffocating. Each day was a delicate balancing act, a tightrope walk between wanting to protect her children and fearing that her struggles would inadvertently harm them.

Mara's anxiety did not only affect her—it rippled out, reaching her children in ways she could not always see or control. When anxiety kicked in, when the intrusive thoughts flooded her mind, she worried not just about herself but about what her fears might do to her children.

She feared that, without meaning to, she was teaching them to see the world through a lens of caution, skepticism, and dread. Every time she raised her voice in a moment of stress, every time she withdrew when sadness overwhelmed her, she could see confusion in their eyes, a quiet question of why their mother sometimes seemed so distant or guarded.

Mara longed to be the mother they deserved and give them a sense of security and joy, but she often felt chained to her own fears and experiences. Life had taught her to expect the worst and shield herself from potential pain, but she worried this approach was teaching her children the same. She did not want them to grow up with that same heavy armor, going through life constantly bracing for disappointment and hurt.

Mara became a sort of "helicopter parent," always hovering over what her children were doing. Imagine a child whose life had been inconsistent, whose caregivers were unreliable or unhealthy. Experiencing such unpredictability left her with deep anxiety and a need to control everything in her environment. Now she was an adult, and everything around her had to be right and under her control. Her past traumas made her cautious and vigilant, while the heavy responsibility she felt to break generational patterns drove her determination to protect her children. This vigilance translated into strict rules and constant supervision. However, she did not fully understand the negative effects this pattern of parenting had on her children.

Mara rarely let her kids spend the night at others' houses unless she knew the parents well. Even in those rare instances, she remained on high alert, often checking in to ensure everything was all right. She was particularly cautious about who was around her daughters. No man was allowed to stay in their home except Mike. This was a mother determined to prevent her daughters from experiencing the same pain and trauma she had endured.

This rule stemmed from fear of potential harm and a strong desire to create a safe environment for her children.

Her own experiences heavily influenced her approach to parenting. This meant setting boundaries that sometimes felt suffocating for her kids. Mara's protective nature often led to conflicts as her children struggled with the lack of freedom. However, Mara believed that these measures were necessary to ensure their safety and well-being.

For her children, it was a confusing and frustrating time. They saw their friends' enjoying freedoms that they could only dream of. They struggled to understand their mother's fears, seeing them as irrational and overbearing. This often led to feelings of resentment and rebellion.

Mara's heart would ache, knowing that her restrictions made her children feel isolated. Despite the anger and frustration from her kids, Mara never wavered. She believed that her vigilance was necessary to keep them safe. She would often explain, "I'm doing this to protect you," though the words rarely seemed to ease their resentment.

This disciplinary approach at times led to tension between Mara and her children, especially as they entered their teenage years. Sleepovers, parties, and even simple things were frequent sources of conflict.

When they acted out, Mara responded with anger, struggling to manage her emotions because she had not yet learned how to parent in a healthy way. Frustration frequently drove her to yelling, cursing, and at times, resorting to physical discipline. Each outburst brought a painful realization: she was repeating the same harmful behaviors she had endured in her own childhood. This realization brought with it a profound sense of guilt; she felt like a failure, trapped in the same cycles that had haunted her for so long. This epiphany hit Mara hard. Despite her best intentions and vows to be different, she began to witness the same patterns of anger, trauma, and emotional disconnection surface in her own parenting.

Mara's perfectionism added another layer of difficulty to her relationship with her children. Her need to keep the house spotless stemmed from her chaotic upbringing, where order and control felt unattainable. For Mara, a tidy home symbolized stability and safety, but this rigid standard was impossible for her children to meet.

The tension it caused left little room for emotional openness, making it difficult for her to connect with her kids on a deeper level. By focusing so much on the external, Mara avoided confronting the deeper emotional wounds from her past, unintentionally creating a barrier between herself and her family.

Though Mara carried deep wounds from her past, her love for her children was unwavering. She was determined to be present for them in ways her own family had never been for her. Mara showed up for every game, every performance, and every road trip, becoming her children's number one supporter—especially during their formative years leading up to high school.

Since she struggled to connect emotionally with her children in the way she desired, Mara found other ways to bond with them. Laughter became her bridge, a way to close the emotional gap without delving into the deeper feelings she found so difficult to express. They often watched their favorite TV shows and movies together.

This was how Mara expressed her love—by being there for her children and finding creative ways to connect with them. Even when the weight of her unhealed emotions lingered in the background, she remained committed to giving her children the love and support she had always dreamed of receiving herself.

During her struggles, Mara kept her children active and engaged in sports and activities. On their trips together, they would sing songs and share stories to pass the time.

One special tradition Mara shared with her children involved gathering broomsticks and singing church songs. They would roll on the floor laughing, singing loudly, and playing makeshift instruments, creating joyful memories together.

In moments of faith, especially when Mara was expecting a miracle from God and needed His intervention, she would lead her children in a chant: "You got to name it!" Mara would start the call, and her kids would shout, "Claim it!" Then she would say, "Believe it!" and they would finish with, "Receive it!"—all chiming in with joy. This tradition became their source of strength. Whenever bad weather or a tornado was looming, they would gather in a circle, holding hands and praying for it to pass over them.

Even though she had not yet fully experienced a personal relationship with the Lord, deep down Mara knew that He was always with her. Just as He had been with her through many dark nights, she could feel His presence steadying her when everything else was uncertain.

Through the guidance of the Holy Spirit, the Lord helped Mara recognize these patterns and see the areas where she had fallen short in her parenting. She began to realize that her inability to show affection, coupled with her relentless perfectionism, was taking a toll on her children. The smallest things—an unwashed dish, a forgotten chore, a raised voice—could set her off. It was not about them, not really. It was the weight of everything else—years of unhealed trauma, anger buried under expectations, and a life that had demanded more than it gave.

Mara carried frustration she did not always understand. There were days when anxiety wrapped around her chest so tightly that even laughter felt like a threat. And in that state, irritability became her constant companion.

Her children did not always know which version of her they would get—the warm, playful mother who laughed during movie nights and made-up silly dances and faces, or the sharp, irritable woman who snapped over unfinished chores or too much noise in the house.

They walked on eggshells, not because they feared her, but because they did not understand her. One moment she was smiling, the next she was overwhelmed, her tone sharp, her patience gone.

It reminded her of her own childhood. Her Aunt Sarah had been the same—exploding over the smallest things, like the time Mara spilled pennies on the floor. The sound of them scattering had barely faded before the shouting began. No pause. No breath. Just immediate rage. In those moments,

Mara froze. Her heart would pound, her eyes go wide, and a deep sense of shame would settle in—not just because of the mess, but because of what it seemed to say about her.

That message she received over and over again: that mistakes were not just accidents—they were flaws in her character. Every forgotten task, every misplaced item, every childish misstep was treated like a personal failure. Love felt conditional. Safety felt earned. In her mind, mistakes equaled rejection.

So, she grew up believing that mistakes made you unlovable.

And now, even as an adult, even as a mother, that belief still lived in her. It whispered lies in her ear when her children messed up. It made her forget they were just kids. It made her react as if their small slip-ups were threats to her stability, when really, they were just learning—just as she once was. She hated it. Hated how the chaos inside her leaked out into the lives of the people she loved most. But knowing it and changing it were two very different things.

But as she sought the Lord's wisdom, Mara realized that parenting from a foundation of love rather than fear was possible. This shift changed everything. Although four of her children were already older, it was not too late. Her healing still mattered.

As Mara faced the weight of her anxieties and the constant need to control every detail of her children's lives, she began to seek the Lord's guidance. She realized that she could not let worry rule her heart any longer. Slowly, she learned how to let anxiousness and fear release their hold on her. To do this, she relied on her faith in God, allowing the Holy Spirit to guide her. She understood that she was not the savior of her children, nor could she carry the weight of their lives alone. She learned to release control to Him, trusting His guidance. The more she prayed and reflected on Scripture, the more she felt safe and able to let go.

She held onto verses such as Philippians 4:6-7:

Be careful for nothing; but in every thing by prayer and supplication with thanksgiving let your requests be made known unto God. And the peace of God, which passeth all understanding, shall keep your hearts and minds through Christ Jesus."

And 1 Peter 5:7:

Casting all your care upon him; for he careth for you."

Even when it felt as if her life had been stripped away from her—that all her struggles, losses, and hardships had left her alone—she began to recognize that God had been with her every step. Through every doubt, fear, and trial, He carried her, never abandoning her. Gradually, she could see how He had protected her and guided her, even in the moments that had once felt unbearably dark. Some days, worries still crept in, and she felt the pull of anxiety. Yet, in those moments, she would pause, pray, and worship, reminding herself that God was in control. She would quietly say, "Lord, let Your will be done," lifting her heart in praise and surrender. Each time she did, she felt a profound peace wash over her, a reassurance that she was not alone, and that her children—and her life—were held safely in His hands. Worship became a way for her to release fear, trust His plan, and center her heart in His presence.

She started to notice the way her words sounded when she spoke with kindness rather than frustration. She observed how her children responded when she approached them with patience instead of anger. Mara was learning to see her children as they truly were, not through the lens of her own past hurts...

Each day, she made the choice to release a bit more of the anger that had once gripped her and let go of the hurt that had shaped her responses. She was not perfect; some days, she stumbled.

There were days when the old patterns crept back in.

Sometimes, Mara would still find herself triggered—swept up suddenly and painfully in the emotional echoes of her past. It was not always the noise or the mess. More often, it was the invisible things—the moments when she felt unheard, unseen, dismissed. When someone ignored her boundaries. When her children brushed off her request. When a sigh, an eye-roll, or a quick remark left her feeling like she didn't matter.

Her body would react before her mind could reason. Her heart would race, her chest would tighten, and that familiar ache of rejection would rise up—sharp and immediate. It was not just about the moment in front of her. It was old pain, resurfacing. Deep-rooted fears whispering lies: *They do not respect you. You are not important. You are failing again.*

And in those moments, she would react—not always in anger, but in defense. A harsh word. A withdrawn silence. The impulse to control or correct before she could even name what she was feeling.

In those moments, she would snap—or shut down—or say things she did not mean. Afterward, the guilt would settle heavily on her shoulders. She would spiral, quietly condemning herself, telling herself she had not changed at all—and at times, others reminded her of this too.

In the past, Mara would let that guilt pull her down into depression and sadness. But now, she went to the Lord. Even when she broke down, she no longer stayed there. She returned to her Lord and Savior—the only One who truly saw her heart.

She would often let out loud, broken cries of tears, sometimes just a whisper:
"I'm sorry. I failed again."

To everyone else, she seemed fine, but inside, she screamed:
"Lord, I need you. Please forgive me."

And every time, He met her there.
Not with shame. Not with distance. But with a gentle voice that reminded her,
"I already forgave you."
"When you gave it to Me, I removed it."
"I don't even remember it anymore."

That kind of grace undid her. It softened the shame. It reminded her that love was not withdrawn when she messed up. That she didn't have to earn her place in His heart.

She began to realize that guilt was not from God. Guilt kept her trapped. His forgiveness set her free.

Mara still journaled, still brought her raw, unfiltered thoughts to God—confessing not just her actions, but the deep ache beneath them. And little by little, her past lost its grip. Not because she forgot it, but because He had already redeemed it.

In God's strength, she could rewrite the narrative for her family.

Little by little, she was transforming into the mother her children needed, and in doing so, she was creating a legacy of love, compassion, and healing for the next generation.

She apologized to her children, acknowledging the ways she had fallen short as a mother. She learned to let go of her perfectionism, choosing instead to show love through patience, kindness, and humility. As she found space to breathe, she was able to repair and rebuild those relationships—and keep them.

As she works to be a better steward of her role as a mother, she strives to show her children the love of God, both in private and public. In relationships, especially within families, inconsistencies between public and private behavior can lead to confusion and emotional distance. For example, a caregiver may display kindness, patience, and support in public settings—such as at work, in church, or among friends—but then behave indifferently, impatiently, or even harshly at home.

This inconsistency can cause those in their care, such as children, spouses, or other loved ones, to feel as though they are not as valued or loved in the private sphere, leading to emotional hurt or alienation.

If they see their care givers' love as something that is only for public display, they may struggle to understand the true meaning of love—unconditional and consistent.

Jesus, however, demonstrates unwavering, unconditional love—He is the same yesterday, today, and forever Hebrews 13:8. His love is not conditional on our actions or behavior. The love we show to those we care for should reflect the love Jesus has for each of us. He did not love in public and then behave differently in private.

His love was consistent, whether He was speaking to crowds or spending time alone with His disciples. Jesus showed His love by His actions, His sacrifice, and His willingness to walk alongside us in our struggles. We are called to mirror that love in our relationships with those we care for.

The Balance of Discipline and Grace

Mara had always believed that discipline meant control. If her children obeyed quickly and without question, it was a sign she was doing her job well. She clung to the phrase she had heard all her life: "Spare the rod, spoil the child." What she did not understand was that the rod was never meant to hurt—it was meant to guide. Like a shepherd's rod, it was a tool of love, not fear.

She remembered the times when her words came out sharper than she intended, when her tone was harsher than she wanted. Discipline, she began to learn, was not about punishment alone. It was about shaping the heart. The rod, the correction, was to teach—not to break.

Discipline without grace created fear, and fear was the enemy of love. The words of 1 John 4:18 echoed in her heart: "There is no fear in love: but perfect love casteth out fear." Mara wanted her home to be filled with that kind of love—love that corrected but did not crush, love that shaped rather than shamed.

She saw how quickness to anger or frustration only pushed her children away, creating walls instead of bridges. God's Word reminded her, "Fathers, provoke not your children to wrath: but bring them up in the nurture and admonition of the Lord" Ephesians 6:4. Discipline was meant to be patient and nurturing, not harsh and punishing.

Mara began to ask herself if she was shaping her children's hearts or simply controlling their actions. Was her discipline rooted in love, or driven by fear?

She started to explain the reasons behind her expectations instead of issuing commands without explanation. Rather than simply saying, "Do this," she would say, "We do this because it helps us respect each other and take care of what we have." This small shift invited cooperation instead of rebellion.

Mara learned that authority without empathy created silence and distance. When discipline was balanced with compassion, it fostered connection and trust. Proverbs 22:6 whispered hope: "Train up a child in the way he should go: and when he is old, he will not depart from it." Loving, respectful guidance planted seeds that would grow deep.

She also discovered that parenting was not only about shaping children—it was about being shaped herself. Every moment of tension, every challenge, every mistake was an invitation to grow in grace. To lead with humility. To discipline without damaging.

But to do this well, Mara had to lay down the heavy bags she carried—the fear of failure, the guilt from past mistakes, the pressure to be perfect. She had to trust that God could use even her flaws to teach her children something beautiful.

Mara did not get it right every day. She still raised her voice too often, got overwhelmed, and doubted herself. But she was learning. Learning that discipline without grace builds walls; authority without empathy creates silence; and love paired with truth transforms.

And in that slow, holy work, her home began to change. Not into a perfect place, but into a safe one. Where truth and love walked hand in hand. Where discipline guided but never crushed. And where grace made room for everyone to grow.

Emptying the Emotional Baggage

Mara had always believed that if she just loved her children hard enough, stayed involved enough, and protected them fiercely, they would grow up unscarred. But what she had not expected was how her own unhealed wounds would show up — not just in her private thoughts, but in how she responded to her children's struggles.

She did not realize, at first, that she was parenting from fear — fear that they would make the same mistakes she did, or worse, suffer the same pain. It was a fear so deep-rooted that it shaped her reactions more than she wanted to admit.

When Fizzle did not make all A's and Mara grounded him, it was not just about grades. It was about her fear of him falling behind, of the world not giving him second chances. She wanted to protect him from failure, but her punishment sometimes made him feel like he was a failure.

When Blue got into trouble at school and Mara took away her long-awaited Justin Bieber tickets, it was not out of cruelty — it was heartbreak. Blue had looked forward to that concert for months. But Mara did not know another way to say, "You matter, and I need you to take life seriously." What she did not realize was that her daughter needed understanding, not shame. She needed connection, not consequences alone.

Lady, bright and beautiful, found herself labeled the biggest flirt at school. Mara's reaction was swift — she pulled her from school completely. She wanted to shield her from judgment, from making decisions that would haunt her. But what Lady needed was guidance, not exile. Mara did not yet know how to walk her through the pain without letting her drown in it.

Aqua often talked back, and Mara took it as defiance. But underneath that attitude was a young girl overstimulated by life, full of emotions she did not yet have the tools to manage. Aqua was not disrespecting her mother — she was overwhelmed. She did not feel seen. But Mara, burdened by her own past, interpreted Aqua's intensity as rebellion instead of a cry for help.

And then there was JJ. Gentle, bright, and curious — but sometimes dishonest. He would say he was reading his Bible or doing something responsible, but Mara would later discover otherwise. She did not always respond with grace. She had been taught that a lie meant you were broken, and she feared what dishonesty might mean for his future. But what JJ needed was a space to tell the truth without fear, to make mistakes and still be loved.

Each child was different. Each one was trying to find their way. And Mara — still healing, still learning — sometimes took their choices as reflections of her failures.

"If they mess up, it means I have failed as a mother."
"If they fall, it must be because I did not raise them right."

These thoughts haunted her. She did not yet know how to separate their journeys from her identity.

But God did. And slowly, Mara started to see what was really happening: she was still carrying her past into her parenting. The perfectionism, the fear, the overreaction — it was not about her kids. It was about the baggage she never laid down.

So she began to release it — not all at once, but bit by bit. She forgave herself for the mistakes she had made in anger, in fear, in exhaustion.

She brought her regrets to God and asked Him to show her how to parent with grace, not guilt.
She realized her children did not need a perfect mother — they needed a present one. A mother willing to listen. To slow down. To try again.

And as she learned this, she changed.
Not overnight.
But with each honest apology.
With each time she chose conversation over punishment.
Each moment she stopped herself from yelling and instead asked, "What is really going on in your heart?"

She started to learn what love looks like without the weight of baggage.

Because Mara's story was not about perfection.
It was about transformation.

Her children still made mistakes.
She still made mistakes.
But now, the home was not filled with the echo of anger — it was filled with healing, with hugs after hard talks, with the courage to begin again.

This is what it means to empty the emotional baggage.
To name the hurt.
To stop letting fear be the loudest voice in the room.
To let grace take the lead.
And to trust that God can use even brokenness to build something beautiful.

For Mara, overcoming the challenge of trusting others was often difficult, especially after the betrayal and hurt she experienced from trusted adults and others in her life.

Trust After Betrayal from Trusted Adults

Betrayal by those we trust leaves wounds that cut deeper than most. For Mara, this betrayal did not come from strangers, but from people her family had trusted—people who should have protected her, but instead caused harm. That pain did not stay buried in her past; it seeped into her parenting, her relationships, and her sense of safety in the world.

She wrestled with why rebuilding trust felt so difficult. It was more than just a personal struggle—it was a battle to break cycles that threatened to repeat themselves across generations. Mara knew she had to learn how to balance protecting her children from harm while allowing them the freedom to grow into secure and independent individuals.

Children see adults as protectors by nature—parents, family members, close friends—people who are supposed to be safe. When those protectors become the source of pain, it causes confusion and fear that can last a lifetime. Mara's mother and Aunt Sarah had believed in these relatives too, never imagining they would be the ones to betray that trust. But the truth was undeniable.

Mara carried these lessons close when it came to Naomi, who had violated her as a child. She refused to let her children visit Naomi's house alone or stay overnight. Some might call it strict, but for Mara, these boundaries were essential shields, protecting her children from harm she knew all too well.

Yet, Mara also understood that parenting out of fear alone could be dangerous. She saw how unresolved trauma could turn into a cage, isolating children instead of empowering them. Finding balance meant learning to recognize real threats without letting old wounds shape every decision.

Protecting children meant teaching them to be aware and resilient—not making them afraid of the world. Mara worked to create spaces where her children could share their feelings openly and learn to trust again. She knew that shielding them did not mean cutting them off from connection.

It was difficult to tell the difference between rational and irrational fear. Rational fear grounded itself in real dangers. Not allowing her children around someone with a history of abuse was a necessary act of protection. But irrational fear, fed by past pain, whispered lies—that no one could be trusted, and that safety was impossible.

Mara found herself caught between these fears. She was right to protect her children from unsafe individuals. Yet sometimes, those fears began to consume her, making her decisions driven more by pain than by caution. The line between protection and prison grew thin.

Healing became her most urgent work—not just for herself, but for the future of her family. Only by tending to her own wounds could Mara learn to discern when fear was a friend and when it was a foe. Only then could she teach her children to trust again, to walk bravely in a world that was both beautiful and broken.

Breaking the Cycle

Mara knew that breaking the cycle meant more than protecting children from harm—it meant facing her own past and carrying out healing that could ripple through generations. Whether children were still at home or grown and walking their own path, the work of restoration was never truly finished.

Healing began with acknowledging the pain carried inside, even when it was difficult to speak aloud. Mara understood she did not need to relive every detail, but admitting, "This happened to me, and it shaped me," was the first step toward freedom. In the quiet moments of her heart, she found comfort in Psalm 147:3: "He healeth the broken in heart, and bindeth up their wounds."

But some of the wounds were tangled too deeply for her to sort through alone. Eventually, Mara came to see that courage was not just in what she faced by herself—it was also in asking for help. Sitting with a trusted Christian counselor became a sacred space where she could begin untangling years of silence, shame, and sorrow. Proverbs 15:22 whispered to her, "Without counsel purposes are disappointed: but in the multitude of counsellors they are established." Healing, she realized, was never meant to be a solitary path.

Trust was fragile and had to be rebuilt again and again, no matter the age of the child. Mara learned that open, patient communication formed the foundation for that trust—whether around the family table or across the miles in a phone call. Ephesians 4:29 reminded her to speak life: "Let no corrupt communication proceed out of your mouth, but that which is good to the use of edifying."

Teaching children about their bodies—their own to protect and honor—was a truth that held across all seasons of life. Whether encouraging a young child to say "no," or supporting an adult child in setting boundaries, Mara held to the truth of 1 Corinthians 6:19: "Know ye not that your body is the temple of the Holy Ghost…?" She wanted her children to know their worth, their voice, and their right to say no.

Building a village of trust meant surrounding her family with safe, faithful relationships—friends, mentors, and leaders whose actions matched their words. Mara knew trust had to be earned slowly, especially when the past had taught her to be wary. Proverbs 27:17 echoed in her soul: "Iron sharpeneth iron; so a man sharpeneth the countenance of his friend." Her children needed sharpening, not sheltering—encouragement, not isolation.

Balancing freedom with protection was a delicate dance. Mara was learning how to become comfortable letting her children go without being controlled by fear. When her heart felt anxious, she would whisper the words of Psalm 56:3: "What time I am afraid, I will trust in thee." Learning to trust God with her children—especially as they became older—meant surrendering control. She reminded herself that releasing them was not giving up, but handing them over to the One who loved them more than she ever could.

When a parent's life has been marked by chaos and unpredictability, it can be easy to believe that control equals safety. Not because they want to be controlling, but because the world has felt so unsafe that they believe only strict protection will keep their children from harm. Mara wrestled with this often. But little by little, the more she trusted God, the more she was able to let go. Sometimes the hardest part of parenting is the surrender—to release what is most precious and allow God to do what only He can do.

She also realized some wounds came not from what was done—but from what was left undone. The silence. The coldness. The emotional distance. Breaking that silence meant fostering honest, heartfelt conversations and refusing to let fear or shame build walls between hearts. Jesus' words in John 13:34-35 became her compass: "A new commandment I give unto you, That ye love one another; as I have loved you... By this shall all men know that ye are my disciples, if ye have love one to another."

This was Mara's ongoing work—not just for her children, but for herself. To face her past with courage, to keep setting healthy boundaries, to nurture trust slowly, and to build a family life where love and safety walked hand in hand. It was a messy, imperfect process—but it was also a story of hope and healing still unfolding.

Invisible Scars of Good Intentions

Long after Mara escaped the physical violence and chaos of her past, she found herself facing a different kind of struggle—one that was quieter, harder to name, but equally damaging. She had learned how to survive. She had learned how to protect. But she had never learned how to be emotionally present, especially for those she loved the most.

Mara never intended to cause harm. In fact, she worked tirelessly to be everything her children needed. She provided, she disciplined, she kept the house in order. But in the midst of all that doing, something essential was missing: her emotional presence.

She began to realize that being physically present was not the same as being emotionally available. She would sit beside her children, nodding at their stories, while her mind wandered to unpaid bills, unfinished chores, or the next problem to solve. When they reached for her, they were often met with a distracted "uh-huh," a tired sigh, or silence. She had no idea how deeply that silence could echo in a child's heart.

Her children, confused and hurt, began to retreat. They stopped sharing. They stopped trying. They still loved her, but they did not feel safe enough to come close. Mara wondered why they were pulling away, unaware that her emotional absence was slowly creating the very disconnection she feared most.

She had thought that avoiding conflict was love. That silence was peace. That tough love was strength. But now, looking back, she saw how often she had minimized their feelings, brushed aside their sadness, or expected them to "get over it" without offering comfort.

Mara's own childhood had never taught her how to sit with pain—her own or anyone else's. No one had modeled affection or taught her to express love with words or tenderness. Physical affection felt foreign. Encouragement did not come naturally. When her children failed or broke down, she responded with frustration rather than grace, assuming they should know how to bounce back. But they were not learning resilience; they were learning fear.

She also set high standards for her children, believing it would prepare them for life. But what they often felt instead was pressure. Expectations without empathy. Structure without softness. When things went wrong, Mara struggled to comfort them. Instead of offering reassurance, she often responded with silence, withdrawal, or disapproval.

It was never intentional. She thought she was doing the right thing—being strong, holding it together, setting an example. Life had taught her that love meant sacrifice, not softness; that strength meant never letting emotion get in the way of doing what is right. So she raised her children with order, with rules, with the constant reminder to "do better," "try harder," "be good."

She believed this was love. In her mind, structure meant safety. Correction meant care. But to her children, it did not always feel that way.

They heard her words—but not her heart. They felt her expectations—but not her embrace. They saw her discipline—but not her delight.

As they grew, they began to associate "love" with performance. They learned that approval came when they behaved, that affection was hidden behind achievement. And without realizing it, they carried that same lens into their view of God.

When they heard people speak about the Lord Jesus, they thought of more rules. More demands. More chances to disappoint. They knew all about His truth—but not about His tenderness. They could quote verses about sin—but not about grace. They could recite commandments—but not feel the comfort of His presence.

And so, they pulled away. Not because they rejected *Jesus Himself,* but because they never really knew His heart. They confused the voice of correction for the voice of condemnation. They did not realize that the same Lord who speaks truth also knelt down to wash feet. That the same One who calls for repentance also restores with compassion. That His rules are never without relationship—His truth never without love.

Years later, some of them began to see. They met others who spoke of Jesus not as a distant Master, but as a gentle Shepherd. They read His words again and saw what they had missed before—eyes full of mercy, arms open wide. And they began to understand: The love they longed for was never absent—only misunderstood. The discipline they feared was meant to protect, not punish. And the God they once thought was hard and distant was actually the Father they had been longing for all along.

As Mara's heart softened and she leaned into healing, she began to see these patterns for what they truly were: echoes of her own unmet needs. Her emotional absence had not been cruelty—it had been survival. But survival had outlived its purpose. Now, it was time to live, to love, and to learn a different way.

She did not have all the answers, but she began to ask better questions. What would it look like to truly listen? To speak gently? To offer affection even when it felt awkward? To apologize when she missed the mark?

Little by little, Mara began to show up—not just in body, but in heart. She chose to hug more. To listen longer. To speak softer. She stopped trying to be the perfect parent and started learning how to be a present one.

It was not about grand gestures. It was about showing up when her children were hurting. Celebrating their small wins. Sitting beside them in silence when words were too much. And most of all, reminding them through her actions that their feelings mattered. That they mattered.

Many parents, like Mara, do not realize the power of their quiet habits. It is not about being perfect—it is about being present. Choosing to pause and listen. Offering affection even when it feels unfamiliar. Speaking with kindness, even in stress. These choices may seem small, but they have the power to heal what silence once hurt.

Through the grace of God and the quiet work of the Holy Spirit, Mara began to understand that true healing was not only about ending cycles of abuse—it was also about rebuilding what was quietly broken. And sometimes, what is broken the most is what was never said, never shared, never felt.

Mara's story is not just one of survival, but of awakening. Awakening to the power of emotional presence. Awakening to the truth that love is not just about protection—it is about connection.

Where Love Learns to Speak

For Mara, silence was never just the absence of words—it was a heavy, invisible weight that shaped her childhood and lingered into adulthood. When conflict arose, instead of hearing comfort or understanding, she was met with cold distance. Family members would shut down or turn away, leaving Mara alone in the quiet, aching for validation that never came. This pattern repeated itself so often that silence became synonymous with punishment, leaving wounds deeper than any harsh words ever could—reminding us that "a soft answer turneth away wrath" Proverbs 15:1, yet Mara rarely received such gentleness.

Mara came to understand that this silent treatment wasn't just a family issue; it could appear anywhere—in friendships, romantic relationships, even at work. When silence was used to punish or control, it shattered trust and left her feeling powerless. She learned it was a toxic pattern no one should accept.

Over time, Mara realized that silent treatment carved deep grooves in her heart. As a child, she believed it was her job to fix the broken emotions of others, to keep the peace by walking on eggshells and hiding her own feelings. This need to "fix" became a shadow she carried well into adulthood. If someone around her was upset, she instinctively blamed herself, bending over backward to regain approval, even when it cost her own happiness. She came to understand the wisdom of "letting your speech be always with grace, seasoned with salt," Colossians 4:6 but struggled to live it out.

This coping pattern spilled into her parenting. Mara struggled to set healthy emotional boundaries with her own children. When they were upset, she felt compelled to smooth things over quickly, fearing that discomfort meant something was wrong. She found herself explaining her choices over and over, trying to make sure her intentions were clear—yet, in doing so, she sent an unspoken message: feelings should be fixed fast, not simply felt.

Friendships, too, felt complicated. Mara often gave more than she had, trying to make others happy, apologizing when no apology was needed, and saying "yes" when her heart whispered "no." This left her feeling drained and sometimes resentful, though it was hard for her to see the cause. Setting boundaries felt like a risk—what if a friend got upset or left?

Romantic relationships brought an even tougher challenge. The silence Mara knew so well taught her to avoid conflict at all costs. She learned to suppress her own feelings, put her partner's needs first, and stay silent rather than rock the boat. This "peacekeeping" cost her her voice and sometimes her sense of self. The fear of abandonment made her vulnerable to partners who were emotionally unavailable or controlling, deepening the wounds silence had already opened.

At work, Mara noticed the same pattern. She was hesitant to speak up, afraid to upset supervisors or colleagues. Criticism felt like confirmation she had failed, and she often took on more than her share, desperate not to disappoint. Over time, this eroded her confidence, leaving her anxious and exhausted, trapped in a cycle of trying harder to earn approval she never truly felt she deserved.

Mara learned that silence carries many meanings. Sometimes it is a weapon, wielded deliberately to control or punish—ignoring calls, refusing to speak, or turning cold during disagreements. This kind of silence isolates and wounds, breaking trust and leaving those on the receiving end feeling rejected and confused.

But silence can also be a sanctuary—a needed pause to gather thoughts, cool heated emotions, and prepare for honest conversation. The difference lies in intention and communication. When someone says, "I need time to think," it opens space for healing rather than harm.

For Mara, recognizing these differences was a breakthrough. She began to set boundaries, speak her truth, and seek help when the silence felt overwhelming. Healing was neither quick nor easy, but each step forward was a quiet victory—a promise that the silence no longer had to define her story.

The Armor That Isolates

Mara's relationships were deeply affected by a lifetime of emotional wounds—not just from childhood, but from a long pattern of neglect, betrayal, and abuse that followed her into adulthood. From early experiences of being overlooked and unheard to painful relationships marked by manipulation and abandonment, each layer of trauma left her more guarded, more uncertain of love. These experiences shaped the way she connected with others, teaching her to protect herself before anyone else could hurt her.

Within her family, Mara found a rare place to be herself. She was funny, quick-witted, and had a gift for making everyone laugh. Her humor could light up a room, even on the hardest days. This was where she felt safest—where she could drop her guard and simply be Mara.

But outside that circle, things were different.

Mara was guarded, shy, and often acted as though she had everything under control. She masked her vulnerability with humor and a confident front, carefully hiding the fears she carried deep inside. While she longed for connection and love beyond her family, her past had taught her that such love might never be truly safe.

She rarely let anyone outside her inner circle see the real her. The thought of revealing her true self—flaws, fears, and all—felt too risky. When people tried to get close, Mara often pulled away or sabotaged the relationship before it could deepen. Dating, especially, came with anxiety. She would make plans, sometimes even go on dates, but then cancel at the last minute or slowly drift away.

Mara feared every man was the same—someone who would eventually hurt or abandon her. The idea of letting someone in was terrifying. So, she chose to walk away first.

Her emotional walls were not built to reject love—they were built to protect her from being hurt again. She mistook her guardedness for strength, but in truth, it only deepened her isolation. Even when she tried to reach out, fear held her back. Trusting others fully felt impossible.

This cycle was not her fault. It was a survival skill she had learned as a child—a way to stay safe from emotional pain. But survival is not the same as living.

Over time, Mara began to see that the strategies that once protected her were now keeping her alone. Healing meant learning to move from survival to self-compassion—and slowly, to the courage of letting others in.

Understanding the Cycle

This cycle is often rooted in experiences of emotional disconnection, fear of rejection, fear of abandonment, perfectionism, and unresolved trauma from. These patterns shape how we parent our children, relate to our spouses, and navigate life's challenges.

Without awareness and healing, we may unknowingly repeat the very behaviors. What is familiar can feel "normal," even if it is painful. This is how generational trauma continues—until someone recognizes it and chooses to do the hard work of change.

These subtle patterns are how trauma gets "handed down" from one generation to the next.

Signs of Generational Trauma

Strict, fear-based parenting: Parents rely on punishment, fear, or control rather than understanding and empathy.

Emotional disconnection: Parents struggle to comfort their child when they are sad, anxious, or afraid.

Perfectionism: Children are taught that they must be "perfect" to be loved or accepted.

Anger and irritability: Parents have quick tempers and outbursts, often reflecting unresolved pain from their own childhood.

Avoidance of vulnerability: Children are taught to "be strong" and "never show weakness," even when they need help.

Why Do We Repeat the Patterns of Our Parents?

It may seem strange that we repeat the behaviors of our parents, even if we disliked how they treated us. But there is a reason for this: Familiarity feels safe, even when it is painful.

The brain naturally seeks out what feels familiar, even if it is uncomfortable.

From a young age, our brains absorb everything around us. We learn how love looks, how conflict is handled, and what it means to feel safe. If love came with conditions, like being "good" to receive affection, the brain registers that as normal. If emotions were ignored or criticized, we may learn to hide our feelings or dismiss them in others. These early lessons create mental "scripts" about how relationships should work.

This is not a sign of failure. It is the brain following the patterns it was taught. Without awareness, these patterns show up in adult relationships and parenting. A person raised by emotionally distant caregivers might end up with an emotionally distant partner — not because they want it, but because it feels familiar.

These patterns often repeat in parenting. People may catch themselves saying or doing things they once swore they would never do. This happens because the brain follows old, deeply rooted pathways.

The good news is that change is possible. Through neuroplasticity — the brain's ability to rewire itself — we can create new pathways. But change takes effort, patience, and self-awareness. The first step is recognizing your patterns. From there, you can challenge them and develop new ways of thinking and relating.

As believers, we can lean on the power of Jesus Christ to break these cycles. Scripture reminds us in Romans 12:2 , *"And be not fashioned according to this world: but be ye transformed by the renewing of your mind, that ye may prove what is the good and acceptable and perfect will of God."* This verse highlights the importance of renewing our minds, which aligns with the concept of neuroplasticity.

Through faith, prayer, and reliance on God's strength, we can overcome old patterns that no longer serve us. **2 Corinthians 12:9** says, *"And he hath said unto me, My grace is sufficient for thee: for my power is made perfect in weakness. Most gladly therefore will I rather glory in my weaknesses, that the power of Christ may rest upon me."* This reminds us that even when change feels hard, God's grace gives us the strength to keep going.

Over time, new pathways form, and with compassion for yourself — and faith in Jesus Christ — you can break free from old patterns and build healthier, more loving relationships.

How We Break the Cycle

Self-Awareness and Clarity

The first step to breaking the cycle is recognizing the patterns in your own behavior and responses. Reflect on your actions and ask yourself:

What patterns from my childhood am I now repeating in my relationships or interactions?

How do I respond when someone expresses emotions or needs? Am I empathetic, dismissive, or avoidant?

Do I try to control situations or people to maintain peace, or do I allow others to think and feel for themselves?

How do I handle conflict? Do I avoid it, overcompensate, or address it directly with respect and honesty?

When I feel triggered, do I take a moment to reflect, or do I react based on old wounds?

Grace Over Guilt

Many of us struggle with emotional challenges because we were never taught how to care for our hearts in a godly way. The Bible shows us that God is our perfect Father, who comforts, heals, and restores us (Psalm 68:5, Isaiah 66:13). If no one comforted you as a child, you may not know how to comfort yourself—or others. But God invites us to learn from Him how to nurture our souls and extend grace to ourselves and others.

When you feel hurt:
Don't ignore your pain or harden your heart Psalm 34:18. Instead, bring your hurt to the Lord in prayerPhilippians 4:6-7 and comfort yourself with His promises. Just as God comforts the brokenhearted 2 Corinthians 1:3-4, you can learn to offer yourself that same compassion.

When you make mistakes:
Remember God's grace is greater than all your sins 1 John 1:9. Instead of condemning yourself, offer forgiveness and kindness as God does through Christ Ephesians 4:32. Confess your faults, but do not dwell in shame—live in the freedom of His mercy Romans 8:1.

When you feel overwhelmed:
Cast your cares on the Lord because He cares for you 1 Peter 5:7. It's right to ask for help and to rest, as God commands us to observe Sabbath rest Exodus 20:8-10 and to find peace in Him Matthew 11:28-30. Taking care of your well-being honors God's design for your life.

By practicing this biblical "reparenting," you rebuild a sense of security rooted in God's love Romans 8:38-39. You break free from cycles of self-neglect and harsh self-judgment and grow into the new creation God has made you to be (2 Corinthians 5:17.

Set Boundaries and Let Go of Perfectionism

Trauma often grows in places filled with control, perfectionism, and shame. To break free, we must release the belief that you—or anyone else—must be perfect. Scripture reminds us:
"All have sinned and fall short of the glory of God" Romans 3:23. No one gets it right all the time—not you, your child, or your parents.

Perfectionism is a heavy burden that keeps us trapped in shame and fear. Instead, God calls us to rest in His grace and freedom 2 Corinthians 12:9.

Setting Boundaries
Set healthy limits with yourself and others to avoid burnout and overextending. Boundaries are acts of self-respect and honor God's design for rest (Matthew 11:28).

Seek Professional Help
Seeking professional help is one of the most powerful steps you can take to heal. Unfortunately, many cultures and communities attach stigma to therapy, perpetuating harmful beliefs such as:

"Something is wrong with you if you need therapy."

"You should just deal with it."

"Others have it worse, so you shouldn't complain."

These beliefs prevent many people from accessing the support they need. As a result, countless individuals silently struggle with pain, anxiety, and unresolved trauma. Therapy is not a sign of weakness—it is a courageous step toward self-awareness and healing. A professional therapist can help you unpack the layers of generational trauma, understand your triggers, and develop healthier coping strategies.

Remember, healing is not about comparing your struggles to others. Your pain is valid, and you deserve support no matter what others may have told you. Seeking help is an act of strength and self-respect.

Lean Into God's Love

Unlike human love, which is often conditional, God's love is unconditional. He does not expect perfection, nor does He shame us when we are afraid or weak. His love is consistent and unwavering. Leaning into His love is the first and most essential step toward healing from the pain and patterns passed down through generations.

Biblical Steps

Prayer and Meditation

Regular prayer can help you release burdens and fears to God. Ask Him for wisdom in identifying unhealthy patterns, strength to resist them, and grace to forgive those who hurt you and seek forgiveness from those you have hurt.

Practical Steps for Prayer:

Start with Gratitude: Acknowledge God's unwavering love.
"Thank You, Lord, for Your unconditional love. Thank You that You never leave or forsake me."

Repentance: Confess any sin, unforgiveness, or patterns you've participated in, and ask God to heal them.
"Lord, I repent for any sinful patterns I've carried—whether from my own actions or the generational sins passed down. I ask for Your forgiveness and Your help in breaking these cycles."

Forgiveness: Ask for the grace to forgive those who have hurt you, and to release them into God's hands. Also, ask for forgiveness from those you may have hurt.
"Lord, I choose to forgive those who have hurt me, whether intentionally or unintentionally. I release them to You, and I trust that You will heal my heart. If there are any relationships where I have caused pain, I ask for Your forgiveness, and for the opportunity to make things right."

Confession and Release: Lay down the pain, wounds, and toxic patterns that have been passed down.
"Lord, I release the trauma from my past, from my family's past, to You. I no longer want to carry this burden."

Petition for Strength and Wisdom: Ask for God's wisdom to recognize these patterns and the strength to resist them.
"Please give me wisdom to see the areas in my life where I need healing. Help me to walk in Your strength and break free from the patterns that have bound me."

Trust in His Will: End your prayer by declaring trust in God's healing process.
"I trust that You are working all things together for my good, and I believe that healing is coming."

Meditation on Scripture:
Reflecting on scripture will help guide your thoughts toward God's promises. Meditate on verses like:

Psalm 34:18 – *"The Lord is close to the brokenhearted and saves those who are crushed in spirit."*

Isaiah 61:3 – *"To provide for those who grieve...to bestow on them a crown of beauty instead of ashes, the oil of joy instead of mourning, and a garment of praise instead of a spirit of despair."*

Let God's Word sink deeply into your heart and let it replace the old, negative patterns with His truth.

2. Study Scripture

Dive deep into the Bible for guidance and encouragement. Verses like 2 Corinthians 5:17 remind us, "Therefore, if any man be in Christ, he is a new creature: old things are passed away; behold, all things become new." Your identity in Christ gives you the ability to start fresh.

Key Scriptures for Healing:

2 Corinthians 5:17 – *"Therefore, if anyone is in Christ, the new creation has come: The old has gone, the new is here!"*

Ephesians 1:7 – *"In Him we have redemption through His blood, the forgiveness of sins, in accordance with the riches of God's grace."*

Your identity in Christ means you are no longer bound by the past. You are a new creation, and God offers you the grace to break free from generational trauma.

3. Community: The Body of Christ

Healing also happens in the context of community. Surround yourself with fellow believers who can support and encourage you. The Church is not just a place for worship, but a place for healing, growth, and support. Find people who can pray for you and walk alongside you in your journey.

Scriptural Encouragement:

Romans 12:15 – *"Rejoice with those who rejoice; mourn with those who mourn."*

Galatians 6:2 – *"Carry each other's burdens, and in this way you will fulfill the law of Christ."*

Your church family can be a source of strength, helping you to carry the emotional burdens that come with healing. Don't hesitate to ask for prayer or support from those around you.

Speak Life and Break the Curse

Declare the truth: Break the cycle by speaking truth over yourself and your family. Declare blessings, not curses. Speak words of life over your children, affirming their worth and identity in Christ.

Pray against strongholds: Pray for deliverance if spiritual strongholds such as generational sin or curses exist. Seek prayer support from your church community or a spiritual leader to help you break free from these chains.

Be Patient and Persistent

Expect setbacks: Healing is a process, and there may be times when old patterns resurface. Be patient with yourself.

Breaking a cycle that has persisted for generations does not happen overnight.

Celebrate progress

Recognize and celebrate the small victories along the way. Each step toward healing and growth is a step toward breaking the cycle.

Breaking generational trauma is a legacy of love. Your children will not have to "earn" love through perfection or obedience. They will know they are loved because they exist.

Each time you offer compassion instead of criticism, patience instead of anger, and love instead of fear, you are creating a new path.

Yet, healing requires more than breaking free from generational patterns—it also demands confronting the allure of quick fixes.

Quick fixes are tempting because they promise immediate comfort, but they fail to provide lasting freedom. Mara had to face the reality that her healing journey was not about avoiding pain but about confronting it with courage, patience, and faith.

Breaking Free from Quick fixes

Life often tempts us with quick fixes and short-term solutions that promise relief but end up deepening our struggles. These choices can keep you trapped in a cycle of pain. Mara withdrew from others, using isolation as a shield to avoid the vulnerability of human connection. When loneliness became too heavy, she turned to toxic relationships—seeking comfort and validation in places that only left her feeling more unworthy and drained. These struggles did not just hurt her in the moment; they reinforced her deepest fears about herself, making the idea of healing feel impossible.

These unhealthy coping mechanisms can feel like survival tools in the moment, but over time, they only add to the weight we carry. Let us explore some of the most common traps and how they affect us:

Temporary Pleasures

We all crave escape sometimes. Whether it is binge-watching TV shows, scrolling endlessly on social media, or indulging in other fleeting comforts, these activities might numb the pain for a while. But afterward, we are often left feeling more disconnected and emptier, especially when we start comparing ourselves to others online.

Alcohol and Substance Use

When emotions become too overwhelming, it is easy to reach for a drink or other substances to dull the pain. While these may offer temporary relief, they can quickly lead to dependence, leaving us feeling even more lost and disconnected.

Toxic Relationships

Sometimes, we seek validation from people who do not genuinely care for us. Whether it is a draining friendship or an unhealthy partnership, staying in these relationships can magnify feelings of inadequacy and loneliness.

Overworking

Throwing ourselves into work can seem noble, even productive, but it is often a way to avoid dealing with emotional pain. The constant push for achievement can lead to burnout and a deep sense of emptiness.

Excessive Perfectionism

Setting unattainably high standards can create a relentless cycle of stress and self-criticism. When we inevitably fall short of perfection, the feelings of failure and inadequacy grow even stronger.

Isolation

Pulling away from others might feel like a way to protect ourselves from hurt, but isolation often intensifies loneliness. Without connection, it's even harder to seek support or begin healing.

These temporary fixes may provide momentary relief, but they drain energy and leave a person feeling more disconnected from themselves and their loved ones. Each day turns into a battle with fear, anxiety, and self-doubt as one struggles to maintain a facade of normalcy while these habits silently undermine well-being.

It is important to understand that these fleeting comforts do not bring lasting change. You might feel temporary relief, but once the effects fade, the emptiness remains, and the weight of the issues only deepens.

Seeking God for healing and restoration was the first step for Mara, but it was crucial to seek professional help to address the deeper root causes of these unhealthy patterns.

The journey to healing is not linear, but with patience and compassion, it is possible to break free from these cycles. You can learn to see yourself as worthy, capable, and deserving of love, success, and peace. The path toward healing comes from

God through a relationship with His Son, Jesus Christ. This connection, which goes beyond a general sense of faith, is deeply transformative.

No Perfect Love in Fear

Reflecting on Mara's traumatic experiences and her longing for true love, it was clear that these two were far apart. She deeply desired to know what true love felt like, but she could not—for two key reasons.

First, Mara had not allowed herself to experience God's love, and she did not love herself enough. Without God's love, every other kind of love remains incomplete. If only she had opened her heart to the love of Christ, she might have seen past the harsh words her partners often used against her. Instead, she let her identity and worth be defined by the actions and opinions of others. She forgot that God had already given her a spirit of love, power, and a sound mind. Fear became easier to accept because it was what she had always known. When someone has been wounded by trauma and rejection, fear can feel like safety. Walls are built—and Mara had built them too. Her life had become defined by defensiveness—guarded, suspicious, and unable to receive the very love she craved.

Fear had become Mara's default. It protected her from emotional wounds, yet in doing so, it also kept her from the love that could truly heal her. She believed love was dangerous, something to be feared, because it often brought rejection and pain. Yet the Bible promises a different truth: perfect love casts out fear 1 John 4:18. Mara had not fully embraced that love, so she remained trapped, unable to step into the freedom God's love offered.

God's perfect love is unconditional and unchanging, unlike the flawed love Mara had known. It does not depend on performance or past mistakes—it is freely given, waiting for her to accept it. When she began to understand this, her perspective slowly changed. She no longer measured her worth by harsh words or sought validation in toxic relationships. She started to see that she was God's creation, beautifully and uniquely made Ephesians 2:10.

As Mara opened her heart to God's love, she grew less defensive and more able to receive love from others. She forgave herself for past mistakes and began forgiving those who had hurt her Ephesians 4:32. Forgiveness unlocked the chains of fear, allowing God's love to transform her from the inside out. In time, she experienced the peace of God that transcends understanding Philippians 4:7. Love became a source of healing and strength, not pain. Her life was no longer defined by fear but by the perfect love of God.

Fear can hold us captive, but God's perfect love drives out that fear and sets us free. True healing begins when we accept His unconditional love, forgive ourselves and others, and let that love fill every part of our lives.

Has your story looked like Mara's? Have painful experiences made you doubt that true, godly love exists?

If so, it is time to return to your first love—Jesus. John 14:6 says, "I am the way, the truth, and the life. No one comes to the Father except through me."

Let Him love you. Let Him show you that you are worthy of true, holy love. You do not have to stay in places where you are mistreated, abused, or manipulated just to feel loved. That is not what God has for you.

God's love removes fear. His love restores, heals, and empowers.

So look to Him. Let His perfect love cast out the fear that has been holding you back.

> BE STRONG AND OF A GOOD COURAGE, FEAR NOT, NOR BE AFRAID OF THEM: FOR THE LORD THY GOD, HE IT IS THAT DOTH GO WITH THEE; HE WILL NOT FAIL THEE, NOR FORSAKE THEE.
> DEUTERONOMY 31:6 KJV

Identity Crisis—Embracing Your Worth in Christ

Imagine living each day feeling like you are not enough. That is where Mara was for years—stuck in a painful cycle of self-doubt and shame. She felt like she was constantly falling short, and her heart was weighed down by the belief that she was never good enough, no matter what she did.

Have you ever experienced the crushing weight of self-doubt? Mara's mind was a battlefield, with relentless negative thoughts screaming at her:

"You're not good enough." Whenever she compared herself to others, it was like a knife twisting deeper, making her feel worthless.

"You're a failure." Every mistake and misstep seemed to confirm her worst fears—that she was destined to disappoint and fall short.

"You're used up." The sense of being spent and exhausted, with nothing left to give, made her feel hollow and depleted.

These were not just passing thoughts but crushing weights that stole her joy and hope. They felt like a relentless storm cloud that followed her, obscuring any glimmer of self-worth and leaving her in a dark, dismal place.

It could have been fair if Mara's hurt and wounds were merely emotional. But hey, no! Even her physique was a source of torture. Mara had always been self-conscious about her lips. They were full, and while some might have considered that a blessing, it was a source of endless taunts for her. "Why do your lips look like that? If you put on lipstick, you will look like a clown!" they would jeer, their words cutting deep.

It did not stop there. Even when Mara tried to laugh it off and pretend it did bother her, the comments came from all directions. In school, they would yell, "Hey, Grace Jones!" someone would shout, referencing the famous singer known for her striking features, but not in a flattering way.

Others would mockingly call her "Woodstock," referring to the Peanuts character with distinctive bird-like features, drawing a comparison to her curly hair that did not always curl perfectly.

In middle school, Mara was also teased about her body, with cruel remarks about being flat-chested. Mara would even use tissues to pad her bra to make herself appear different, hoping it would help her fit in and escape the relentless taunts.

At home, she would stand in front of the mirror, her fingers tracing the outline of her lips. She wondered why they could not be smaller and like everyone else's. She longed to blend in, to be invisible, so no one would have anything to say about her. But no matter how hard she tried, the hurtful words echoed in her mind, reinforcing the idea that she was different in a way that was not celebrated, but ridiculed.

Have you ever felt like Mara? Have you ever been taunted, criticized, or belittled by people close to you, like friends, classmates, family, or a romantic partner? Have their words followed you, leaving emotional scars that impact how you view yourself? These negative comments can feel like a weight, shaping your thoughts and feelings for years. Mara once believed those voices, allowing them to define her. But over time, she began to ask herself: What if those voices weren't telling the truth? What if my worth isn't defined by others' opinions?

We often carry the pain of criticism, especially when it's from people we care about. When these moments occur, it's important to remember: Your value is not determined by how others treat you, and it's possible to heal and rebuild your sense of self.

Mara realized that she needed to set boundaries in her relationships. Setting boundaries isn't about rejecting people but protecting your peace.

When someone's words or actions hurt her, she began to respond with kindness and clarity: 'When you say that it hurts me. I need to be treated with respect.' If the other person responded with care, such as apologizing and working toward change, Mara knew the relationship was worth nurturing. However, if the person dismissed her feelings, Mara understood it might be time to reassess the relationship, especially if it continued to harm her emotional well-being.

She found her answer in the verses of Psalm 139 and read them aloud: "Thou didst cover me in my mother's womb. I will give thanks unto thee; for I am fearfully and wonderfully made" Psalm 139:13-14.

At that moment, she realized she was more than the sum of her imperfections. Fearfully and wonderfully made, she was a child of God, loved beyond measure.

The words washed over her, soothing the wounds that had festered for so long. As she meditated on the scripture, a new understanding began to take root in her heart. She realized that her identity was not defined by her appearance but by who she was in Christ.

Beloved, let Christ heal you. Outward beauty is fleeting—it would fade with time. But a woman who fears the Lord, who knows and believes who she is in Christ, would always be valuable.

Negative thoughts can be relentless, but God's Word reminds us to put on the full armor of God daily. It is not enough to stand guard every other day; we must be vigilant each day, arming ourselves with His truth. Every lie and attack must be met with the shield of faith, the sword of the Spirit, and the power of His Word.

Just like Mara, it is high time you focus on your inner qualities that truly matter. Also, pray for strength to let go of hurtful words from the past and to embrace the truth of your actual worth in Christ. Your outward appearance does not define you, but the fruit of God's Spirit in you does. The love, joy, peace, patience, kindness, goodness, faithfulness, gentleness, and self-control you exhibit distinguish you from the rest of the world.

The journey ahead would not be easy, and the voices of doubt would still try to creep in, but now she had something more substantial to hold on to. And with that, she began to see herself not as the world saw her but as God did, which is what matters.

As Christians, we often grapple with identity crises, especially when we are navigating life without truly understanding God's purpose for us. It can feel overwhelming when we find ourselves bombarded with instructions and messages dictating who we should be or what we must do. Amid the noise and chaos, it is natural to feel a sense of inadequacy, particularly when we struggle to meet the expectations set before us.

Apostle Paul reminds us in 1 Peter 2:9, "But ye are an elect race, a royal priesthood, a holy nation, a people for God's own possession, that ye may proclaim the excellencies of him who called you out of darkness into his marvelous light." This verse speaks to how special we are to God.

Or maybe you do not see yourself as special. Like Mara, you are special to God; that is why, against all odds, He has called you out of the crowd and into the light of His truth.

It took Mara a series of repeated heartbreaks, pain, all kinds of abuse, and torture before she realized and embraced who God said she was chosen, loved, and cherished.

Like Mara, people's hurtful and demeaning words have clouded your sense of judgment. Each time you try to remind yourself of your identity in Christ, your past comes knocking at your door, reminding you of all the horrible experiences you were subjected to.

Do you enjoy hearing any of that? It is time you rise and silence those voices. They have overstayed their welcome! Each time they come, remind yourself that you are loved, cherished, and chosen by God to carry out His works. Your identity is in Christ. No matter what happens, do not let anyone take that truth from you.

No one truly befriends you or chooses to be in your life because of your appearance. People want to be around you or in your life because of how you make them feel—through how you treat others and your genuine character. It is crucial to understand that healing from the negative impact of taunts and deceit is vital.

These hurtful comments and deceptions are tools of Satan, who is described in John 8:44 as "the father of lies" He aims to distort the truth and undermine your self-worth with falsehoods and deceit. In times when you feel overwhelmed by these lies, it is essential to counter them with the truth of God's Word. For instance:

Lie: You are a failure.
Truth: God's power defines Your worth and capabilities, not by your perceived failures.
I can do all this through him who gives me strength.
Philippians 4:13

Lie: "You'll never be forgiven for your past mistakes."
Truth: God's forgiveness is complete and unconditional.
   If we confess our sins, he is faithful and just and will forgive us our sins and purify us from all unrighteousness.
1 John 11

Lie: "No one will ever truly love you."

Truth: God's love for you is unwavering.
But God demonstrates his own love for us in this: While we were still sinners, Christ died for us.
     Romans 5:88

Remember, the lies of Satan are meant to lead you astray and keep you in bondage. By embracing God's truth and allowing it to renew your mind, you can overcome the negative impacts of deceit and embrace God's healing.

You are not just anyone; you are a beloved child of God. The Bible confirms this in the book of Romans, which says that God's Spirit testifies with our spirit that we are children of God. Most importantly, if God created you in His image and likeness, who are you if you are not His child?

There is freedom and hope in discovering your true identity in Christ. You are not defined by your past or the opinions of others; instead, you are defined by the unshakable truth of who you are in Him. Remember the words of

> BEHOLD, WHAT MANNER OF LOVE THE FATHER HATH BESTOWED UPON US, THAT WE SHOULD BE CALLED CHILDREN OF GOD; AND SUCH WE ARE. 1 JOHN 3:1

Breaking Free from Comparison: Celebrating Your Individual Journey

Mara often reflected on her relationship with the Lord, realizing that it is highly individualized. It's easy to fall into the comparison trap, especially when we look at others and wonder why their lives seem more blessed or prosperous. Even Peter, a great apostle who did remarkable things for God, fell victim to this comparison. Instead of focusing on his own mission, he became concerned with what was happening to John. The Lord redirected him, emphasizing the importance of focusing on his own calling.

In John 21:20-22, Peter, curious about John's future, asks Jesus about him. Jesus replies, "If I want him to remain until I come, what is that to you? You follow me!" This illustrates that each person's path is unique and designed by God, and we should focus on our journey instead of comparing ourselves to others.

Mara recognized that comparison often leads to feelings of jealousy or inadequacy, creating an unhealthy perspective on our blessings. She understood that most people do not see the struggles or sacrifices others have faced to achieve their successes. Instead of comparing herself to others, she learned to celebrate her own journey and focus on her relationship with the Lord.

Galatians 6:4 reminds us, "But let each man prove his own work, and then shall he have his glorying in regard of himself alone, and not of his neighbor." This verse encourages us to focus on our own actions rather than what others are doing.

Hebrews 12:1-2 states, "Wherefore, seeing we also are compassed about with so great a cloud of witnesses, let us also lay aside every weight and the sin which doth so easily beset us, and let us run with patience the race that is set before us, looking unto Jesus the author and perfecter of our faith." This verse urges believers to stay focused on their own race, not distracted by the paths of others.

Mara made it a point to remind herself not to look to the right or the left but to keep her eyes fixed on Jesus. To help maintain this focus, she often took breaks from social media and other distractions. These breaks allowed her to focus on what God was doing in her life, rather than comparing herself to others.

As time went on, Mara started to notice a transformation in her heart. She stopped looking at other people's lives as a yardstick for her own. Instead, she began to celebrate her own growth, no matter how small the steps seemed. She realized that comparing herself to others only distracted her from the work God was doing in her life.

In the quiet moments, Mara learned to cultivate a spirit of gratitude. She would pause throughout her day, recognizing the blessings she had—both big and small. When she started seeing her life through the lens of thankfulness, the yearning for what others had faded away. She understood that contentment was not found in what others possessed, but in recognizing the richness of her own life, designed by God.

Social media, which had once been a source of temptation to compare, became less of a challenge. Mara decided to take intentional breaks, using that time to refocus on her relationship with God. She curated her social media feeds to follow people who encouraged her and lifted her up spiritually, rather than contributing to feelings of inadequacy. These small changes helped her find balance, allowing her to stay grounded in her own journey without being distracted by the polished highlights of others' lives.

Over time, Mara's mindset shifted. Instead of seeing someone else's success as a threat to her own, she learned to view it as inspiration. She could celebrate the victories of others, knowing that their achievements didn't diminish the plans God had for her. She saw their progress not as a comparison to her own life, but as a reminder that God is at work in all of His children, each with a unique purpose.

When you spend time alone with the Lord and build a relationship with Him, He begins to reveal the plans and purposes He has for you in His Kingdom. By abiding in Him, your path becomes clearer, and He equips you to take the necessary steps toward fulfilling His purpose for your life. Along the way, God brings healing and restoration, walking beside you every step of the way.

You no longer have to compare yourself to others. In God's eyes, you are uniquely created with a purpose specifically designed for you. His plans for your life are perfect, and as you trust Him, He will lead you into a life of fulfillment and peace. Rest in the assurance that His grace is sufficient, and His love is enough.

Redefining Intimacy in God's Love

Mara's understanding of intimacy was deeply shaped by her past. As a child, moments that should have fostered security and emotional warmth instead brought confusion and pain. Intimacy became something she associated with vulnerability and rejection, not safety or love. These experiences left her numb, unsure of what a healthy connection looked like.

In her adulthood, this unresolved hurt manifested in a detached view of intimacy. For Mara, it became an outlet rather than an act of love—a way to momentarily silence the emotional chaos within. She did not know how to connect on a deeper level because the idea of vulnerability felt too dangerous. Intimacy had always been tied to fear, rejection, and inadequacy.

Romans 5:8 further revealed this to her: "But God commendeth his own love toward us, in that, while we were yet sinners, Christ died for us." Even in her brokenness, God loved her. His love was not dependent on her being perfect or free from her past—it was always there, constant and unwavering. Knowing she was loved unconditionally, Mara learned to trust again, not in people, but in God, who would never fail her.

Through this profound revelation, she experienced freedom from her past, and intimacy became holy, reflecting God's design for closeness and connection. Mara's heart was no longer bound by the lies of rejection but by the truth that God's love conquers all pain, rejection, and fear.

Through Christ's love, Mara finally found healing and learned that true love starts with knowing how deeply God loves her. With this foundation, she could embrace healthy, God-honoring intimacy built on trust, respect, and the love that only comes from the Father.

Mara realized that true intimacy was not meant to harm or diminish her; it was meant to reflect the love of God—a love that heals and builds up rather than tears down. God's love can heal the most profound pain. Through His grace, Mara found the strength to move beyond.

This love gave her the courage to believe in herself, to hope for true intimacy, and finally, to see herself as worthy of love. For the first time, Mara began to believe she was worthy of love. This understanding gave her the courage to hope for relationships that reflected the unconditional love of God, built on mutual trust, respect, and emotional connection.

True intimacy is more than physical—it is about being seen, known, and loved, first by God and then by others.

No Greater Love

There is no greater love than the love of God, the kind that would compel Him to lay down His life for those He cherishes. As Jesus said, "Greater love hath no man than this, that a man lay down his life for his friends" John 15:13. This divine love, immeasurable and profound, was what Mara discovered as she walked through her healing journey with the Lord.

The Lord was so patient with Mara on her healing journey. He did not judge her or condemn her for her shortcomings; He simply guided her with His grace and love, leading her to become the best version of herself—the woman He had called her to be.

In the depths of her healing journey, Mara discovered a love unlike any she had known. It was a gentle, tender love that never shamed her. He allowed her to grow at her own pace, to see truth she once could not bear to face. He guided her with a deep, immeasurable love, one that confirmed what she already suspected: He was her Lord, her Savior, and her first love.

In His presence, Mara found a love that transformed her without a single harsh word. There was no condemnation, no belittling, no crushing guilt. Instead, He walked beside her, step by fragile step, teaching her to trust, to hope, and to believe in the goodness He had placed within her. The Lord was infinitely patient, knowing her every fear, understanding her sensitivities. He knew how fragile her heart could be, and rather than force change, He nurtured it with kindness and compassion.

Even when Mara stumbled into sin, He did not turn away. He met her there, in that very place of brokenness, saying softly, "I am right here. I am not going anywhere." These words wrapped around her soul, calming her trembling spirit. She realized in that moment that no one could ever love her more than God. What she wanted, what she needed, was to be loved as He loved—patiently, wholeheartedly, without reservation.

His understanding astonished her. His patience undid her defenses. His kindness drew her nearer and nearer to His heart. This was love that healed, love that built trust. As she experienced it, Mara changed. No longer desperate for human approval, no longer caged by shame, she grew confident in the love that had first created her.

After knowing the Lord in this way, Mara could never settle for lesser loves that demanded her worthiness or found fault at every turn. She had tasted a love that was patient and kind, gentle and understanding—one that truly saw her, valued her, and never abandoned her. This love was supernatural and sustaining, a reality more powerful than anything she had dared to imagine. Having experienced such love, she knew she never wanted to lose it, no matter the cost.

Those who entered Mara's life afterward found a woman softened by grace. She carried a new gentleness, a calm assurance. She had been loved at her weakest, at her most vulnerable, and she had emerged stronger and more compassionate than before. She lived now as a testament that when the Lord pours out His patient, unwavering love, the human heart cannot help but bloom.

In His love, Mara discovered something beyond words. It was a deep friendship, a holy intimacy that transcended human understanding. It was not merely a story of self-improvement or personal growth, but a profound encounter with the living God who chose to love her completely. Nothing could ever match the sweetness of that truth.

Mara knew, beyond all doubt, that this love—patient, enduring, unconditional—had changed her forever. And in that knowledge, she found peace.

Guidepost: Abiding in His Love Daily

As Mara continued her journey, she came to understand the truth of Jesus' words: to love the Lord with all her heart and to love others as herself Matthew 22:37-39; Mark 12:30-31. When the Lord reshaped her heart, this command became the guiding principle of her life. At times, Mara would still slip into impatience or judgment, but the Lord would gently remind her, "Remember how I have loved you." In recalling His patient, gracious love, Mara learned to extend that same compassion to others, offering understanding where once she might have offered harshness.

If God had loved her so tenderly even as she struggled, how could she not give others that same mercy as they walked their own paths of healing? It was not always easy, but holding fast to the patience and kindness He had shown her made it possible. True transformation meant loving as He loved—patiently, gently, wholeheartedly.

Mara also realized that this was a continuing journey. Some days would be harder than others, yet she knew who her anchor was. The Lord's words echoed in her mind: "Pick up your cross and follow Me," and "Put on the full armor of God." She understood that staying connected to Him daily was not merely a suggestion but a necessity. Allowing even a day or two of drifting away from His presence gave the enemy more room to cause doubt and fear. Scripture warned her that the adversary prowled like a roaring lion, seeking to devour, and Mara saw clearly that she had to remain closely connected to the Source of her strength daily.

By abiding with the Lord each day, Mara guarded her heart against the enemy's tactics. This daily devotion kept her mindful of His patient, compassionate love. Rooted in Him, Mara rediscovered how to love as He did—offering the same tenderness, patience, and grace to others that she herself had so freely received.

After His Own Heart

Mara often wondered why David was described as a man after God's own heart. It puzzled her how someone so flawed, who had committed grievous sins, could still be so deeply loved and admired by the Lord. Mara longed for that same closeness with God. She yearned to be regarded as someone who sought after God's own heart. Her prayers frequently reflected this desire, and she would ask for wisdom, guidance, and revelation from the Holy Spirit to understand the secret behind David's relationship with the Lord.

Mara began to uncover profound truths about David's life and heart. The Holy Spirit would guide her to key passages, illuminating the essence of what made David unique. It was not that David was sinless or perfect—far from it. The Bible records many of David's sins, including his adultery with Bathsheba 2 Samuel 11 and his orchestration of Uriah's death 2 Samuel 11:14-17. Yet, what set David apart was his response to sin. David had a repentant heart.

In Psalm 51, written after the prophet Nathan confronted him about his sin with Bathsheba, David's repentance shines through. He cries out to God, saying:

"Have mercy upon me, O God, according to thy lovingkindness: according unto the multitude of thy tender mercies blot out my transgressions. Wash me thoroughly from mine iniquity and cleanse me from my sin. Create in me a clean heart, O God; and renew a right spirit within me" Psalm 51:1-2, 10.

David's prayer reveals a deep awareness of his sin and an earnest desire to be cleansed and restored to right standing with God. His plea to be purged with hyssop Psalm 51 alludes to Old Testament purification rituals, signifying his longing for spiritual cleansing. Mara saw in these verses the evidence of a heart that sought to be reconciled with God, no matter the cost.

Theologically, David's life illustrates the principle that God values a contrite and humble heart over outward perfection. Isaiah 66:2 declares, "These are the ones I look on with favor: those who are humble and contrite in spirit, and who tremble at my word." Mara realized that God's approval of David wasn't based on his achievements or moral perfection but on his willingness to repent and return to God wholeheartedly.

In her study, Mara also found parallels between David's life and the teachings of Jesus. In Luke 18:10-14, Jesus tells the parable of the Pharisee and the tax collector. The tax collector, standing at a distance and unwilling even to lift his eyes to heaven, prays, "God, have mercy on me, a sinner." Jesus commends this man, saying he went home justified before God. Like David, the tax collector exemplifies the attitude God desires: humility, repentance, and faith in God's mercy.

Mara began to apply these lessons to her own life. She learned that being "a person after God's own heart" didn't require perfection but a willingness to acknowledge her shortcomings and seek God's forgiveness and guidance.

Her prayers became more heartfelt and unfiltered, mirroring David's psalms.

> LORD, SEARCH MY HEART AND KNOW ME. REVEAL ANY AREA WHERE I'VE STRAYED FROM YOUR WILL. HELP ME TO TURN BACK TO YOU WITH ALL MY HEART. CREATE IN ME A PURE HEART, O GOD, AND RENEW A STEADFAST SPIRIT WITHIN ME." PSALM 51:1-2, 10,

Over time, Mara experienced a deeper intimacy with God. Through Scripture, prayer, and the work of the Holy Spirit, she came to understand that repentance wasn't just about confessing sin; it was about turning her whole heart back to God. This realization brought her peace and joy, knowing that, like David, she too could be a person after God's own heart. Remember, God's grace is always sufficient for those who turn to Him with a contrite heart.

Called to Purity

After experiencing a series of failed relationships, each leaving Mara more wounded than before, she reached a point of exhaustion. Each relationship felt like a cycle of longing, disappointment, and heartbreak. The relationship with Mike was especially painful. She had invested so much hope and energy into it, only to be left feeling even more disconnected from the kind of love she longed for.

During a time of deep prayer and quiet reflection, the Lord began to speak to Mara. As she spent time with Him, seeking healing and understanding, God revealed how her past relationships had affected her ability to connect with a man who truly loved God—and, in turn, could truly love her. The Lord gently showed Mara that her struggles with trusting and connecting with others were tied to the emotional wounds from her past, including her unresolved fears of abandonment, rejection, and unworthiness.

One day, during her quiet time with the Lord, Mara felt Him calling her to embrace a life of abstinence. This was not presented as a punishment, but as a sacred invitation to embark on a journey of healing and spiritual growth. The Lord revealed that celibacy would provide her with the space to focus on surrendering her heart fully to Him, allowing Him to restore and reshape her life according to His purpose.

Through prayer and reflection, Mara realized that her commitment to abstain from sex wasn't just about avoiding relationships—it was a way to ready her heart for the kind of love God truly desired for her.

The Lord showed her that this season of abstinence would help her cultivate purity—not just of the body, but of the heart and mind. It was an opportunity to deepen her relationship with God, align her life with His will, and create a foundation for a future relationship built on mutual love and respect.

One day, during her quiet time with the Lord, Mara felt Him calling her to embrace a life of abstinence. As she listened to this call, she realized that abstinence was the key to breaking free from unhealthy relationship patterns. It would give her the strength to heal from past hurts, build her identity in Christ, and learn to value herself the way God values her.

Mara started to understand that abstinence was not about closing herself off from love, but about preparing herself for the kind of relationship that would honor God and her own worth. She embraced this call, trusting that, in God's perfect timing, He would bring the right person into her life, someone who would cherish her as she cherished God.

Purity, in its true and most accurate biblical sense, is not just the absence of physical sin or impurity, but a lifestyle of honoring God with one's body, mind, and heart. It is about aligning one's thoughts, actions, and desires with God's will, respecting the sanctity of the body as His temple, and living in a way that reflects His holiness and righteousness. Purity encompasses both sexual and spiritual aspects of life, including how we relate to others, the choices we make, and how we steward our hearts and bodies.

In Scripture, purity is often connected with holiness. 1 Thessalonians 4:3-5 says, "It is God's will that you should be sanctified: that you should avoid sexual immorality; that each of you should learn to control your own body in a way that is holy and honorable, not in passionate lust like the heathen, who do not know God." This highlights that purity is not just about avoiding certain behaviors but also about pursuing a life of holiness, controlled desires, and honoring God in everything we do.

Purity is important to God because it reflects His character. God is holy, and He calls His people to be holy as well. In 1 Peter 1:16, God commands, "Be holy, because I am holy." Purity, particularly in relationships, demonstrates a commitment to God's plan for love, marriage, and sexuality. When we live in purity, we are better able to experience the fullness of God's love, grow spiritually, and remain free from the consequences of sin.

Purity also protects us emotionally, spiritually, and physically. 1 Corinthians 6:18-20 warns us to "flee from sexual immorality...Do you not know that your bodies are temples of the Holy Spirit, who is in you, whom you have received from God? You are not your own; you were bought at a price. Therefore, honor God with your bodies." Engaging in sexual sin or impurity can create emotional and spiritual scars, disrupt our intimacy with God, and damage relationships. Purity safeguards our hearts from unhealthy attachments, soul ties, and the consequences of sin that can affect our mental, emotional, and physical well-being.

The effects of purity are profound. First, purity fosters a closer relationship with God. By choosing to honor Him with our bodies and lives, we open ourselves to His guidance and blessings. Second, purity strengthens our character. It builds self-discipline, honor, and integrity, qualities that are foundational to living out God's will. Third, purity allows us to experience true love in relationships. When we honor God with our bodies and live by His standards, we attract relationships that are rooted in mutual respect, trust, and God-centered love. Hebrews 13:4 says, "Marriage should be honored by all, and the marriage bed kept pure, for God will judge the adulterer and all the sexually immoral." When we keep our relationships pure, we preserve the sanctity of marriage and honor God's design for love and intimacy.

Ultimately, purity is about trusting in God's plan and living in a way that brings glory to Him.

Two Shall Become One

Soul ties refer to deep emotional, spiritual, and sometimes physical connections formed between individuals, often within the context of close or intimate relationships. These bonds are not solely emotional but can also carry a spiritual dimension, influencing how a person thinks, feels, and behaves even after a relationship has ended. The Bible references the profound connection created through sexual intimacy in 1 Corinthians 6:16 "What? know ye not that he which is joined to an harlot is one body? for two, saith he, shall be one flesh." This verse underscores the lasting impact of sexual union and the depth of connection it establishes. These connections may cause emotional struggles, spiritual confusion, and difficulty moving forward after a relationship ends.

Living a life of purity—whether in thought, action, or relationships—can help guard against forming connections that may be spiritually or emotionally harmful. Purity is often emphasized in the Bible as a way to protect one's relationship with God and maintain emotional and spiritual clarity. For instance, 1 Corinthians 6:18 advises: "Flee fornication. Every sin that a man doeth is without the body; but he that committeth fornication sinneth against his own body." This highlights the unique impact of sexual sin and the importance of exercising caution in forming deep, intimate bonds.

Reflection

Reflect on how past or current relationships have influenced your emotional, mental, and spiritual well-being. Do they reflect God's love, healing, and freedom? Are there recurring behaviors (manipulation, control, or sin) in these relationships that prevent you from growing in Christ? Ask yourself if God is calling you to set stronger boundaries to protect your heart, your body, and your spirit. Turn to God's Word, prayer, and support from other believers to heal from emotional wounds and sexual sin. Understand that God can redeem all situations, and no relationship or situation is beyond His power to heal.

A Powerful Prayer for Freedom from Soul Ties

Heavenly Father, I come before You with a humble heart, seeking Your healing and freedom. Lord, I ask that You break every unhealthy soul tie that has been formed in my life. By the power of Jesus Christ, I sever every connection that does not align with Your will. I renounce any attachment to past relationships, experiences, or desires that have kept me bound. I declare that I am free in Jesus' name.

Lord, I ask for Your protection over my heart, mind, and spirit. I desire to live according to Your Word, knowing that Your plans for me are good. Help me to see myself through Your eyes—as loved, worthy, and whole.

Restoration and Healing

Shattering the Old Expectations

Mara's journey was relatable, marked by a tug-of-war between her desire for growth and the haunting echoes of her past. Each step she took closer to God was a step away from her former self. Yet, the closer she walked toward healing and redemption, the more some people clung to the shadow of who she used to be. The rejection was painful, and at times, it felt like a personal failure. Mara's emotions were torn—she wanted to reconnect and heal, but instead, she was left feeling like her past was being thrown back in her face.

There were moments when the wounds of her past seemed to define her present. Her heart ached as she faced the truth: she had healed, but others were not always ready to accept the new version of herself. People would sometimes hold on to the past, refusing to let go of old hurts.

These dynamics were challenging, as people often fluctuated between accepting her and pushing her away. This left Mara feeling stuck—like she had done everything she could, yet still found herself stuck in cycles of rejection.

Though her heart longed for reconciliation, Mara began to realize that not every relationship could be restored. Healing did not always mean going back. Instead, it often required courage to move forward, leaving behind those who could not embrace her growth.

Sometimes, people distance themselves—whether they are family, friends, or romantic partners—and this can be deeply painful. It is particularly challenging when someone has put in significant effort to grow, heal, and align with the person God has called them to be, yet those closest to them struggle to recognize or accept that transformation. It can feel as though the memory of the person they once were continues to overshadow the individual they are becoming in Christ.

This can leave feelings of guilt, pain, or rejection in its wake, making it hard to reconcile the love you have for them with the emotional distance they create.

It's a painful reality that many of us face, feeling isolated or misunderstood, especially when our growth or change isn't recognized or embraced by others. We may find ourselves questioning our worth, wondering if the love and efforts we've invested are enough, or feeling abandoned because others cannot yet see the new identity we are stepping into through Christ.

They labeled her as a 'holy roller,' unable to see the deep work God was doing in her. Yet, despite the misunderstanding and judgment, Mara found peace in the fact that God's call on her life wasn't based on the approval of others, but on His perfect love and purpose for her."

God's call for us to grow, heal, and step into the fullness of who He has created us to be is not dependent on the recognition or validation of those around us. His love is enough to sustain us, and His peace can help us move forward.

Over time, Mara began to believe that God saw her for who she was becoming, not who she had been. She chose to lean into that truth, allowing it to anchor her as she learned to release the weight of others' judgments. In doing so, she discovered a liberating grace—the freedom to be unapologetically herself, redeemed and whole, regardless of who chose to walk beside her. With a heart anchored in the understanding that "If God be for us, who can be against us?" Romans 8:31, she found comfort in the truth that not everyone would embrace her new life in Christ. Yet, she knew this was a journey between her and God, and His approval was all she truly needed.

Mara had to continually remind herself that she had already been forgiven—through Christ, she was made new. The Bible reminded her of this truth: "If we confess our sins, He is faithful and just to forgive us our sins, and to cleanse us from all unrighteousness" 1 John 1:9. This gave Mara the freedom to stop holding on to guilt and shame. Since God had already forgiven her, it was time for her to forgive herself and stop letting her past define her future.

Sometimes the past would resurface, whether through the words of others or her own inner struggles. But Mara had to make the choice to keep moving forward.

For Mara, part of this healing was learning to pray for those who cut her off or stopped talking to her. She realized that while she could not change people, only God could heal their hearts. In prayer, she would ask God to soften their hearts and help them let go of the past pain that kept them from embracing the new work He had done in her. But she also had to trust in God's timing.
Their healing may take months or even years.

Mara's baby brother, Anthony, is still holding on to some unresolved pain. Mara prays today for reconciliation and healing.

Mara and their mother, out of love and concern, had offered help when they saw Anthony faltering in his early adulthood. They tried to step in, to offer support, hoping to guide him in a direction that would bring peace and stability. But Anthony didn't see it that way. He felt betrayed. He saw their help as interference, as a reminder of all the ways he had fallen short. The love they offered him, he took as judgment.

In his pain and anger, Anthony cut ties with them. Mara, her mother, and Kenneth off and on. She longed for the brother she once knew—the one who had laughed with her, who had shared dreams and fears. Now, all she had was silence. But today he has reconciled with their mother. Mara continues praying and believes the Lord will bring restoration to Anthony.

But she had learned not to let the rejection of others derail her progress.

Her journey was not defined by the people who chose to cut her off or hold on to old wounds—Mara's new identity was found in Christ, and that truth gave her the strength to keep moving forward.

For anyone struggling with the same pain, Mara would say: Do not let the past hold you hostage. You have been forgiven, and you can forgive yourself. Trust in God's perfect timing and His ability to heal both you and the hearts of others.

Keep moving forward in your healing, and do not let others' rejection stop you from embracing the new life God has for you. God's love is always greater than any hurt, and His peace will sustain you through it all.

When others cannot or refuse to see your growth, it becomes essential to surround yourself with people who support and encourage the person you are becoming. These relationships offer a foundation of positivity and strength, helping to nurture continued growth and healing.

However, healing sometimes also means making peace with separation. Accepting that not everyone will accompany you on your journey allows space for new relationships that align with your purpose and the person you are becoming.

Mara knew that holding onto resentment over their actions would hinder her own healing. She sought God's help to release any lingering frustration or pain she felt from their choices. She asked the Lord to remind her that their struggles were not a reflection of her worth or effort, but a testament to their need for healing and His grace.

She also forgave herself for any guilt she carried—guilt that whispered she had not done enough or been enough for them.

Mara understood that just as He had guided her through her darkest moments, He was working in their lives, even if she could not see it. Isaiah 55:8-9 reminded her, "For my thoughts are not your thoughts, neither are your ways my ways," declares the Lord. "As the heavens are higher than the earth, so are my ways higher than your ways and my thoughts than your thoughts."

Mara's decision to release control and trust in God's timing freed her from the burden of trying to fix everything. Instead, she focused on her own growth and on creating a home filled with love, support, and understanding.

The enemy thrives in strongholds of bitterness and pain, seeking to use these wounds to hinder growth and healing. It is crucial to remember that the true battle is not against people but against the spiritual forces at work behind situations of conflict or hurt.

Sometimes, the enemy uses individuals or circumstances to distract or discourage, but with God's grace and wisdom, it is possible to rise above and respond with love, prayer, and forgiveness. Recognizing this truth allows for a deeper perspective and the ability to fight spiritual battles with faith and trust in God.

> *FOR THE WEAPONS OF OUR WARFARE ARE NOT OF THE FLESH,*
> *BUT MIGHTY BEFORE GOD TO THE CASTING DOWN OF*
> *STRONGHOLDS.*
> *2 CORINTHIANS 10:4*

Blessed be God, even the Father of our Lord Jesus Christ, the Father of mercies, and the God of all comfort; Who comforteth us in all our tribulation, that we may be able to comfort them which are in any trouble, by the comfort wherewith we ourselves are comforted of God.

Mara's story encourages us to embrace God's peace, extend His love to others, and trust in His power to transform even the most hardened hearts. With God's grace, broken relationships can be restored, and lives can be renewed.

> *BLESSED BE GOD, EVEN THE FATHER OF OUR LORD JESUS CHRIST,*
> *THE FATHER OF MERCIES, AND THE GOD OF ALL COMFORT; WHO*
> *COMFORTETH US IN ALL OUR TRIBULATION, THAT WE MAY BE*
> *ABLE TO COMFORT THEM WHICH ARE IN ANY TROUBLE, BY THE*
> *COMFORT WHEREWITH WE OURSELVES ARE COMFORTED OF GOD.*
> *2 CORINTHIANS 1:3-4*

Prayer Against Discord and For Unity

Gracious Father,

We stand on Your promises today, believing in the power of Your Word. According to Ezekiel 36:26, "And I will give you a new heart, and a new spirit will I put within you; and I will take away the stony heart out of your flesh, and I will give you a heart of flesh." Lord, we ask You to renew our hearts, make them tender toward one another, and fill us with Your Spirit so we may walk in unity and peace.

We recognize, Lord, as 2 Corinthians 10:4 declares, "For the weapons of our warfare are not of the flesh, but mighty before God to the casting down of strongholds. In faith, we come against all forms of discord, division, and strife that try to break the unity you desire for us.

We ask that You bind us together with love and humility. Where there is misunderstanding, bring clarity. Where there is bitterness, bring forgiveness. Where there is division, bring reconciliation. Lord, help us place our trust in You and in who You are—the God who transforms hearts and brings peace.

In Jesus's name, amen.

May God bless you as you trust Him for unity and peace, believing He can tear down all strongholds of discord.

AND ABOVE ALL THESE THINGS PUT ON CHARITY, WHICH IS THE BOND OF PERFECTNESS. COLOSSIANS 3:14

In the Hands of the Savior

Sometimes, Mara would always be anxious if others were mad at her. It was an automatic response she had developed over the years — a quiet panic that would creep in whenever someone's tone shifted or their words felt sharp. Her mind would race with questions: *"Did I do something wrong?" "Are they upset with me?" "What can I do to fix it?"* It was exhausting, and yet, it felt so normal.

For most of her life, Mara believed it was her job to keep the peace, to make sure everyone around her was happy, even if it came at the cost of her own peace.

It started in childhood, where love and approval often felt conditional. If she failed to meet certain expectations, the warmth she craved would turn cold. She grew up in a home where emotions were unpredictable, often overwhelming, and rarely constructive.

Her Aunt Sarah, burdened by unresolved pain of her own, struggled to channel her emotions in healthy ways. Anger erupted like sudden storms, fierce and unpredictable, while long silences chilled the air with an unspoken tension.

For a young child, it was like walking through a minefield, each step uncertain, each interaction fraught with the heavy burden of trying to decode moods and avoid triggering another eruption.

As a result, she learned to read people's emotions like a radar system, scanning for any sign of anger, disapproval, or frustration. If she sensed it, she would go into "fix-it mode," trying to smooth things over, even if she was not the one who caused the problem.

But over time, the weight of carrying other people's emotions became overwhelming. It wasn't confined to her home life — it seeped into her relationships with family, friendships, and even her work.

If a family member spoke to her in a harsh tone, she would spend the rest of the day replaying the moment in her mind, wondering how she could have done things differently. If a sibling seemed distant, she would question if she had upset them somehow, even if nothing had happened.

This cycle continued until Mara realized something life-changing: *It was not her job to be everyone's savior.*

This revelation did not come overnight. It came through prayer, reflection, and a deeper understanding of God's word.

It was a way to free herself from carrying the emotional weight of other people's choices. This is when she began to see that not every negative emotion or reaction from others was about her. Sometimes people were upset because of their own issues, not because of something she did. Slowly, she stopped asking, *"Are they mad at me?"* and instead asked, *"Is this mine to carry?"* Most of the time, the answer was no.

Mara found peace in the words of Matthew 11:28-30 *"Come unto me, all ye that labour and are heavy laden, and I will give you rest. Take my yoke upon you, and learn of me; for I am meek and lowly in heart: and ye shall find rest unto your souls. For my yoke is easy, and my burden is light."*

Her heart softened as she realized that she did not have to carry the burden of other people's emotions. She did not have to "fix" their sadness, anger, or frustrations. Her only role was to love them and pray for them. It was God's job to heal their hearts, not hers. Her prayers were powerful, but they were not a substitute for God's work. She could love people without losing herself in their storms. She could stand firm, knowing that God was in control.

The hardest part of her journey was learning to walk away from the "fixer" role. It meant accepting that she might not always get closure. It meant realizing that she could not force people to change, apologize, or be kind. But she also learned that closure did not come from them — it came from God.

Whenever the urge to "fix it" arose, she leaned on Proverbs 3:5-6 *"Trust in the Lord with all thine heart; and lean not unto thine own understanding. In all thy ways acknowledge him, and he shall direct thy paths."*

This verse reminded her that she did not have to understand why people acted the way they did. She did not have to make sense of it. She just had to trust God. When people walked away from her, she did not chase them anymore. She did not beg for their love or explanation. Instead, she prayed for them. She whispered their names in prayer, saying, *"Lord, I place them in Your hands."*

The peace that came with this was unlike anything she had felt before. For so long, she had been weighed down by the responsibility of other people's feelings. Now, she was free. Free to love, free to pray, and free to let go. She was able to see people through a lens of love rather than fear.

Her heart no longer carried the heavy burdens of others' choices. She had placed them in God's hands, and in return, He gave her peace.

Father Forgive Them

How could someone ever get over something that hurts so deeply, done to them by someone so close? The Bible acknowledges that the ones who might betray you are sometimes the people closest to you.

> YEA, MINE OWN FAMILIAR FRIEND, IN WHOM I TRUSTED, WHO DID EAT OF MY BREAD, HATH LIFTED UP HIS HEEL AGAINST ME.
>
> PSALM 41:9

Hurt and betrayal often come from the least expected sources. The very places where you sought love, and warmth can shatter your heart in ways you never imagined. Trusting someone deeply, believing they would be your strength, only to have them expose the harsher truths of human nature, is a wound unlike any other. It leaves you questioning everything, forcing you to pick up the pieces and heal on your own.

No one ever wants to confront hurt. Yet, regardless of when it happens—at any age or through any form—it has an uncanny way of piercing deep into the core of your being, leaving you vulnerable and wounded.

The lasting power of betrayal, hurt, and abuse lies in how they linger. Even years after the incident—long after the perpetrator has likely moved on or forgotten—the memory remains vivid. The words still echo in your heart, and the actions replay in your mind repeatedly.

But it does not stop there. Pain takes root, influencing your thoughts, emotions, and even the way you see the world. It shapes your life, altering your expectations and interactions. If you let bitterness take hold, it does not just remain within—it spills over, causing you to hurt others as well.

When individuals inflict pain, it often stems from their own unresolved issues and personal suffering. This behavior can be a misguided attempt to cope with frustration or emotional turmoil.

From this place of hurt, we may question God's love, asking, "If God truly cared about me, why would He allow this person to hurt me this way?" Where was God when I had to face this terrible pain that I did not bargain for?

These are dark moments that can challenge our faith. Yet, even in those times, God assures us that He is with us.

He will walk through the hurt and give you beauty for ashes, as stated in Isaiah 61:3: "To appoint unto them that mourn in Zion, to give unto them a garland for ashes, the oil of joy for mourning, the mantle of praise for the spirit of heaviness; that they might be called trees of righteousness, the planting of the Lord, that he might be glorified." Some moments in our lives are so dark that it is hard to see past them; it is tough to understand why we must go through such painful times.

But John 1:5 tells us, "And the light shineth in the darkness; and the darkness apprehended it not." This Light, of course, is Jesus Christ.

The Bible makes many references to our Savior as our Illumination. "Your word is a lamp unto my feet, and light unto my path" Psalm 119:105. Even in our darkest hour, we have the Light that will shine through. We can go to the Word and witness His glory, leaning on Him when we cannot make it through on our own.

But how does knowing this help us when we are feeling vulnerable, betrayed, and rejected?

God took on human form, lived among us, and showed us His glory through His life, death, and resurrection. By becoming flesh, Jesus made God's love and truth accessible to us in a tangible way.

> "AND THE WORD BECAME FLESH, AND DWELT AMONG US, AND WE BEHELD HIS GLORY, GLORY AS OF THE ONLY BEGOTTEN FROM THE FATHER FULL OF GRACE AND TRUTH" JOHN 1:14.

When we feel vulnerable, rejected, or lost, it's comforting to know that Jesus, the living Word, is the Light that guides us. Even in our darkest moments, we can turn to Him for strength, knowing that He cares for us. The most painful moments in our lives allow us to increase our faith by trusting the Lord and knowing He will take care of us. "casting all your anxiety on him, because he careth for you" 1 Peter 5:7.

Only by the grace of God and through the loving example of His Son is true forgiveness possible. No matter how deep the hurt is, forgiveness is within reach. Yes, it may be painful, and you might want to bury the hurt deep without addressing it, but God will bring it forward to perfect the forgiveness. You will need to revisit the moment of damage so that true healing can begin.

Forgiveness is a work that Christ will start in you when you are ready. The first step is your willingness. When you forgive, you free yourself from the burden and pain of the incident. You release yourself from the hardship of holding onto resentment, breaking free from being a prisoner to the past. Forgiving those who hurt you, just as God forgave you for Christ's sake, leads to personal growth and a conscience free from offense.

We may be affected by the consequences of the generations before us, but we do not have to be permanently cursed to live that way. We can be more than conquerors through the help of the Great Redeemer.

In the ultimate example of forgiveness, Jesus, after enduring immense suffering, betrayal, and betrayal by those closest to Him, called out from the cross, "Father, forgive them, for they know not what they do" (Luke 23:34).

Jesus, in His deepest moment of hurt—after being betrayed by one of His disciples, abandoned by His followers, mocked, and crucified—still chose to forgive. His words on the cross weren't just for those who physically hurt Him in that moment, but they were for all of humanity, for every sin and offense ever committed. Jesus was not only calling for forgiveness for others, but He was demonstrating how we, too, should forgive when faced with hurt and betrayal.

His plea, "Father, forgive them," was not conditional upon whether the offenders deserved forgiveness, but rather a reflection of His divine love and grace. It teaches us that forgiveness is not about excusing the offense but about releasing the power of the offense over us. Jesus knew the cost of forgiveness—His own suffering and sacrifice—but He also knew that forgiveness was the path to healing, restoration, and freedom.

Understanding this profound act of forgiveness on the cross is key to embracing forgiveness in our own lives. When we struggle to forgive, remembering that Jesus, in His pain, forgave His tormentors, we can find the strength to forgive those who have hurt us.

Through Christ's example, we are called to forgive not out of our own strength, but by relying on God's grace to help us let go of resentment and embrace the freedom that comes from releasing the weight of unforgiveness. We can be more than conquerors with the help of the Great Redeemer.

A Heart Restored by Grace

Mara's mother and Mara's Aunt Sarah experienced incredible transformations through the power of God's love. Mara's mother, once trapped in the grip of alcohol addiction, was set free.

She was baptized and joined a church, and the Lord began healing her increasingly each day. For much of Mara's childhood, her mother struggled to express affection, struggling to give hugs or say, "I love you." But now, she has become a source of love and stability, especially with her grandchildren.

Mara's mother has shown up for her in ways she never could, offering emotional and financial support during hardship. When Mara needed help most—raising her children and returning to school for her master's degree—her mother was there. She helped babysit the kids and provided the support Mara needed to finish her education. Mara is incredibly grateful, knowing she could not have made it without her mother's love and strength.

Mara sees that the Lord worked powerfully in her mother's life, bringing lasting change when needed. Mara witnessed the incredible transformation in her mother's life. This transformation was not just powerful—it was deeply personal, a testament to the power of God's grace and redemption. Glory to God for showing that He can change anyone who surrenders to Him. His love is unfailing, and He waits for us with open arms even when we stray. No sin is too deep or pain too great for Him to heal because He already paid the price at the cross.

Forgiveness without Reconciliation

Mara has chosen not to engage directly with the other men who violated her. Instead, she has forgiven them in her heart. This is a powerful example of how forgiveness can happen even without reconciliation and how it is freeing oneself from the burden of anger and resentment.

From a biblical perspective, forgiveness is a commandment from God, even when the offense is deep. In Matthew 6:14-15, Jesus says, "For if ye forgive men their trespasses, your heavenly Father will also forgive you. But if ye forgive not men their trespasses, neither will your Father forgive your trespasses." Forgiveness is not necessarily about excusing or condoning the actions of others but about releasing the grip that their sin has on your heart.

Allow God's love to heal the brokenness and trusting that God will bring justice, as it says in Romans 12:19, "Avenge not yourselves, beloved, but give place unto the wrath of God: for it is written, Vengeance belongeth unto me; I will recompense, saith the Lord."

Forgiving from the heart without necessarily reconnecting or reconciling with the offender can still bring freedom. As Ephesians 4:31-32 reminds us, "Let all bitterness, and wrath, and anger, and clamour, and evil speaking, be put away from you, with all malice: and be ye kind one to another, tenderhearted, forgiving each other, even as God also in Christ forgave you."

Mara's ability to forgive those who never apologized shows her strength in Christ. She let go of bitterness not for their sake but for her own spiritual and emotional well-being, releasing the weight of anger to embrace the peace of Christ.

Beyond Understanding

Mara's journey toward healing was filled with emotional challenges, especially connected to painful memories from her childhood. Two relatives, Tony and Naomi, had deeply wounded her through abuse. Though Tony passed away years ago, the impact of those experiences still shaped her path toward forgiveness and restoration.
Mara had not had contact with Tony since she was a young girl, and she never heard from him again after that incident.

In her heart, she often wondered if Tony had ever found redemption, if he had ever realized the harm he caused. She would never know. The unanswered questions weighed on her, but she chose to forgive Tony through her faith in God, even without closure.

Naomi, Tony's wife, was a different story. Naomi had been part of Mara's life when she was young, and while they never spoke about what happened, Mara maintained a distant relationship with her. Mara never brought it up. Over the years, by the time she became an adult and had healed, Naomi, now is elderly. Being older, Mara chose not to bring up the offense to Naomi, who had been the one who had abused her. Mara had spent years reconciling her emotions privately with God, finding a measure of peace through faith and reflection.

Mara's decision not to confront Naomi about the abuse was shaped by several complex and deeply personal reasons. Over the years, Mara had worked through her pain, finding peace through her faith and self-reflection, and she felt that reopening old wounds might not provide the healing she sought. Confronting Naomi in her old age seemed unlikely to bring the closure or understanding that Mara had hoped for.

As Naomi aged, Mara saw how fragile her mental and emotional state had become. The woman who had once been a source of pain was now a person who struggled with the clarity of thought. Mara understood that attempting to address the past with someone whose memory might be slipping or whose reactions could be unpredictable would only complicate things further. It was possible that Naomi, in her confusion, wouldn't even remember the harm she had caused or might reject the very notion of her wrong doings. The thought of having Naomi dismiss or deny the hurt Mara had carried for so long was an unbearable prospect.

Mara prayed that God would lead Naomi to repentance. She knew Naomi had been complicit in the silence surrounding the abuse and that this silence had once deepened her hurt. But instead of holding onto bitterness, Mara surrendered it all to God, trusting that only he could heal her wounds and bring justice perfectly. She realized that seeking revenge or forcing Naomi to admit her role in the silence was not the answer.

Mara had learned, perhaps painfully, that some conversations, particularly those about the deepest scars, were not always worth having if the outcome would only perpetuate more harm. Her peace, after all, had not come from Naomi's acknowledgment or apology—it had come from God's gentle work in her heart. Through prayer and surrender, she had found the strength to forgive and the grace to heal, even without the closure she once thought she needed. Her peace was no longer dependent on others but rooted in the One who makes all things new.

You will keep in perfect peace those whose minds are steadfast, because they trust in you. **Isaiah 26:3**

As Mara reflected on Romans 8:28, she held onto the belief that "And we know that to them that love God all things work together for good, even to them that are called according to his purpose." She rested in the knowledge that her healing came from the Lord.

Mara believed the Lord would deal with Naomi in his way and time. Today, Naomi has a relationship with the Lord and regularly attends church and Bible study. They occasionally check in with each other through phone calls and occasional visits. Glory be to God—He forgives and brings even those who think they've committed the worst sins back to Him, offering them grace and redemption.

Guidepost: Learning Forgiveness

Forgiveness is about letting go of the negative feelings that something has caused you or that you caused others. It is about relieving yourself of the bitterness or hatred you may be feeling toward somebody, especially someone close to you because it is not healthy to hold on to those negative emotions. They will just eat at you from the inside until you either break down or explode.

Forgiveness is not always easy—especially when you're still around the people who once hurt you, and their words or actions continue to wound you. It can be painful to forgive when the same hurt happens again and again. If someone refuses to change or seek help, it may be necessary to set healthy boundaries or distance yourself for your own peace. Sometimes people truly do not see how their behavior affects others.

Forgiving others can feel impossible, especially when they seem undeserving. But remember this: none of us were deserving either. We were all born into sin, yet God, in His great mercy, forgives anyone who confesses their sins and places their trust in His Son, Jesus Christ. Through Him, we learn what true forgiveness looks like.

The journey to forgiveness was difficult. Mara grappled with the bitterness and pain that had taken root in her heart for years.

Romans 6:14 reminded her, "For sin shall not have dominion over you: for ye are not under law, but under grace."

This profound truth helped Mara see that forgiveness is an act of grace, not a response to the law. It is about releasing the burden of anger and allowing God's love to heal the wounds.

Mara also realized the hypocrisy of expecting God's grace for herself while holding others to the law. She understood that asking God for His grace and forgiveness while demanding strict justice for others was unfair. Matthew 6:14-15 taught her: "For if ye forgive men their trespasses, your heavenly Father will also forgive you. But if ye forgive not men their trespasses, neither will your Father forgive your trespasses."

But if you do not forgive others, your Father will not forgive your sins. This conviction drove Mara to treat others with the same mercy she sought from God.

Mara forgave, and she found herself transformed. The same grace that healed her soul began to mend her relationships. She discovered that forgiveness is about setting others free and liberating oneself from the shackles of past hurts.

Ephesians 4:31-32: "Let all bitterness, and wrath, and anger, and clamour, and evil speaking, be put away from you, with all malice: And be ye kind one to another, tenderhearted, forgiving each other, even as God also in Christ forgave you."

Colossians 3:13: "Bearing with one another, and forgiving each other, if any man hath a complaint against any; even as the Lord forgave you, so also do ye."

> BUT GOD COMMENDETH HIS OWN LOVE TOWARD US, IN THAT, WHILE WE WERE YET SINNERS, CHRIST DIED FOR US.
>
> ROMANS 5:8

God will help you release resentment until your heart is completely free.

She remembered what had happened, but the memories no longer hurt her. Instead, her heart softened, and she began to pray for those who had wronged her, as Jesus instructed. She blessed them and wished them well, and in doing so, she found freedom.

Mara also recognized that forgiveness was a two-way street. She knew it was not enough to forgive those who had hurt her; she also had to seek forgiveness from those she had wronged. This realization was significant for her healing journey. Determined to make amends, Mara reached out to the people she had hurt. She was reminded of the scripture "If we confess our sins, he is faithful and righteous to forgive us our sins, and to cleanse us from all unrighteousness" 1 John 1:9.

Mara expressed her remorse, sincerely repented, and asked for their forgiveness, acknowledging her mistakes. Even if they chose not to accept her apology, she understood that this act was vital for her emotional and spiritual freedom. By taking this step, Mara sought to heal her relationships and free herself from the burden of guilt and regret.

Mara also thought about the people she had wronged in the past but could no longer reach out to directly. Understanding that she could not physically connect with them, she prayed to the Lord.

In her journaling, she reflected on both sides of forgiveness: giving it to those who wronged her and seeking it from those she had hurt. This comprehensive approach allowed her to embrace a fuller sense of healing and reconciliation.

All those heavy emotions—bitterness, resentment, and anger—were released. Mara felt like she had broken another chain that used to bind her to her traumatic past.

Here is something you can do to help. Write the names of people who have hurt you. Keep a journal of your feelings, release the anger, and then give your worries to God. Remember what Jesus said "But I say unto you, love your enemies, and pray for them that persecute you" Matthew 5:44.

Forgiveness vs Trust

You might be wondering, "But what about the people who keep hurting us over and over again? How can we forgive them if they continue to cause the same pain?" I hear you, and it's an important question.

For someone who has endured—and continues to endure—trauma from the same person they love and want to see change, it's essential to protect your emotional, mental, and spiritual well-being. God does not call us to remain in harmful situations, but He does call us to release bitterness and trust Him to bring healing to our hearts. Forgiveness doesn't mean ignoring the pain or allowing continued harm; it means freeing yourself from bitterness so healing can begin.

It is crucial to understand that forgiveness and trust are two different things. Forgiveness is a choice we make in our hearts to release someone from the debt we feel they owe us for hurting us. It does not mean we condone their actions, and it certainly does not mean we forget the hurt.

Trust, on the other hand, is earned over time. If someone repeatedly hurts you, it is natural and wise to set up boundaries to protect yourself. You can forgive someone and still choose not to trust them, especially if their actions continue to cause harm. Trust is built through consistent, respectful behavior, and it is okay to withhold trust from someone who has not shown the ability or willingness to change.

This is where boundaries come in. Boundaries are healthy limits we set to protect ourselves from further harm. Forgiving someone does not mean you allow them to continue causing the same pain over and over.

Like many of us, Mara struggled with setting boundaries, especially with those who consistently hurt her. She believed forgiving meant allowing people back into her life in the same way, but God began to show her that forgiveness. The Lord showed Mara Proverbs 4:23: "Keep thy heart with all diligence; for out of it are the issues of life."

This verse taught Mara the wisdom of guarding her heart. She learned that setting healthy boundaries did not mean she was unloving; she was being wise about how she allowed people to interact with her. God never called her to be a doormat but to be discerning in her relationships.

This required tough conversations and a clear understanding that boundaries are a form of love—not only for herself but also for the other person, as it helps to hold them accountable for their actions.

A practical example of setting boundaries occurred when Mara faced an overwhelming workload with new clients assigned to her caseload. The additional responsibilities led to stress and burnout, affecting her performance and well-being. She found herself stretched thin, trying to meet everyone's needs while neglecting her own health. She realized she had to set clear boundaries to prevent overwork and burnout.

The Lord brought to her mind Matthew 18:15: "Moreover, if thy brother shall trespass against thee, go, tell him his fault, between thee and him alone: if he hears thee, thou hast gained thy brother." She understood that while she could support her clients and coworkers, she needed to recognize her own limits.

By communicating her capacity and setting realistic expectations with her supervisor, Mara was able to manage her workload better. This meant saying "no" when necessary and delegating tasks to ensure she did not compromise her own well-being.

Boundaries also became crucial in Mara's personal relationships. With some family members who repeatedly hurt her, she realized that continuing to allow the same behavior was not what God wanted for her.

The Bible shows us in Luke 17:3-4: "Take heed to yourselves: If thy brother sin, rebuke him; and if he repents, forgive him. And if he sins against thee seven times in the day, and seven times turn again to thee, saying, I repent; thou shalt forgive him." However, when people refused to repent or change, Mara understood she needed to distance herself. She could love them, pray for them, and wish them well, but she did not have to allow them access to her heart in the same way as before. Boundaries became her way of protecting the peace God had given her.

In practice, Mara began to limit how much she shared with people who only sought to tear her down. She learned to say "no" without feeling guilty, trusting that God would honor her decision to maintain healthy relationships. She began prioritizing James 1:5: "But if any of you lacketh wisdom, let him ask of God, who giveth to all men liberally and upbraideth not; and it shall be given him." Mara asked God for wisdom for where to set boundaries and how to enforce them in a loving way.

Forgiveness was always available, but trust and access had to be earned. You might ask how someone earns trust back. It involves seeking help, working on oneself, and actively changing harmful behaviors. Earning trust requires genuine repentance and consistent effort toward positive change, reflecting a new heart and mind.

The Bible advises us to be cautious about surrounding ourselves with those who are troublesome or foolish. Proverbs 13:20 says, "He that walketh with wise men shall be wise; But the companion of fools shall suffer harm." And Proverbs 14:7 advises, "Go from the presence of a foolish man, when thou perceivest not in him the lips of knowledge."

Trust is rebuilt through sincere effort, a demonstrated commitment to change, and choosing to be around those who encourage growth and wisdom.

By setting boundaries, Mara found freedom. She was no longer carrying the weight of other people's behaviors but was instead walking in the wisdom and love of Christ.

Now was the time for Mara to pursue her dream of owning her own business. After praying, she felt God guiding her and telling her it was time to take the leap. Could she really do it? Reflecting on her journey, Mara realized that stepping out in faith had been a constant part of her life since surrendering to Christ. It had not always been easy, but each time she placed her trust in Him completely, she experienced His care and provision. Now, whether she felt ready or not, she knew she had to step out in faith once again.

Strength in Weakness

Mara had started going with J to Bible group after God had saved her life. She was filled with joy and gratitude, determined to change and live for the Lord with this second chance. When Mara told J she wanted to attend Bible study, J was shocked and thanked God all at the same time. Initially nervous in this unfamiliar environment of women and prophets where everyone was encouraged to pray, Mara felt unsure and apprehensive.

During the gathering, the prophet called Mara forward unexpectedly, asking, "You love Him, do you not?" Mara, uncertain of the meaning, nervously replied yes. The prophet continued, "Sometimes He is watching you, and you do not even know it." Mara was puzzled, wondering who might be watching her, especially since the Lord had called her to a life of abstinence. Confused, Mara sought J's help to understand the prophetic message, learning that prophecy can encompass past, present, and future insights.

This journey, guided by insights from the Lord and others in Christ, shaped Mara's understanding of spiritual revelations.

As the Bible study group concluded, Mara was asked to pray, and despite her fears, she found the courage to speak. She noticed someone beside her expressing deep emotional pain, which inspired her to respond.

Trusting that the Holy Spirit would guide her in saying the right words, she took a deep breath and began to pray. As Romans 8:26 reminds us, "And in like manner the Spirit also helpeth our infirmity: for we know not how to pray as we ought; but the Spirit himself maketh intercession for us with groanings which cannot be uttered." Sometimes, the Holy Spirit intercedes on our behalf, even when we do not know what to say.

The prophet then recognized Mara's emerging gift, affirming her as a prayer warrior and intercessor. From that moment on, people often sought Mara out for prayer, and she began to discover and use her spiritual gifts for the Lord's work.

It can be intimidating when the Lord prompts us to use our gifts. All we need to do is take a step of faith, trusting that His power within us activates our abilities. Just like when

Moses was scared to speak, the Lord reminded him that he only needed to express himself.

Discovering and Using Her Gifts

When Mara became a new creation in Christ, she stepped into a journey that would transform her life. At first, she wasn't sure what God wanted her to do or how He wanted to use her. Slowly, He began to reveal the unique gifts He had placed within her—not for her own recognition, but to serve others and bring glory to His kingdom.

Mara remembered 1 Corinthians 12:4-7, which Paul had written:
"There are different kinds of gifts, but the same Spirit distributes them. There are different kinds of service, but the same Lord. There are different kinds of working, but in all of them and in everyone it is the same God at work. Now to each one the manifestation of the Spirit is given for the common good."

The words struck her deeply. Her gifts—whether teaching, encouragement, intercession, or discernment—were not hers to claim. They flowed from the Spirit, and their purpose was to bless others.

She reflected further on 1 Corinthians 12:11:
"All these are the work of one and the same Spirit, and He distributes them to each one, just as He determines."

Mara realized that God gives gifts according to His wisdom and timing. Her part was not to manufacture or demand recognition, but to stay close to Jesus, walk in obedience, and trust Him to work through her. As 1 Peter 4:10 reminded her,
"Each of you should use whatever gift you have received to

serve others, as faithful stewards of God's grace in its various forms."

Through prayer, studying Scripture, and listening quietly for God's voice, Mara's gifts became clearer. Romans 12:6-8 guided her practical steps:
"We have different gifts, according to the grace given to each of us. If your gift is prophesying, then prophesy in accordance with your faith; if it is serving, then serve; if it is teaching, then teach; if it is to encourage, then give encouragement; if it is giving, then give generously; if it is to lead, do it diligently; if it is to show mercy, do it cheerfully."

Mara began to see opportunities where her gifts could make a real difference. Sometimes it was a gentle word of encouragement to a weary friend. Other times, it was careful discernment in prayer for someone facing a difficult choice. She discovered that spiritual gifts flourish when she stays close to God, obeys Him daily, and steps out in faith, even when it feels uncertain.

Faith to Believe

After her healing, Mara reflected deeply on what had happened. She realized that faith was not simply acknowledging God's power—it was stepping into it. It was trusting Him enough to take the first step, even when fear and doubt tried to pull her under. Like Peter stepping out of the boat to walk on water, faith worked as long as her eyes stayed fixed on Jesus. The moment she looked at the waves, she began to sink—not because the miracle stopped, but because her attention shifted.

She understood that faith does not deny the storm; it looks straight through it and sees the Savior standing on the waves. Her healing was not only about her body—it was about her heart learning to trust the Lord completely. God had shown her that faith opens the door for His power to move. The miracle was not about her; it was about Him.

Through her journey, Mara learned that faith is the key to experiencing God's power. It is not about wishing for a miracle; it is about walking in the certainty that His Word is true. Romans 10:17 reminded her: "So then faith cometh by hearing, and hearing by the word of God."

The more Mara listened to God's Word, the stronger her faith grew. The miracle strengthened her not only in body but also in spirit. Her healing became a testimony—a living reminder that when her eyes stay on Jesus, no storm, diagnosis, or fear can stand against His Word. Faith invites believers to trust beyond what they see, to believe in the promises of God, and to move forward with confidence even when the path is unclear.

Gowing in God's Presence

The more Mara spent time in the Lord's presence, the more He began to reveal His purposes through her life. What she once viewed as confusion or burden began to unfold as divine direction. The dreams she used to have—once puzzling and heavy—were no longer random scenes but spiritual insight.

In time, the Lord showed Mara that those dreams were not meant to frighten or confuse her but to guide her in prayer.

They were glimpses into the spiritual realm, where she was being called to intercede for others. What once felt overwhelming became an invitation to partner with God in His redemptive work.

Mara realized that the power did not come from her—it came from the Spirit of God working through her. The Holy Spirit was teaching her how to discern, how to pray, and how to stand in the gap for others with humility and faith.

As 2 Corinthians 4:7 says, "But we have this treasure in jars of clay, to show that this all-surpassing power is from God and not from us."

Every insight, every prayer, every dream was not about her gifting—it was about God's mercy and power reaching others through her obedience. The more she yielded to the Holy Spirit, the more she saw lives touched—not because of her, but because God honors a willing heart.

When she prayed in obedience, people found peace. When she interceded, situations shifted. It was not about recognition—it was about revelation: God is faithful to use those who make themselves available.

Mara's story reminds us that every believer can hear from God and partner with Him in prayer. You do not need a title or a platform—just a heart that listens and responds. God still speaks, still heals, still reveals. He calls us, as He called Mara, to stand in the gap for others, to pray His will on earth as it is in heaven.

Ephesians 6:18 says, "And pray in the Spirit on all occasions with all kinds of prayers and requests. With this in mind, be alert and always keep on praying for all the Lord's people."

Through this journey, Mara learned that the prophetic is not about seeing—it is about serving. It is not about being known—it is about making Jesus known. Her dreams became assignments, her prayers became weapons, and her faith became the bridge through which God brought light into dark places.

And that is where the glory belongs—not to the vessel, but to the One who fills it.

The Promise of Doing Greater Works

Jesus Himself encouraged His disciples that their mission would extend His ministry on earth. In John 14:12, Jesus said:

Very truly I tell you, whoever believes in me will do the works I have been doing, and they will do even greater things than these, because I am going to the Father."

This promise is the foundation for why believers seek and use their spiritual gifts— to reveal Jesus to the world through healing, teaching, deliverance, and the proclamation of the gospel, so that others might come to salvation through Him.

The goal as believers is to:

Grow in relationship with Jesus,

Discover the gifts He has given,

Use them faithfully, empowered by the Holy Spirit,

And actively go make disciples, sharing the gospel boldly.

This aligns perfectly with the Great Commission in Matthew 28:18–20:

Therefore, go and make disciples of all nations, baptizing them... teaching them to obey everything I have commanded you."

The Holy Spirit guides, empowers, and equips every believer to walk in these gifts. Your call is to seek, discover, and serve—knowing the Lord is with you every step of the way.

Answered Prayer

Mara's older brother, Kenneth, started his heart failure journey with a stroke in 2012. No one saw the sudden, terrifying event coming. Just before the stroke, doctors had warned him to slow down and stop working so much. They saw the signs that his body was under immense strain and cautioned him that he could face severe consequences if he did not make changes. But like so many of us, Kenneth pushed those warnings aside, telling himself he was strong enough to manage it.

He had always been a hard worker who prided himself on providing for his family and staying busy. Slowing down did not seem like an option. But then, the stroke hit, and everything changed. The once robust and invincible man was suddenly vulnerable, facing the reality that his heart was failing him. The stroke left him with temporary paralysis for about six months. Soon after, his insurance ran out, forcing him to be discharged from the hospital before he could complete his therapy. With no professional assistance, Kenneth faced a daunting road to recovery. Yet, he refused to give up.

The doctors told him that the strokes had severely weakened his heart, and he was now on the road to heart failure. The weight of their words hung heavy in the air, but Kenneth still found it hard to accept. He had always been able to push through adversity—why would this be any different?

But it was different. His body could not keep up with the demands he had placed on it, and the consequences were undeniable. It was a wake-up call that forced Kenneth to confront his existence like never before.

One day, the doctor told Mara and her family something very distressing.

"He is about to expire," the doctor said.

"What does that mean?" Mara asked, as if in denial.

"I'm about to die," was Kenneth's reply. Now, Mara's denial was intentional. She refused to believe it.

"God has the final say," she said as she and her family joined hands. They prayed together in agreement and asked for the healing power of the Great Physician. Where there is a person or group of people to pray, there is undoubtedly a God to answer. He is the only prayer-answering God.

Within a couple of months, Mara's older brother was transferred to a hospital that put him on a waiting list for a new heart. Shortly after that, in May of 2013, a miracle occurred: an organ was donated.

He underwent a successful heart transplant, an operation that not only saved his life but also transformed it. This experience was a miracle he could not deny, a testament to the power of hope and the incredible gift of life.

Mara's older brother always believed in God, primarily because of his close relationship with his grandparents on his father's side of the family. He still remembered going to church with his Grandma Carrie. Grandma Carrie was special to many, including Mara, and her faith left an impression on Kenneth. Even after the heart transplant that saved his life, Kenneth's faith strengthened even more.

Kenneth's four kids and grandkid were thankful for their extra time with him. After his life-changing experience, Kenneth dedicated his life to God even more and still reads the Bible regularly. He knew that just as a new physical heart had given him life, God's work could bring spiritual renewal to the hearts of everyone involved.

The road was long, but Kenneth's resilience, coupled with the prayers of his family, brought him to a place of healing. With his new heart, Kenneth slowly began to reclaim his life. Though the stroke had left its mark, he had regained much of his strength and mobility. The man who once feared he might never hold his children or play with his grandchild again found himself able to do just that. Each hug and laugh shared with his loved ones were a testament to God's grace and mercy.

Kenneth's life is now a living testimony to the power of God's healing. He enjoys every moment with his children and grandchildren, cherishing their time together. He knows every day is a gift and lives it with gratitude, praising God for the second chance he never thought he would receive. Glory be to God, who restored Kenneth's physical heart and renewed his spiritual one. His story is a reminder that no matter how dire the circumstances, with faith and perseverance, there is always hope.

Do You Still Believe in Miracles?

Has life dealt you such harsh blows that you have lost sight of what God has been doing—and is still doing—in your life? Have trials and tribulations prompted you to doubt the existence of miracles?

This struggle is part of life's cycle. Many people have faced similar challenges, and some, like Job in the Bible, have encountered even worse situations that left them feeling hopeless, helpless, and faithless. Job expresses his despair in Job 30:20: "I cry unto thee, and thou dost not answer me: I stand up, and thou gazest at me." Yet Job remains an outstanding example worth emulating. Amid all he faced, he never doubted God's ability to perform miracles. His unwavering faith in God made all the difference.

In Mark 11:22-24, Jesus encourages us: "Have faith in God. Verily I say unto you, Whosoever shall say unto this mountain, Be thou taken up and cast into the sea; and shall not doubt in his heart, but shall believe that what he saith cometh to pass; he shall have it. Therefore I say unto you, All things whatsoever ye pray and ask for, believe that ye receive them, and ye shall have them." The key takeaway from this scripture is faith—it is the foundation upon which miracles are built. The question remains: "Do you still believe in miracles?"

You may have been praying for a long time, just like Mara, yet it may feel like God is silent or unwilling to answer. However, that perception is not reality. God often works in mysterious ways—ways that no one can fully explain. The creation of the world was a miracle; your very birth was a miracle. While many scientists attempt to explain the wonders of God, none have succeeded in fully understanding them. They often make excuses that reveal their limitations.

God is still in the business of performing miracles today. Have you not heard of women who conceived without wombs? How about those who defied medical logic and conceived after menopause? Can you explain that? When you pray, four things characterize God's answers: your faith, His perfect timing, the motive behind your prayer, and your ability to wait for the answers.

Some people, even Christians, struggle to believe in answered prayers and miracles. Perhaps it is because they cannot physically see God's hand at work in their lives. The saying goes, "Seeing is believing." But as believers, we are called to live by faith, not by sight. We serve an Almighty God who performs incredible acts from heaven, and these miracles are evident in the lives of those who believe.

The Holy Spirit dwells in saved believers; He does not dwell in everyone. He moves us to great works, but He Himself cannot be seen or touched. Despite the inspiring poetry about faith, the footprints of Jesus are not always visible in the sand. This is where faith and hope come into play. Hebrews 11:1 tells us, "Now faith is assurance of things hoped for, a conviction of things not seen." Faith is the substance of what we hope for, the evidence of what is unseen.

Even Jesus' disciples struggled with faith at times. Peter walked on water when he focused on Jesus, but when he looked at the wind and waves, doubt came, and he began to sink. Thomas wanted to see the wounds in Jesus' hands and side before he would believe. John 20:25 records his words: "Unless I see in His hands the mark of the nails and put my finger into the mark of the nails, and put my hand into His side, I will not believe." When Jesus appeared and showed Thomas the wounds, Thomas believed and declared, "My Lord and my God!" John 20:28. Thomas' hesitation demonstrates the natural human desire for physical proof, yet it also underscores the power and necessity of faith. Faith is the substance of what we cannot see, the foundation upon which miracles stand, and the bridge between doubt and belief.

The Bible promises that "My God shall supply every need of yours according to his riches in glory in Christ Jesus"(Philippians 4:19. This is our assurance as believers that the Lord will provide whatever we need as long as we give Him the glory and believe in His Son. Jesus Himself stated in Luke 11:9, "Ask, and it shall be given you; seek, and ye shall find; knock, and it shall be opened unto you." We can be confident that the Lord will provide. His ways are not our ways, and He will fulfill His promises in His own timing. No matter how long the wait, He will come through.

With this confidence, prayers get answered and miracles happen. Recognize them when they occur and give glory to God so that He can fully bless you. When God blesses one person, it can create a ripple effect on those around them, leading to positive changes and breaking generational strongholds.

This is the incredible power of faith and hope. Pray boldly and trust that you will be heard. Praise God when you witness a miracle; you never know what seeds of confidence your testimony may plant in someone else's heart. Even when it feels like the storm is raging and the miracle is out of reach, fix your eyes on Jesus, just as Peter did. Walk forward in faith, knowing that the One who commands the wind and waves is with you—and that with God, nothing is impossible.

Being Set Apart
Shake off the Dust

> *If anyone will not welcome you or listen to your words, leave that home or town and shake the dust off your feet.*
>
> Matthew 10:14

The Lord was strengthening Mara's faith in Him and teaching her how to depend on His voice, even when everything around her seemed to be falling apart. She kept following Him on her new life journey, hoping to one day learn to genuinely love like He does.

God brought Mara to a new job. In this role, she helped people dealing with addiction. As you may recall, Mara had some experience with a person with an addiction, namely Mike, in one of her longest relationships. Through this new job, God gave Mara an understanding of addictions and those who deal with them daily. This was part of Mara's healing journey and learning how to forgive.

The job was rewarding, and Mara was able to heal some. But soon, things began to get rocky at work. Tension grew that Mara did not understand. She started to feel that the people at her job did not like her much.

Mara's growing attraction to her coworker James added a layer of complexity to her commitment to abstinence, which she had maintained for one year at this point. As their mutual interest grew, so did the tension between them. This tension often manifested in minor disagreements fueled by the unspoken emotions they both struggled to control. Despite the growing attraction and the intensity of their interactions, Mara remained resolute in her decision to honor her commitment to the Lord. She knew that giving in to her feelings would compromise her chosen path, and this internal conflict made her even more determined to stay true to her values.

Mara's dedication to her faith, even in the face of temptation, underscores the complexities of navigating relationships while remaining true to her convictions. This commitment can become even more challenging when emotions are involved. Her journey illustrates the inner conflict many have encountered when trying to uphold their values amid emotional and relational challenges.

When James tried to show Mara things about the job, since he had been there longer, Mara was uncomfortable being around him. When she and James had small disagreements, she would become enraged and slam doors in his face. Those temper tantrums from her childhood returned that old defense mechanism was kicking back in.

The relationship triggered Mara's fear and anxiety. But James would always come to talk to her afterward and calm her down. James often commented and told Mara he liked her hair and would give her note cards to show how much he appreciated her work. Even though they were obviously attracted to each other, he was just a good friend.

"You cannot be getting angry like that," James said one day. Mara smiled.

"I know."

"Your husband will come once you change." And after saying that, James paused and looked up to the sky. "You know that, right?" He said with his eyes still pointing at heaven.

"Yes," Mara said, "I need to change my attitude." Then he sighed with relief that Mara understood her shortcomings, which kept her from her future spouse, whom the Lord had promised her.

"Your husband's going to love to watch sports," James said. He would often tell her things about her future husband. Mara did not know how he knew these things.

Despite their attraction, Mara and James knew their relationship was not meant to go anywhere. It was somewhat of a torture to be in this situation at a job that sparked her anger with a coworker she was so attracted to.

So, she started praying for God to remove her from that job. Mara's attraction to James seemed innocent at first. Their conversations and mutual respect created a bond that felt unique. However, as James was married, Mara struggled with conflicting emotions. Mara began to wonder if James was experiencing challenges in his marriage, as he rarely spoke about his personal life except for his daughter.

Deep down, Mara heard a small voice saying, "Mara, I would never give you a married man." She knew that nothing good could come from being with someone who was married, as it did not align with God's Word. Mara knew the Lord would never bring something together that contradicted His Word.

Recognizing the need to set boundaries, Mara decided to look for another job. She knew she could not follow her fleshly desires after the Lord had called her to abstinence, viewing this situation as one of her first tests and steps toward healing. Mara stayed away from work events involving James, understanding deep down that she was honoring God.

Despite never being intimate with James, Mara could not fathom how she had developed feelings for him. This experience was unprecedented for her, as she always believed physical intimacy was a prerequisite for such emotions.

Mara opened her Bible, seeking guidance many times when she was in a challenging situation: "But a man who commits adultery has no sense; whoever does so destroy himself. Blows and disgrace are his lot, and his shame will never be wiped away" Proverbs 6:32-33 NIV.

Mara knew she had to make a choice—either continue down this path of emotional turmoil or take a stand to honor God's Word. Galatians 6:7-8 says, "Be not deceived; God is not mocked: for whatsoever a man soweth, that shall he also reap. For he that soweth unto his own flesh shall of the flesh reap corruption; but he that soweth unto the Spirit shall of the Spirit reap eternal life."

In the end, Mara learned that true fulfillment and happiness come from living a life that honors God. It is powerful reminder that while temptation can be strong, the long-term pain and loss of straying from God's commands are far more significant by staying true to her faith, Mara paved the way for a future filled with God's blessings and the promise of a God-ordained spouse.

Through this experience, God taught her to trust in and pull closer to Him in challenging situations. He also showed her that she still had work to do on herself and needed to learn how to regulate her emotions and anger. The lessons were invaluable but did not stop her from applying to other employers.

This was where Mara had to rely on her faith rather than her senses, as her trust in God was first put to the test. Mara had been struggling at her new job. While it provided a chance to heal and regain some stability, it was not the place she had prayed for. The environment felt heavy—some coworkers were unkind, and others made her feel out of place.

She prayed constantly, crying out to the Lord to guide her. She asked Him to help her resist temptation and to show her the way out of the confusion and discomfort.

During her prayers, Mara received an interview for a position that aligned with her purpose—a job connected to the field that had helped her through school. She saw this as a glimmer of hope, but she did not want to make any decisions without clear confirmation from God.

The days leading up to the interview were filled with anxiety and tears. Mara poured her heart out in prayer, asking the Lord if it was time to leave her current job. One day, as she waited anxiously to hear back, she opened her Bible. Her eyes fell on Matthew 10:14: "And whosoever shall not receive you, nor hear your words, when ye depart out of that house or city, shake off the dust of your feet."

It felt as though God was speaking directly to her. The verse echoed her feelings of being unwelcome and reminded her that she did not have to stay where she was not accepted or where her values felt compromised. As she read further, she came across 1 Corinthians 10:13: "There hath no temptation taken you but such as man can bear: for God is faithful, who will not suffer you to be tempted above that ye are able; but will with the temptation also make the way of escape, that ye may be able to endure it."

This verse brought her even greater clarity and peace. God was reminding her that He would not let her face more than she could handle and that He always provided a way out of difficult situations. Mara took this as her confirmation.

In faith, she submitted her two-week notice, even though she had not yet heard back about the new job. The very next day, she received an email offering her the position. Overwhelmed with gratitude, she knew this was God's answer to her prayers.

It is amazing how God meets us in our struggles, providing direction when we cry out to Him with all our heart. Mara's story is a testament that God's plans are always for our good.

Overcoming Temptation

Mara had been walking a new path for a year, committed to abstinence and deepening her faith. Yet, she found herself in the middle of an unexpected battle. At her new job, she grew attracted to James, a kind coworker who was married. This attraction stirred a confusing storm inside her heart—feelings she hadn't anticipated and wasn't sure how to handle.

Temptation, Mara learned, often begins quietly—in the heart and mind—long before it shows in actions. She realized her feelings for James were tied to something deeper: a longing for love, affirmation, and acceptance that she hadn't fully recognized before. The compliments James gave her and the kindness he showed met an emotional need she had carried for years. But Mara knew that acting on these feelings would go against everything she had committed to with God.

The tension between Mara and James made things harder. Sometimes, small disagreements flared into angry outbursts, echoes of defense mechanisms Mara had developed in childhood. Yet James was patient; he would calm her down gently, reminding her that the future her heart longed for was still waiting—a promise she believed God had given her.

Through prayer and reflection, Mara recognized the importance of setting boundaries. She began to distance herself from James, avoiding situations where her emotions might overwhelm her. It wasn't easy. The pull of her feelings was strong, but her desire to honor God was stronger.

Whenever Mara felt tempted or confused, she turned to the Bible. Verses like Proverbs 4:23 reminded her of the consequences of straying from God's ways, while Galatians 6:7-8 encouraged her to sow to the Spirit rather than to the flesh.

Prayer became Mara's refuge. She poured out her heart to God, confessing her struggles, asking for strength, and surrendering her desires. She found comfort knowing that God was faithful and would never let her face more than she could bear. As she prayed, Mara sensed God guiding her toward a new opportunity—a different job aligned with her calling and purpose.

This new job wasn't just a career move; it was part of her healing journey. It helped her focus her energy on serving others and fulfilling God's plan for her life. Mara learned to replace wandering thoughts with purpose, letting God fill the void temptation once tried to occupy.

Mara's story is one many can relate to—the tug-of-war between desire and devotion, flesh and spirit. But it is also a powerful reminder that temptation doesn't have to define us. Through God's strength and guidance, we can stand firm, set healthy boundaries, and choose what honors Him.

For anyone struggling with temptation—whether lust, addiction, or any other challenge—Mara's journey offers hope. With honest prayer, reliance on God's Word, and practical choices, it's possible to overcome the strongest desires. Temptation may come, but God always provides a way out, a path to peace, and the strength to keep moving forward.

While the enemy sought to drag Mara back into her past and trap her in a web of emotions, God granted her victory because she sought His face. Temptations are an inevitable part of your journey with God, and your faith will be tested. The Bible even encourages you to *"count it all joy when ye fall into divers temptations; knowing this, that the trying of your faith worketh patience"* James 1:2-3.

Using temptation as an excuse to return to your past is invalid. You have the power to resist temptation or to let it overcome you. Remember, *"There hath no temptation taken you but such as is common to man: but God is faithful, who will not suffer you to be tempted above that ye are able; but will with the temptation also make a way to escape, that ye may be able to bear it"* 1 Corinthians 10:13.

You do not have to fight alone—for God has already equipped you with strength through His Spirit. Victory comes not through your own will, but through remaining close to the One who has already overcome the world.

Often, we find ourselves sliding back into the pit God pulled us out of, struggling against the rush of emotions that try to keep us trapped. This is when you must cling to your salvation, knowing God is not your enemy but your ally who helps you overcome evil. These are the moments to keep your eyes on God and draw closer to Him.

When fighting temptation, ask for His help. God assists us in overcoming addictions to drugs, alcohol, sex, lust, pornography, adultery, wrong relationships, and more. The battle is not won by our strength alone. We must die to ourselves daily, putting on the full armor of God.

Putting on the full armor means sitting with God every day—praying, reading the Bible, and worshipping Him by giving thanks for what you have now and what is yet to come.

God provides signs and speaks to us continuously. Do not wait until the damage is done to reach out. Call on Him before you feel tempted and pray for strength to face the troubles ahead.

Mara finds strength in her faith, particularly through Bible verses like 2 Corinthians 12:10: "For when I am weak, then I am strong." She believes the strength to resist temptation comes from her Lord and Savior, Jesus Christ. Though healing is a process, she understands that the reward far outweighs every tear shed during her nights of crying. This perspective gives her hope and clarity as she continues her journey.

"And let us not be weary in well-doing: for in due season, we shall reap, if we faint not" Galatians 6:9. The Lord knows it won't be easy. Mara often felt like she was barely hanging on, but God never failed her.

Whenever Mara reached her breaking point, God was there. At just the right moment, He would send someone her way with a word of encouragement or whisper the right words into her heart, reminding her she was not alone.

Whether a friend, a scripture speaking directly to her situation, or an unexpected opportunity, God always made His presence known. Even in the most difficult moments, when Mara felt overwhelmed, God opened doors of hope. He reminded her He was walking with her every step, carrying her through trials and giving her strength to keep going.

FINALLY, BE STRONG IN THE LORD AND IN THE STRENGTH OF HIS MIGHT. PUT ON THE WHOLE ARMOR OF GOD, THAT YOU MAY BE ABLE TO STAND AGAINST THE SCHEMES OF THE DEVIL.

EPHESIANS 6:10-11

Are You Ready for What You're Asking For?

Healing is a deeply personal and transformative journey, one that can be both difficult and empowering. When you are in the process of healing, it is easy to unknowingly attract people who are also in the same emotional place. You may find yourself drawn to people who, just like you, are not fully healed, not emotionally available, or not ready for the kind of relationship you truly want or deserve.

For Mara, this truth became real in a way she did not expect. As she worked through her own struggles and tried to heal, she found herself in situations where she was attracting men who were not ready for a real, committed relationship. They were emotionally distant, some even married or still carrying their own emotional burdens. She realized that, in a way, these relationships reflected her own emotional state. At the time, Mara did not fully understand it, but she was unconsciously drawn to people who were not able to give her what she needed because, deep down, she was not yet fully prepared either.

It is easy to believe that you are ready for a relationship simply because you want one. However, if you are still dealing with unresolved fears or emotional pain, you may continue to attract people who are also struggling. It is as if your heart and your actions quietly signal to others that you are not yet ready for the depth of connection you desire.

Mara came to understand that to be ready for the right kind of relationship, she needed to do more than just hope for it. She needed to allow Jesus, her Healer, to work deeply within her heart. She had to let Him uncover the roots of her pain, the fears, and the scars hidden beneath the surface. This process was often painful, but it was necessary. Jesus was the one who could bring true healing, not only on the outside but in the deep places of her soul. He had to prepare her, shaping her into the person she was asking Him to bring into her life.

We often pray for things—healing, love, or new opportunities—but we are not always prepared to receive them. Are we willing to become the person who can sustain that blessing? When we pray for restoration or relationship, it is important not only to ask but also to prepare our hearts and lives to be ready for what we desire.

Mara's story reminds us that before you ask God for something, you should ask yourself, "Am I preparing myself to be what I am asking God to receive?" Are you allowing Him to heal the broken places within you and to work on your character so that you can become the person you need to be for the blessing He is preparing for you? Whether it is love or a new opportunity, this is a hard truth, but an important one. God does not simply give us what we want; He shapes us so that we are able to carry and sustain it.

If you are asking for a healthy, loving relationship, you must first let Him heal you so that you can be emotionally and spiritually ready for that kind of connection. If you are asking for a new opportunity, trust that He will first prepare you with the strength and wisdom needed to step into it. God desires to give you the desires of your heart, but He also desires to prepare you for them, so that when they arrive, you are ready to fully embrace and sustain them.

You Shall Not Be Burned

"When thou passest through the waters, I will be with thee; and through the rivers, they shall not overflow thee: when thou walkest through the fire, thou shalt not be burned; neither shall the flame kindle upon thee" Isaiah 43:2.

Mara walked through a lot of fire for over thirty years and built up a lot of anger, but God was healing her from those burns. A big part of this process was her new position. Even though the pay was lower than any other job she had worked in the previous ten years, she took the position by faith. She felt in her heart that the Holy Spirit was telling her it would be worth it in the end.

For the first few months, the new job went well. They worked with Mara's school schedule, and she even got some of her hours counted toward her degree. Mara thought she was finally working with people she got along with and who were not looking down on, judging, or deciding they did not like her based on false perceptions.

But it did not last. Soon enough, some of Mara's coworkers began being mean to her. They spoke with Mara's clients behind her back and told them to write up grievances about her. Mara was getting in trouble for things she was not trained to do. Her coworkers said they were tired of covering for her so she could go to school. Things got so bad that eventually, Mara cried every day she had to go to work. Her schedule was being tampered with. She felt she was being mistreated because of her race and did not understand how people could be that way in this day and age.

Just when Mara felt like she was starting to get ahead in life, mistreatment from others brought back depression and tears again. She did not know what to do. When she was finally called to the office and put on a letter to meet expectations, that is when she knew something had to be done.

Mara wrote a letter to Human Resources because she wanted to discuss some untrue accusations thrown at her. They set a date for her to meet with HR, but she still did not feel good about any of it.

Right before seeing a client one day, Mara was in her office crying. She worried about losing her job and credit hours for school. A sudden knock at her door caused her to sit up quickly and wipe the tears from her eyes.

"Come in," Mara said, trying to sound like she had not been crying. The door opened, but it was not her client. It was a lady named Jewels; someone she had never seen working at the job before.

"Are you okay?" the lady asked her.

"Yes," Mara said, followed by some sniffling.

"What's wrong?"

"I don't understand why this is happening." Without knowing who she was, Mara began briefing her about what was going on in her life and the discrimination she at work.

"They did me the exact same way at my last job," Jewels said. She and Mara shared a moment of silent understanding. Then the lady continued. "We're gonna say a prayer, and God is gonna work it out."

They prayed together and asked God to intervene according to His will. Then the woman gave Mara some advice. She told her to take all her notes and information, bring them to the Equal Employment Opportunity Commission (EEOC), and file a complaint. She told Mara to do this before coming back to work.

Mara had piles of notes about the incidents. Mother always told her to keep a paper trail. It was one of the good influences she had on Mara's life. The following day, Mara woke up early and went to the EEOC. She met with Grace, told her what had happened, and showed her the extensive notes she had taken regarding the incidents.

"I definitely think you have a case," Grace said.

"But my meeting with HR is in a couple of days," Mara explained.

Grace looked Mara in the eyes and said, "You will graduate and finish school. I am sending them an email, and they will receive it before that meeting." Grace's words and confident voice filled Mara with a measure of strength that eased her anxiety.

When she walked into the meeting with HR, the dynamic was completely different from what she expected. It was all "Hi! What is going on?" How can we help you? And nobody said much beyond that. There was no more talk about how Mara had to meet certain expectations or change her schedule.

Once again, Father God came through with a messenger named Grace. You know how the saying goes: He is not always on our time, but He is always on time. His timing is always best, and He fights for those who love Him.

"And we know that to them that love God all things work together for good, even to them that are called according to his purpose" Romans 8:28.

However, after the triumphant meeting, the road got bumpy again. As if what happened was her fault, they moved her to a location further away from her home. Mara's employer sent her to their more diverse office.

This made Mara angry, but she played along because she needed to pay the bills and acquire hours for school. The situation made Mara realize that she never wanted to work for another company again. From the moment of that realization, Mara began asking God to make a way for her to own her own business one day.

Things were not looking so great for Mara. She was a single mother of five children, attending school, working full-time she struggled to make ends meet. Her bills were piling up, and her credit was suffering. The weight of her financial situation often left her feeling depressed and anxious.

Mara's job added to her struggles, particularly at the new office. Despite her efforts to remain friendly and kind, she faced coldness from her colleagues, including those of her own race, whom she had hoped would understand and relate to her.

No matter how much she tried, they refused to engage with her, and she constantly tried to please others, sacrificing her happiness. It was exhausting. The more Mara tried to win people over, the more frustrated and overwhelmed she became.

Healing the Inner Child: Surrendering to God's Strength

As the personal attacks felt more frequent, Mara's patience wore thin. Every time someone ignored her efforts or made her feel small, she noticed a familiar pain rising inside of her—one she had felt many times before.

It was Mara's inner child, still carrying the wounds of her past experiences with rejection. Throughout her upbringing, she faced numerous injustices, often feeling unprotected, overlooked, and undervalued. These deep-seated hurts resurfaced, triggering her desire to defend herself and stand for what was right.

When a coworker or anyone crossed her professionally, Mara would react strongly, sending long emails and attempting to prove herself. But deep down, her reactions were not just about the present situation—they were about that unhealed part of her that still felt powerless and abandoned, just as she had felt as a child. By fighting back, defending herself, and trying to be heard, Mara only worsened the situation and pushed herself further from peace.

Mara realized that her responses, rooted in anger, fear of rejection, and her past traumas, were not bearing the fruit of Christ. The Lord was calling her to love her enemies and pray for those who wronged her, a command she found incredibly difficult. "But I say unto you, Love your enemies, and pray for them that persecute you" Matthew 5:44. This felt impossible because Mara was trying to defend her present self and that wounded child within her who had never received protection or justice.

Mara slowly began to understand that she had been trying to manage these conflicts within her own strength and according to her own will. "Beloved, avenge not yourselves, but give place unto the wrath of God: for it is written, Vengeance belongeth unto me; I will recompense, saith the Lord. But if thine enemy hunger, feed him; and if he thirst, give him to drink: for in so doing thou shalt heap coals of fire upon his head. Be not overcome of evil, but overcome evil with good" Romans 12:19-21.

Mara realized that her inner child's wounds were influencing how she interacted with people now. Instead of reacting out of that place of pain, she needed to surrender those past hurts to God and trust that He was the one who would protect and vindicate her. Jesus's teaching in Matthew 5:46 challenged her: "For if ye love them which love you, what reward have ye? do not even the publicans the same?" (Matthew 5:46) challenged her. Mara knew that loving only those who were kind to her was not enough. God was calling her to be set apart.

Controlling Your Emotions

The Bible says much about controlling your emotions and avoiding aggressive behavior. "A fool uttereth all his anger; but a wise man keepeth it back and stilleth it" Proverbs 29:11. You cannot control what people say and do to you, but you can control how you react to them.

Feeling anger is a normal part of life—it does not make you sinful. Scripture acknowledges this in *Ephesians 4:26*:

"Be ye angry, and sin not: let not the sun go down upon your wrath."

This verse reminds us that while anger itself is a natural emotion, what matters most is how we handle it. Being mindful of your feelings allows you to pause, reflect, and choose a response guided by wisdom rather than emotion. When you recognize anger early, you can manage it before it leads to words or actions you'll regret.

Proverbs 29:22 warns,

"An angry man stirreth up strife, and a furious man aboundeth in transgression."

Anger can easily escalate into conflict if left unchecked. Acting *reactively*—lashing out in the heat of the moment—often leads to more pain and misunderstanding. Acting *proactively* means taking a step back, inviting God into the moment, and choosing peace over provocation. You might take a deep breath, say a short prayer, or walk away for a moment before responding. These small acts of self-control protect your relationships and your own spiritual well-being.

Paul also offers practical guidance in *Ephesians 4:31–32*:

"Let all bitterness and wrath and anger and clamor and slander be put away from you, along with all malice. And be ye kind one to another, tenderhearted, forgiving each other, even as God also in Christ forgave you."

Unresolved anger can grow into bitterness and resentment if we let it linger. By releasing these emotions and choosing kindness, we open our hearts to healing and peace. Holding on to anger only weighs us down. As *1 Corinthians 13:5* reminds us, love "keeps no record of wrongs."

Letting go—even in small ways—is the first step toward peace.

It is important to understand that these are not switches you can just turn on and off. Healing is a process. Especially if you have been holding on to resentment or any kind of negative energy, it will take time to change the habits of your mind. You will gradually achieve this by reading the Word of God daily and trying your best to be more like Jesus every day.

God sent Mara a supervisor who taught her how to communicate in a healthy, assertive way. To do this professionally, she had to learn to manage her emotions. One time, Mara became frustrated when a colleague failed to complete a task that could potentially impact a client. Unfortunately, her anger spilled over into a group chat visible to all her coworkers, revealing her emotions to the entire team.

Her supervisor called her into the office and empathized.

"I understand that you are passionate about your job and what you believe in," the supervisor said, "but you have to find a way to use logic when communicating rather than emotion." He told her to find healthy coping skills to manage her emotions and then come back to communicate in a healthy way.

Mara occasionally struggled with how she dealt with her emotions and anger. Whenever she got upset, she would talk to her supervisor. Mara was very thankful to this supervisor because he helped her professionally with something she could take into her personal life. Later in life, Mara learned to calm herself down through prayer and journaling. These practices became lifelines, allowing her to slow down and think more logically and clearly.

As she matured, she realized the importance of finding healthy ways to deal with her emotions rather than reacting impulsively. Her journey to emotional healing was long, but through God's grace and practical habits, she discovered that processing emotions is crucial to living a peaceful, fulfilling life.

For Mara, prayer was more than a ritual—it was a way to connect with God and share her deepest thoughts and feelings. It was a space where she could pour out her heart, knowing God was listening and offering her peace in return. When she felt overwhelmed, prayer became a tool to calm her mind and reset her perspective. Philippians 4:6-7 was a verse that spoke to her heart: "In nothing be anxious; but in everything by prayer and supplication with thanksgiving let your requests be made known unto God. And the peace of God, which passeth all understanding, shall guard your hearts and your thoughts in Christ Jesus."

Whenever Mara felt hurt or upset, instead of acting out in anger or frustration, she would turn to God in prayer, which helped her avoid being swept away by her emotions.

Journaling was another key to her emotional healing. Writing down her thoughts allowed her to process them in a safe space. Journaling gave her the chance to reflect on her feelings, identify what bothered her, and saw patterns in her emotional responses. She understood herself better and saw how God worked in her life. By writing down her prayers, fears, and hopes, Mara could look back and see her progress, giving her peace and clarity.

By learning to pause, process, and reflect, she grew more intentional in how she responded to situations that once triggered emotional outbursts. As she worked through her emotions, Mara found that it was vital to acknowledge them instead of pushing them aside. Ignoring emotions only led to them resurfacing later, often with more intensity.

She realized that by confronting her feelings head-on, she could manage them better and prevent them from controlling her. Processing emotions also helped Mara improve her relationships. She started approaching conflicts and difficult conversations with a clear mind, allowing her to communicate more effectively. In Proverbs 16:32, she found wisdom that reminded her of the value of self-control: "He that is slow to anger is better than the mighty; and he that ruleth his spirit, than he that taketh a city."

Love Your Enemies

As Mara prayed, she came to understand that the same God who created her — the Lord she prayed to and the Jesus who taught her to love her enemies — were one and the same. His love was personal, constant, and unchanging. "What do I need to learn from this experience, God?" Mara finally asked. "Love my enemies?" And God told her that, yes, she was right.

The next lesson the Lord taught Mara was profound: how to love her enemies and pray for those who wronged her. This was an incredibly challenging journey for Mara, who had grown accustomed to defending herself and battling feelings of anger and offense. Mara, feeling the weight of being hurt and wronged by others, cried out to the Lord, "Lord, how am I supposed to love people who are hurting me and doing me wrong?"

Gently, God reminded her through His Spirit, "Mara, love is easy when it is returned. Any person can love those who love them back. But I call you to something higher: to love even those who have hurt you." He guided her to Luke 6:32-33 "For if ye love them which love you, what thank have ye? for sinners also love those that love them. And if ye do good to them which do good to you, what thank have ye? for sinners also do even the same."

"Mara," God was helping her to see, "even the world's standard is limited. Evil people love those who love them, but I ask you to rise above that. True love does not seek reward; it blesses, forgives, and prays for those who persecute you." Jesus Himself modeled this perfect love when He prayed on the cross for those who were crucifying Him: "Father, forgive them; for they know not what they do" Luke 23:34.

Through these lessons, Mara understood that love was not just a feeling for the kind or friendly. Love, as God defines it, was a choice — an action — and sometimes the hardest, most powerful form of love is the one given to those who do not deserve it. As Mara sought God's guidance, He led her to meditate daily on 1 Corinthians 13:4-7 "Love is patient, is kind; love is not jealous; love does not brag and is not arrogant, does not behave itself unseemly; seeketh not its own, is not provoked, taketh not account of evil; rejoiceth not at unrighteousness, but rejoiceth with the truth; beareth all things, believeth all things, hopeth all things, endureth all things."

These verses became Mara's daily reminder that love, as God defines it, goes beyond feelings and circumstances. It is how we choose to treat others, even when they do not deserve it. Love is not conditional or based on how others treat us — it is rooted in Christ's example and His power working through us.

Another verse she was led to meditate on was 1 Peter 4:8 "Above all things being fervent in your love among yourselves; for love covereth a multitude of sins." This verse showed Mara that love, when done earnestly, has the power to heal. It covers offenses and brings reconciliation. She learned that her role was not to defend herself or seek revenge but to trust in God's love to heal the hurt and make things right.

Imagine the struggle of setting aside years of hurt and betrayal to pray for those who caused pain. It required Mara to confront the spirit of anger and offense that had gripped her heart for so long. It was not just about tolerating or ignoring her enemies; it was about actively seeking their well-being and blessing them despite their actions against her.

In Matthew 5:44, Jesus commands His followers: "But I say unto you, Love your enemies, and pray for them that persecute you." This goes beyond human instinct or societal norms — it is a call to transcend personal hurt and embody a love that reflects God's unconditional grace and mercy. Romans 12:14 reinforces this by urging believers to "Bless them that persecute you; bless, and curse not." It challenges Mara and all who read her story to respond to adversity with acts of kindness and words of blessing rather than retaliation.

By choosing to pray for her enemies, Mara found a renewed sense of peace and freedom from the burden of bitterness. Her journey inspires us to consider how we respond to those who wrong us, urging us to embrace forgiveness and compassion as instruments of God's love in a broken world.

Mara's success was because of her diligence in learning to manage her emotions and communicate in a healthy, assertive way. This lesson required Mara to lean on God for guidance, especially in interacting with her colleagues and others. Mara prayed for wisdom to navigate inconvenient situations with humility and grace. She started working on her character and how she responded. Mara made a habit of asking God for guidance, especially when she did not know what to say. With time, her conversations became more peaceful and productive.

The investigation into her discrimination claims dragged on, but Mara stopped fixating on it. She barely heard updates and chose to trust God with the outcome rather than stress over what she couldn't control. Mara's story reflects the real-life journey many of us face in learning to balance our professional lives with our faith, surrendering our insecurities and need for control to God.

Mara had once struggled with a lack of appreciation, leading to moments where she did not show up or did not put forth her best effort. She found it challenging to give her best when she felt unrecognized. However, she came to understand that her true worth was not determined by others' acknowledgment, but by her identity in Christ.

But God, in His wisdom, helped her see that her work, no matter how unappreciated by others, was ultimately an offering to Him. In Colossians 3:23-24, the Bible reminds believers: "And whatever you do, do it heartily, as to the Lord and not to men, knowing that from the Lord you will receive the reward of the inheritance; for you serve the Lord Christ."

This verse helped Mara realize that when she worked, even in moments when others might not notice, she was serving God. Her efforts were not in vain, for the Lord saw everything, and He would reward her for her faithfulness.

Additionally, in Ephesians 6:7. "With good will doing service, as to the Lord, and not to men." This verse further solidified Mara's understanding that her labor was not merely for human approval, but for God's glory. It was a reminder that when she worked, her actions were an expression of her love and faith in God.

By changing her perspective to focus on serving God rather than seeking external validation, Mara found renewed purpose and strength. Her work became a way to honor Him, and in doing so, her efforts were no longer tied to the recognition of others, but to the eternal value of serving the Lord.

Stepping Out in Faith

Mara had completed all her hours for school and graduated with her master's degree. She felt it was time to step fully into her calling and start her own business for God's glory. The Lord had already provided opportunities for her, and Mara was ready to embrace this next step of faith.

Throughout her life, the Lord had asked Mara to step out in faith, and each time, He had proven Himself faithful. Leaving old habits behind, stepping away from relationships, and trusting Him in moments of uncertainty had always led to growth and deeper reliance on God. Every challenge reminded her that His plans were greater than her fears or doubts.

One of the most significant moments came when the Lord told Mara to leave her job to start her own business. She had asked God for guidance and prayed for the opportunity to follow her calling. Despite uncertainty, Mara stepped out in faith, trusting that God's plan was greater than her own. She paused and asked, "Are you sure, Lord?" He answered gently but clearly, "My plan is better." Mara knew it was time to move on, but fear and doubt tried to hold her back.

One evening, Mara went out to dinner with a friend of her youngest daughter. Mara usually did not take time for herself; she was always busy, but that night felt different. During their conversation, the woman revealed that she had an opening in her business and suggested that Mara could seize this opportunity while also receiving referrals. Mara felt an overwhelming sense that this meeting was divinely orchestrated—a clear sign of God's presence and guidance in her life.

Confident in the Lord's direction, Mara stepped out in faith and submitted her two-weeks' notice. Shortly after, the very job that had once seemed ready to let her go surprised her. They offered her the option to stay part-time with flexible hours and even increased her pay. Glory to God! This showed how God honors faithfulness and walks with those who obey Him.

Even with this offer, Mara's heart was not at peace. She prayed earnestly, seeking God's confirmation. His voice was clear: she needed to leave completely. Though the new business had barely covered expenses, Mara obeyed. She trusted God, spending time with Him daily, studying His

Word, and praying like she was speaking with a close friend: "Speak, Lord, for your servant is listening," she would say.

Not even a few days after leaving, Mara received a call offering a major contract that more than doubled her income within six months. Her business flourished in ways that could only be described as miraculous, demonstrating God's favor and perfect timing. All glory went to Him.

Mara's journey is a testimony that when we follow God's calling, step out in faith, and give Him the glory, He opens doors that no one else can. Even when the world sees risk, God's plan is perfect. Luke 1:37 reminds us, "For no word from God shall be void of power." Proverbs 3:5-6 reinforces this truth: "Trust in the Lord with all thine heart; and lean not unto thine own understanding. In all thy ways acknowledge him, and he shall direct thy paths."

By following her calling and trusting God completely, Mara not only built a successful business but also provided a living testimony of His faithfulness. Her obedience, courage, and devotion allowed God to shine through her life, showing that His plans are always greater than our own.

Finding Approval in His Guidance

Not everyone will cheer you on or support your decisions, and that is something Mara had to come to terms with. She often sought approval from others before making a decision, rather than trusting that if God had called her to something, His approval was all that mattered.

If you are struggling with making a decision, seeking the Lord's guidance is essential. Sit with Him, pray, and reflect on His Word. Remember, God has the final say in all matters.

While seeking advice and input from others can be valuable, Let God's voice be the one that directs your path. When you believe God has called you to a particular path, trust He will provide confirmation and be with you every step of the way.

Overcompensating to Earn Love and Acceptance

Mara often cried out to God in frustration and weariness. People in her life seemed to love her only when she was useful to them—if she said or did the wrong thing, they would withdraw, ignore her, or dismiss her entirely. Their affection felt conditional, earned only through her constant giving, pleasing, and self-sacrifice.

This pattern left Mara hollow and depleted. She worked tirelessly to keep others happy, hoping for the validation of their love. Yet time and again, she felt used, unappreciated, and abandoned the moment she failed to meet their expectations.

Why did Mara overcompensate? Deep down, she feared rejection and craved acceptance, believing her worth depended on what she could do for others. Many people struggle with this same cycle—giving excessively in order to earn love—because they have not yet experienced unconditional acceptance. This often leads to exhaustion, self-blame, and emotional emptiness.

Even worse, Mara blamed herself, thinking, "Maybe I'm not enough. Maybe I'm the problem." But over time, she learned to turn to the Lord—not as a last resort, but as her foundation. Unlike people, God's love is constant and does not depend on performance or pleasing others.

Giving with Balance: Rooted in God's Love

The Lord calls us to love Him first with all our heart and soul, and then to love others as ourselves Matthew 22:37-39. This is the foundation for all healthy giving. When our love for God is strong, our generosity toward others flows naturally—not out of fear, obligation, or the need to earn approval, but from a heart filled with His grace.

"Each one must give as he has decided in his heart, not reluctantly or under compulsion, for God loves a cheerful giver." — 2 Corinthians 9:7.

When we give in this way, we are cheerful givers. Our time, energy, and resources are shared freely because we first give to ourselves the same love, acceptance, and grace that God gives. But if we overcompensate—giving out of a sense of duty, fear, or a desire to be needed—we risk frustration, anger, and resentment. Over-giving without joy drains us and undermines the very love we hope to share.

Healthy giving is not about exhaustion or approval; it is about reflecting God's love. By grounding ourselves in His love first, we can give to others generously, joyfully, and without resentment, trusting that our worth does not depend on what we do for anyone else.

Unlike people, the Lord never turned Mara away. She never fully understood the depth of His love. Even when she failed, when she felt unlovable, or feared He would leave her like everyone else, He never did. He had promised that He would never leave or forsake us, and He kept that promise. Yet she often questioned His love, unsure if it was real. Still, she sang to Him, pouring out her heart in praise and trust, even in her doubts.

Mara would lift her voice in worship, singing to the Lord, "Why do You love me like You do?" Her question was not born of doubt but of awe—a wonder at the depth of God's love. Instead of feeling burdened by thoughts of unworthiness, she allowed herself to be overwhelmed by His grace.

Each note she sang became a prayer, a melody of gratitude that rose from her heart. In worship, she felt the weight of rejection and hurt fall away, replaced by the comfort of His presence.

As she sang, she was not asking for answers anymore. She was simply basking in the mystery of a love so great; it surpassed her understanding.

Say this prayer if you, too, are waiting on God to send the right people into your life. Trust that He hears your heart's cry and will bring the right people to encourage, uplift, and walk alongside you in His perfect timing.

Dear Heavenly Father,
Send people into my life who will love me like You do—unconditionally.

Surround me with those who won't give up on me when I fall short, who will offer compassion and understanding instead of rejection.

Teach me to seek approval only from You and help me love myself as You love me.

Amen.

Mara stopped running on empty, learning instead to fill her heart with God's truth.

She leaned into God's love and began to release her need to prove her worth to others. As she reflected on her thoughts and patterns, she longed to understand why she had acted the way she did—and why she had always sought approval from others. She didn't want to stay trapped in the same cycles. She sought understanding, not to shame herself, but to heal, to learn, and to respond differently.

Know Your Whys

Mara sat quietly, alone with her thoughts. There were no curtains softening the light, no background noise except the quiet of the moment. She remembered the Holy Spirit's gentle whisper: **Know your whys.** The words weighed on her heart, urging her to look back at her past choices and uncover their true motives. Why had she done the things she had done? Why did she continue making certain decisions?

As a child, she had eagerly signed up for every school talent show, joined the drill team, and embraced any opportunity to perform. At the time, she told herself it was because she loved the stage, the thrill of dancing, singing, and hearing an audience's applause. Yet was that entirely true? Even then, part of her craved more than the performance itself. She longed for approving nods, admiration, and the sense of being special. It was not wrong to enjoy performing—God gives gifts for a reason—but she now wondered if her deepest motive had been the validation that followed the final bow.

In adulthood, Mara considered the moments she posted pictures on social media, capturing herself in a flattering outfit or announcing a job promotion. Why did she share these things? Did she genuinely want to keep friends and family updated, or was she hoping to gather likes and complimentary comments? Did she yearn for that boost to her sense of worth, even if it was fleeting? The excitement of positive feedback often faded quickly, leaving her questioning her significance when responses were fewer than she expected.

Mara also examined her career decisions. The promotions and extra projects—did she truly love the work, or was she chasing recognition and approval? Was her driving force the satisfaction of a job well done, or the admiration of coworkers and superiors? At times, she realized, her "why" had been entangled in a desire to be seen as competent, valuable, and indispensable, rather than a calling from God or a true passion for the task at hand.

Scripture reminded her that God cares about the heart. As 1 Samuel 16:7 states, "…the Lord seeth not as man seeth; for man looketh on the outward appearance, but the Lord looketh on the heart." Knowing her why mattered because it showed whether her actions were rooted in love, purpose, and authenticity, or in a hunger for acceptance and praise. It was not about never enjoying applause or never posting another picture again. It was about understanding what fueled her decisions. Did she find her worth in human responses, or in who God said she was?

Galatians 1:10 challenged her thinking: "For do I now persuade men, or God? or do I seek to please men? for if I yet pleased men, I should not be the servant of Christ." This verse pressed Mara to recognize that if her goal was to please people, she would stray from her devotion to Christ's calling. Colossians 3:23 further guided her: "And whatsoever ye do, do it heartily, as to the Lord, and not unto men." God desired that her efforts and intentions come from a heart that sought to honor Him, rather than impress others.

The Holy Spirit's whisper was an invitation to freedom and truth, not a condemnation of her past. If as a child she had performed partly for applause, now she could celebrate her gifts simply because God delighted in seeing her use them. If she had pursued work accolades for validation, she could now seek excellence while resting in God's unconditional love and calling for her life.

It would take time, prayer, and courage. Mara understood this. She might still struggle when considering a volunteer project or deciding whether to share something online. Yet now she had a tool: the question, "Why do I do what I do?" This question could guide her toward motivations rooted in genuine love and purpose, rather than a restless chase for human approval.

Romans 12:2 encouraged her: "And be not conformed to this world: but be ye transformed by the renewing of your mind…" Understanding her why would transform not only her decisions but her heart as well. It would free her from the silent chains of people-pleasing and external validation. It would allow her to step fully into the person God created her to be, delighting in who she was without constantly measuring herself against others.

Mara knew her future choices would not always be perfect, but they could be more honest. When she said yes to a project, it would be because she believed in it, not because she sought praise. When she posted a picture, it would be to share a moment of beauty or joy, not to accumulate compliments. When she used her gifts, it would be in gratitude to the One who gave them, not to prove her worth.

As she reflected, Mara felt more aligned with God's truth. Jeremiah 17:10 reminded her: "I the Lord search the heart, I try the reins…" God already knew her motives, and now He invited her to know them too. In embracing this understanding, Mara stepped into a more authentic, God-centered life, guided by a deeper, purer "why."

It is easy to slip into patterns of seeking approval, validation, or a sense of worthiness from others. Consider your own life: Why do you say yes to certain commitments? Why do you post on social media? Why do you work as hard as you do? Are your efforts rooted in love, sincerity, and a calling you believe God has placed on your heart, or are they driven by a quieter yearning to be seen, praised, or accepted?

When you begin asking yourself, "Why do I do what I do?" you open a door to greater authenticity. Instead of feeling trapped by the opinions of others, you can find freedom in knowing that God fully loves and values you—no performance, applause, or "likes" required.

Take time to pause and pray before making decisions. Ask God to align your intentions with His purposes.

This kind of self-examination, guided by Scripture and the Holy Spirit, may lead you toward a more authentic life. As you learn your "whys," you can offer your gifts, words, and actions as true expressions of who God created you to be—serving and sharing not from insecurity, but from a secure place of love, purpose, and faith.

Wise Counsel

God answered her prayer by leading her to a therapist who understood her struggles and deeply respected her faith. This therapist became pivotal in Mara's healing journey, helping her unearth the deep-rooted issues that had affected her for so long.

Through therapy, Mara was gently guided to confront her deepest fears rooted in childhood. Together, she and her therapist explored the emotional wounds that had shaped her understanding of love, worth, and trust. As Mara began to look closer, she realized that her fear of abandonment had created an anxious attachment style. She longed for closeness and reassurance, constantly seeking signs that she was loved and safe.

But because of this pattern, Mara often found herself drawn to men with an avoidant attachment style — men who seemed emotionally unavailable or uncomfortable with intimacy. At first, their independence felt magnetic; she mistook their calm distance for confidence. Yet as the relationship deepened, her need for connection clashed with their fear of vulnerability.

This created a painful push-and-pull dynamic. The more Mara reached out for closeness, the more these men pulled away to protect themselves from being overwhelmed. And the more distant they became, the more anxious and desperate Mara felt. Both were caught in a cycle driven not by a lack of love, but by fear — fear of being hurt, rejected, or not enough.

What neither realized was that both were emotionally unavailable in different ways. Mara was unavailable to herself — she looked for validation outside of her, rather than within. The men she was drawn to were unavailable to others — they kept emotional walls up to avoid feeling exposed. In truth, both longed for connection but were trapped in opposite coping mechanisms born from similar wounds.

Healing began when Mara could see this clearly: it wasn't that she was unlovable, nor that the men she was drawn to were incapable of love. They were simply two sides of the same coin — both shaped by fear, both trying to protect their hearts the only way they knew how. Understanding this helped her shift from blame to compassion — for herself, and for those she once tried so hard to fix.

Therapy helped Mara learn **tools for managing depression, anxiety, and PTSD**.

From a young age, Mara felt invisible. No matter how hard she tried, she could never earn the attention or approval of those around her. She performed in talent shows, completed every school project perfectly, and went out of her way to please—but recognition rarely came. This left Mara with a deep sense of unworthiness.

Even as a child, her mind raced with automatic thoughts: "I am not enough. I must try harder. Maybe if I do this perfectly, she will love me." These thoughts stirred fear, sadness, and anxiety in her body. Her chest tightened, her heart raced, and a small spark of anger often rose, directed at herself for being "too sensitive."

Her protective behaviors emerged naturally:

Overstriving: Taking on more than she could handle to prove her worth.

Withdrawing: Pulling back emotionally, afraid any misstep would push others away.

Self-criticism: Echoing the unspoken judgment of her mother.

Anxiety or frustration: Feeling tense, defensive, or restless.

Even as an adult, small triggers could awaken these old fears. A friend's quiet tone, someone forgetting a commitment, or a subtle critique could ignite the familiar sense of inadequacy.

But now, Mara was learning to pause and take every thought captive 2 Corinthians 10:5. When her mind whispered, "I am failing; I am not enough," she practiced gently reframing it: "I am fearfully and wonderfully made" Psalm 139:14. When anxiety rose, she prayed, "Lord, I choose to bring this fear to You and see this moment through Your eyes" Philippians 4:6. Slowly, each thought, fear, or self-judgment became an opportunity to renew her mind (Romans 12:2) instead of reacting automatically.

Therapy gave her the tools to understand the cycle of thoughts, feelings, and behaviors. She learned to notice triggers, recognize automatic reactions, and respond differently. For instance, when she felt the familiar tightening of fear after a friend forgot a plan, she would pause and ask herself what was really happening inside her—and how she could choose a different response.

Thought: "They don't care about me."

Feeling: Anxiety, sadness, slight anger.

Behavior: The old Mara would withdraw or overcompensate.

New Response: "Maybe they are busy. My worth is not defined by this. God loves me."

Outcome: Calmer, more peaceful, able to respond with grace.

She realized that her worth was not something she needed to earn; it was freely given by God.

Yet it was God's love that healed her at the deepest level. Through prayer and Scripture, Mara began to hear the truth: "My grace is sufficient for you" 2 Corinthians 12:9, "Do not be anxious about anything, but pray about everything" Philippians 4:6, and "Come to me, all who are weary and burdened, and I will give you rest" Matthew 11:28.

Slowly, Mara began to rest. When triggers arose, instead of reacting with fear or overcompensation, she would pause, pray, and renew her mind: "Lord, help me see this moment through Your eyes. I am enough because You love me." She forgave herself for the years spent striving for a love she could never earn from human sources.

Mara's journey was not linear. Old fears, anxiety, and frustration still rose up at times. But each time she took her thoughts captive and reframed them with God's truth, she felt a peace that therapy alone could not provide. Her perfectionism, once her shield, gradually gave way to rest. She was finally learning to live in the truth that she was fully seen, fully loved, and fully enough—not because of what she did, but because of who God said she was.

Mara realized that her anger was not just a reaction to those around her—it was also a defense mechanism. It protected her from harm and shielded the vulnerable inner child within her—the little girl who longed to be seen, heard, and valued. Over time, anger became a barrier that kept her from truly connecting with others.

Through therapy, Mara learned that anger was not her enemy but a signal—a reminder of unresolved wounds. Assertive communication allowed her to express her needs and desires clearly and directly, without compromising her values or disrespecting others. She learned to honor her own voice, just as Proverbs 31:26 says, "She openeth her mouth with wisdom; and in her tongue is the law of kindness." Wise communication, she discovered, is both firm and kind.

Mara's journey offers an important lesson: anger itself is not inherently bad. As Ecclesiastes 7:9 reminds us, "Be not hasty in thy spirit to be angry: for anger resteth in the bosom of fools." By understanding the roots of her anger, Mara began to see it as a signal to pause, reflect, and address deeper needs. Assertive communication empowered her to break cycles of passive silence or explosive aggression, leading to healthier relationships and emotional well-being.

Reflection:
Have you ever stayed silent instead of speaking up, fearing conflict, judgment, or rejection? Such fears often trace back to childhood experiences. Mara grew up in a home filled with tension and chaos. She learned to fight—not only physically, but with words and attitude. Her anger was ever-present, built up from years of frustration and unfair treatment. When she stayed silent, frustrations accumulated until they erupted uncontrollably.

Through therapy, Mara began to understand these patterns. She recognized that both her aggression and her silence were survival strategies. Understanding this allowed her to respond differently, with honesty, clarity, and kindness.

How Do You Become More Assertive?

Recognize Your Fears

The first step is to acknowledge what is holding you back. Are you afraid of being judged, criticized, or rejected? Recognize that these fears are natural but not always accurate. Your voice matters, and you have the right to be heard. Proverbs 29:25 says, "The fear of man bringeth a snare: but whoso putteth his trust in the Lord shall be safe." This verse reminds us not to let fear control us but to trust that God is with us as we learn to speak up.

Acknowledge Your Worth

You have value, and your needs matter. Assertiveness starts with self-worth. If you believe your thoughts, feelings, and needs are less important than others, you will struggle to speak up. Psalm 139:14 says, "I will praise thee; for I am fearfully and wonderfully made: marvellous are thy works; and that my soul knoweth right well." If you see yourself the way God sees you—valuable, loved, and worthy—you will be more confident in expressing yourself.

Practice Saying "No" Without Guilt

People-pleasers often feel guilty saying "no," but learning to set boundaries is essential for emotional well-being. Start with small steps. Practice saying no to small requests, such as an invitation to an event you do not want to attend. Remember, saying "no" to others is often saying "yes" to yourself. Matthew 5:37 says, "But let your communication be, Yea, yea; Nay, nay: for whatsoever is more than these cometh of evil." This verse reminds us of the power of clear, simple communication.

Express Yourself Clearly and Directly

Use "I" statements to take responsibility for your feelings. For example, instead of saying, "You never listen to me," try saying, "I feel unheard when I am interrupted during our conversations." This approach is less likely to make the other person defensive and more likely to lead to constructive dialogue.

Stay Calm and Practice Emotional Regulation

One of the hardest parts of assertive communication is staying calm when emotions are high. When you feel overwhelmed, take a deep breath, pause, and remind yourself that you can communicate from a place of peace, not frustration. James 1:19 says, "Wherefore, my beloved brethren, let every man be swift to hear, slow to speak, slow to wrath." By following this wisdom, you can respond with clarity and calmness, even in difficult conversations.

Hold Firm to Your Boundaries

People may not always like your new assertiveness. If you were always a people-pleaser, people may push back when you start setting boundaries. Stand firm. Galatians 1:10 says, "For do I now persuade men, or God? or do I seek to please men? for if I yet pleased men, I should not be the servant of Christ." Your goal is not to please people; it is to honor God and live with integrity.

If you struggle with passive silence or aggressive outbursts, it is important to know that assertiveness is a skill you can learn. It does not happen overnight, but with patience and practice, you can develop the confidence to express yourself clearly.

Assertiveness allows you to communicate in a way that builds trust, strengthens relationships, and honors your God-given worth. Second Timothy 1:7 says, "For God hath not given us the spirit of fear; but of power, and of love, and of a sound mind." This means you have the strength and authority to communicate with courage and love.

Final Encouragement:

Healthy communication is not about being "nice" or winning an argument. It is about being honest, clear, and kind. Your childhood may have shaped your habits, but it does not define you. You can learn to be assertive, set boundaries, and speak with confidence.

You have a right to be heard. You have a right to be respected. You have a right to be loved. Assertiveness reflects your God-given worth.

For years, the enemy whispered lies to steal her joy, destroy her sense of self-worth, and keep her trapped in the past. But Mara learned to fight back with God's truth. Where there had been shame, there was now dignity. Where there had been sorrow, there was joy. Where there had been fear, there was confidence in her identity in Christ John 10:10; James 4:7; Romans 8:37.

That same freedom is available to you. Even when doubts, fears, or "what ifs" invade your mind, God's peace can settle the storm within. His love fills every broken space, His joy overflows, and His presence brings calm to life's challenges John 14:2.

Step forward with courage. Speak your truth with boldness, patience, and love. Allow God's truth to guide your words, and watch the weight of the past lift as you embrace the freedom, healing, and abundant life He promises.

People Pleasing

Mara often tried to please others, even though she struggled to control her emotions. She feared that if she expressed herself fully—if she became angry, sad, or frustrated—people would judge her, label her as "difficult," or see her as a bad person. Fear of criticism, rejection, or abandonment made her walk on eggshells around others.

Sometimes, this fear worked in her favor: she held back her emotions, silenced her voice, and did what she thought others wanted. People-pleasing became a protective strategy. By staying agreeable, she felt a small sense of safety, believing that if she kept others happy, she would be accepted and avoid conflict.

But the Bible warns against living solely to please people. Galatians 1:10 says, "Am I now trying to win the approval of human beings, or of God? Or am I trying to please people? If I were still trying to please people, I would not be a servant of Christ." Mara had to learn that seeking God's approval mattered far more than seeking human approval.

Other times, emotions built up too much, and she would explode. Then the judgment she had feared all along seemed to come true—people looked at her as if something was wrong. Those moments reinforced the belief that she had to control herself, hide her feelings, and keep pleasing others to be seen as "good" or lovable.

Her people-pleasing was not about being weak or fake—it was about survival. It was a way to manage the fear of being rejected, criticized, or abandoned. Even when it meant suppressing her own needs, silencing her voice, or holding in her emotions, it felt safer than risking disapproval.

Over time, Mara began to discover God's truth. Psalm 139:14 reminded her, "I praise you because I am fearfully and wonderfully made; your works are wonderful, I know that full well." She did not have to earn love or approval—God had already made her worthy. She could express herself honestly, manage her emotions, and still be fully loved and accepted.

Step by step, Mara learned to let go of people-pleasing and fear, discovering that her voice and feelings truly mattered. Colossians 3:23 became her guide: "Whatever you do, work at it with all your heart, as working for the Lord, not for human masters." Pleasing God first, not people, gave her courage and freedom.

The Weight of Overthinking

Mara's greatest struggle was overthinking. It was like being trapped in a maze with no exit, constantly replaying conversations, decisions, and "what-ifs" over and over in her mind. It did not matter how small the situation was—it could be a text message, a comment from a co-worker, or an offhand remark from a family member. Once it entered her mind, it lived there rent-free, consuming her peace and filling her with anxiety.

She would reread texts repeatedly, wondering if she had said the right thing. "Did I come off rude?" "Should I have said something different?" These thoughts would spiral out of control. Her heart would race, her palms would sweat, and she would spend hours questioning herself. The "what-ifs" would stretch far beyond the moment, pulling her thoughts into the future. She would worry about next week, next month, and sometimes even next year. Would she still have the same job? Would people still like her? Would her relationships survive? Her mind became a battlefield where peace rarely won.

Why Do We Overthink?

At its core, overthinking comes from fear and the need for control. We believe if we think long and hard enough, we will be able to avoid pain, embarrassment, or failure. But it only keeps us stuck. Her mind tried to "prepare for battle" by overanalyzing everything to avoid being hurt.

Signs You Might Be an Overthinker

Constantly replaying conversations in your head
Worrying about future events far in advance
Avoiding confrontation out of fear of being

"the badperson"
Rereading texts to make sure you are not misunderstood
Obsessing over other people's opinions of you

If you recognize yourself in any of these patterns, you are not alone. Overthinking is a natural response to uncertainty, but it is not the life God has called you to live.

What Does the Bible Say About Overthinking?

Mara had always been a thinker. Her mind raced from one worry to the next—replaying conversations, imagining worst-case scenarios, and questioning every choice she made. She realized that overthinking was stealing her peace, but she didn't know how to stop it.

One morning, Mara opened her Bible and came across Matthew 6:34: "Take therefore no thought for the morrow: for the morrow shall take thought for the things of itself. Sufficient unto the day is the evil thereof." The words struck her. She realized she had been living a week, a month, even a year ahead, worrying about things that hadn't even happened. God was calling her to stay present, to trust that His provision was enough for today.

Philippians 4:6-7 became her anchor: "Be careful for nothing; but in everything by prayer and supplication with thanksgiving let your requests be made known unto God..." Mara started practicing a small but powerful habit: whenever a thought spun out of control, she paused and prayed. "God, I release this to You. Guard my mind with Your peace." Slowly, she began to notice a shift—her anxious spirals were interrupted by prayer, and a quiet calm started to settle in.

Isaiah 26:3 reminded her that peace comes from trusting God, not from controlling everything: "Thou wilt keep him in perfect peace, whose mind is stayed on thee: because he trusteth in thee." Mara realized that surrender wasn't giving up—it was giving God the space to work while she rested.

She learned to name her fears. "What am I really afraid of right now?" she would ask herself. Rejection? Failure? Embarrassment? Once identified, she could confront them with truth: "For God hath not given us the spirit of fear; but of power, and of love, and of a sound mind" 2 Timothy 1:7.

Mara also learned to challenge her thoughts. She would write them down and ask: "Is this true? Can I control it? Will it matter a year from now?" Overthinking often thrived on things beyond her reach. "Casting down imaginations...bringing into captivity every thought to the obedience of Christ" 2 Corinthians 10:5. became her mantra. Every anxious thought was a thought she no longer had to entertain.

And when her mind began to spiral, she used prayer as a "pattern interrupt." A simple, honest prayer: "God, I release this thought to You. Help me focus on what is true, right, and good." The practice reminded her to turn to God constantly, as 1 Thessalonians 5:17 encouraged: "Pray without ceasing."

Finally, Mara learned to trust God's timing and plan. She remembered Isaiah 55:8-9: "For my thoughts are not your thoughts, neither are your ways my ways, saith the Lord." Overthinking often came from trying to control the next step, but faith taught her to rest in God's wisdom. She realized that peace wasn't the absence of problems—it was trusting God through them.

Slowly, day by day, Mara's mind found rest. She still thought deeply, but now her thoughts were guided by prayer, truth, and trust. Overthinking no longer ruled her—it became a reminder to turn to God, to release, and to walk in peace.

God's Word addresses overthinking, worry, and anxiety head-on. Here are a few key scriptures that speak to this struggle:

Matthew 6:34. "Take therefore no thought for the morrow: for the morrow shall take thought for the things of itself. Sufficient unto the day is the evil thereof."

Overthinking often focuses on the future, but God calls us to stay present. Worrying about a week, month, or year from now is a waste of energy. God's provision is daily.

Philippians 4:6-7. "Be careful for nothing; but in everything by prayer and supplication with thanksgiving let your requests be made known unto God. And the peace of God, which passeth all understanding, shall keep your hearts and minds through Christ Jesus."

Instead of overthinking, God calls us to bring our thoughts to Him in prayer

Final Words of Encouragement

Overthinking is exhausting, but it is not unstoppable. Mara's journey of overcoming it began when she stopped trusting herself and started trusting God. You can do the same. Remember, you do not have to have all the answers today. You do not have to figure out what is going to happen next month, next year, or five years from now. You are not called to have everything figured out—you are called to have faith.

Jesus said, "Come unto me, all ye that labour and are heavy laden, and I will give you rest" Matthew 11:28. Overthinking is a heavy burden, but Jesus offers rest. Lay your worries, doubts, and fears at His feet.

When you are tempted to analyze everything, pause and pray. Release it to God and ask Him to guard your mind with peace.

Isaiah 26:3. "Thou wilt keep him in perfect peace, whose mind is stayed on thee: because he trusteth in thee."
Perfect peace comes from a mind that trusts God, not one that is fixated on trying to control everything. Surrendering control to God gives your mind the space to rest.

You are worthy of peace. You are worthy of a clear mind. You are worthy of love—not because you are "perfect" or "do everything right" but because God says so. Let this be the day you declare: I will no longer be a slave to overthinking. I am free.

Church Hurt and the Search for True Faith

Church hurt can come from various sources, such as trusted leaders, parents, romantic partners, or a community. Perhaps you have experienced this too.

Mara's first brush with church hurt came from trusted church leaders. Seeking comfort and guidance after her traumatic experiences, she turned to a church. Vulnerable and looking for the Lord's guidance, she and her friends reached out for help.

They were directed to an associate pastor's house, where he began making inappropriate sexual advances toward them, taking advantage of their youth and inexperience with the church. This shameful and unacceptable behavior stands in stark contrast to the values of the body of Christ.

The betrayal deeply affected Mara and her friends, leading them to question their faith and the church's integrity. Unfortunately, many individuals engage in such misconduct, tarnishing the church's reputation and showing little regard for those who are not firmly rooted in their beliefs.

Later, Mara experienced additional hurt from the church during her relationship. The Bible was weaponized against her, leading her to feel unworthy of God's love, as if she could never meet His standards. This manipulation not only distanced her from her faith but also intensified her feelings of inadequacy and self-doubt.

As she got older and tried to become part of another church, Mara encountered favoritism and cliques that made her feel unwanted. This disillusionment deepened her mistrust and pushed her further from the church, leaving her perplexed.

Unfortunately, this is fast becoming the norm. This contradiction can be incredibly disheartening and confusing, making it difficult for individuals to trust their faith.

When leaders and community members fail to live up to the standards of love, integrity, and compassion outlined in the Bible, it damages the trust of those within the church.

It tarnishes the image of the church itself. This can lead to feelings of betrayal and push people away from seeking a relationship with God.

It can lead you to question God's love or feel inadequate, as if you can never live up to His standards.

It was not until later in life, when Mara was on the brink of despair that she learned about the true nature of God's love.

Mara found herself in a constant struggle between the expectations of religion and the longing for an authentic relationship with Jesus. Faith had felt like a series of rules for much of her life—tasks to complete to stay in God's good graces. But inside, there was a more profound yearning: one that sought connection, love, and acceptance from God, not based on her performance, but simply because of who He is.

Mara was reminded of 1 John 4:9-10: "In this was manifested the love of God toward us, because that God hath sent his only begotten Son into the world, that we might live through him. Herein is love, not that we loved God, but that he loved us, and sent His Son to be the propitiation for our sins."

Religion, as Mara understood it, emphasized "doing." It was about attending church, obeying commandments, and avoiding sin. Yet, instead of drawing her closer to God, it often left her feeling weighed down and disconnected. Each failure to meet these religious standards seemed to echo that she was not good enough for God's love.

She reflected on how the Bible warned against relying on religion without a relationship. The verse in Hosea 4:6 came to mind: "My people are destroyed for lack of knowledge." Mara realized that she and so many others had been perishing spiritually, not because they attend church, but because they did not know the true heart of God. Legalism and expectations clouded the simple yet profound truth of God's grace.

Salvation and God's love are not rewards for good behavior but are given freely by God's grace. This was a pivotal moment for her—understanding that grace cannot be earned but is a gift freely given.

She also realized that sincere heart change required more than just performing religious duties. Her early experiences with faith had involved ritualistic practices—going to church, reciting prayers, and following rules—but these actions, while important, did not transform her heart.

Mara understood that religion alone could not change her deeply rooted issues. It was a relationship with Jesus Christ that brought genuine transformation.

In her newfound relationship with Jesus, Mara experienced a profound shift. No longer was she bound by the legalistic demands of religion that only highlighted her shortcomings. Instead, she found freedom in the grace offered by Jesus—a grace that healed her anger, hurt, resentment, and sin. Through this relationship, Mara learned that Jesus addresses the root of sin and transforms lives from the inside out. As Jesus said: "The thief cometh not, but that he may steal, and kill, and destroy I came that they may have life, and may have it abundantly" John 10:10.

In our walk with God, it is easy to fall into the trap of feeling like we must earn His love. This mindset, often rooted in religious performance, can leave us feeling disconnected and weighed down. But the truth of the gospel reveals a far greater freedom—one rooted in grace.

When we focus too heavily on religious standards, we may begin to question God's love or feel inadequate. Each failure might echo the false belief that we are "not good enough" for Him. This perspective can lead to burnout and a distorted understanding of faith.

The Bible reminds us in Ephesians 2:8-9. "For by grace are ye saved through faith; and that not of yourselves: it is the gift of God: Not of works, lest any man should boast."

This verse reveals that our salvation and God's love are not rewards for our deeds. They are gifts freely given through faith in Christ. Grace removes the pressure to "measure up" and replaces it with the assurance that God's love is unconditional.

Shifting Your Perspective

God's love is steadfast

> Romans 5:8 reminds us that "while we were yet sinners, Christ died for us." His love for us was demonstrated before we could do anything to deserve it.

Shortcomings are not final

> Grace covers our shortcomings. We do not need to carry guilt; instead, we can turn back to God and trust in His forgiveness.

Faith, not works, is what matters

Obedience and good deeds flow naturally out of a relationship with God, but they are not prerequisites for His love or salvation.

Practical Steps for Embracing Grace

Meditate on scripture

Spend time reading verses about grace and God's love. Passages like John 3:16 and Romans 8:1 can help renew your mind.

Pray for a heart change

Ask God to help you let go of performance-based thinking and embrace the truth of His grace.

Seek support

Join a Bible study group or connect with others who understand and can encourage you in this journey.

Rest in God's presence

Take time to be still and reflect on His love for you, free of any agenda or tasks.

Living in Freedom

Mara needed to understand that once the Lord had set her free, she was truly free indeed. However, many believers struggle to live in the fullness of that freedom. They continue acting as though they are still bound to the same fears, doubts, and attempts to earn God's approval, despite having been released from those burdens by Christ.

For some, this looks like striving for perfection, as though God would love them more if they performed better. They carry guilt and shame for sins that God has already forgiven. They may fear that one misstep will cause the Lord to reject them, even though Scripture assures them otherwise. Jesus Himself said, "If the Son therefore shall make you free, ye shall be free indeed" John 8:36. True freedom means no longer living as a spiritual captive to fear, guilt, or condemnation.

Mara discovered that she did not need to impress God to earn His love. She was free from the burden of trying to gain His favor through works, knowing that His love was already hers. Romans 8:1 states, "There is therefore now no condemnation to them which are in Christ Jesus." This truth meant she no longer had to cower under the weight of condemnation or fear that He would turn away from her if she failed.

The more Mara opened her heart to Jesus, the more she began to experience the freedom of living in relationship with Him. She realized He had called her His friend, not just His servant. As Jesus said, "Henceforth I call you not servants… but I have called you friends" John 15:15. Being a friend of Jesus meant approaching Him honestly, sharing her fears, doubts, and dreams, and trusting that He would respond with grace and love.

When believers refuse to accept the freedom Christ has given, they remain like prisoners who sit inside a cell after the door has been opened. They believe lies, that they must prove themselves worthy of love or that their mistakes define them. Yet the Lord invites them, as He invited Mara, to step out into the light, to walk with Him daily, and to trust that He is present and compassionate.

As Mara embraced this truth, the walls she had constructed around her heart began to crumble. She realized that a relationship with Jesus involved a continual drawing near to Him and a willingness to receive His love and guidance. In this place of trust and honesty, she found true freedom, living as the beloved friend of Christ that God had created her to be.

The Divine Mystery

Mara began to yearn for something more—an authentic, deeper understanding of God, one that transcended the limits of human comprehension. She longed to know the Lord personally, to truly grasp His divine nature, and to understand who He is on a profound spiritual level. Her soul resonated with the promise in Matthew 7:7 "Ask, and it shall be given you; seek, and ye shall find; knock, and it shall be opened unto you." Mara realized that relying solely on natural reasoning would never suffice; she wanted insight that only the Holy Spirit could provide.

As she drew nearer to the Lord, Mara clung to the words of Jeremiah 29:13: "And ye shall seek me, and find me, when ye shall search for me with all your heart." She understood that knowing God in this way required opening herself fully to the Spirit's guidance, allowing Him to reveal truths beyond the limits of ordinary understanding. She recalled Paul's prayer in Ephesians 1:17, where he asked God to give believers "the spirit of wisdom and revelation in the knowledge of him." Mara's heart embraced this prayer, longing for the Lord to unveil Himself in ways that no earthly wisdom could achieve. Embracing the Spirit's teaching, Mara trusted that she could move beyond surface-level knowledge into a transformative relationship with her Creator.

This season of seeking was not without its challenges, but Mara believed that by persistently asking, seeking, and knocking, the Lord would graciously open the door to deeper understanding. It was a journey of faith, carrying her away from the shallows of prior assumptions and into the profound, living waters of divine truth.

Mara's journey into quiet, dedicated time with the Lord—listening, seeking His guidance, and engaging in prayer and Bible study—brought forth profound insights into the nature of Jesus Christ and the Trinity. These discoveries shaped her understanding of faith and deepened her relationship with God.

As she explored the dual nature of Jesus—fully human and fully divine.

The One Who Is Fully God and Fully Man

Mara had always heard that Jesus was God's Son — divine and perfect. But she struggled to understand how the Savior of the world could also be fully human. How could someone who healed the sick, calmed the storm, and walked on water also know what it felt like to be tired, hungry, or heartbroken?

As she studied and prayed, Mara began to see the wonder of what theologians call the **hypostatic union** — one person, two natures: fully God and fully man. This truth was no longer cold theology to her; it became a window into the very heart of Jesus.

He Knows Our Weakness

The verse that first captured her attention was Hebrews 4:15.

"For we have not an high priest which cannot be touched with the feeling of our infirmities; but was in all points tempted like as we are, yet without sin."

It struck Mara that Jesus was not distant or detached. He felt what we feel. Every struggle, every temptation, every ache of the human heart — He knew it firsthand. Yet He remained without sin. In that realization, Mara found comfort: Jesus understands not only in theory but through experience.

The Servant Who Chose Humanity

Next, Philippians 2:6-8 KJV painted a breathtaking picture for her:

"Who, being in the form of God, thought it not robbery to be equal with God:
But made himself of no reputation, and took upon him the form of a servant,
and was made in the likeness of men..."

Jesus chose humility. He laid aside His glory to walk our dusty roads — to eat, to sleep, to weep. He did not come as a king in a palace, but as a servant in poverty. To Mara, this revealed not only His obedience but His heart — the God who stooped low to meet humanity where we are.

"Jesus Wept"

The shortest verse in the Bible became one of the deepest for Mara:

John 11:35 — "Jesus wept."

Here was the Son of God, crying at the tomb of His friend Lazarus. He knew He would raise Lazarus from the dead, yet

He paused to feel the pain of those around Him. In that moment, Mara saw a Savior who didn't rush past sorrow — He entered into it. She began to believe that when she wept, Jesus wept with her too.

The Human Experiences of Jesus

The Gospels gave Mara more glimpses into His full humanity:

Birth and Growth: He was born of a woman, Mary (Matthew 1:25), and grew up under the law Galatians 4:). He learned, worked, and matured just as every human does Luke 2:52.

Bodily Needs: He grew hungry after fasting forty days Matthew 4:2, weary and rested at a well (John 4:6), and thirsted on the cross John 19:28.

Death: He endured the ultimate human experience — death itself. The shedding of His blood John 19:34 was real pain and real sacrifice. Even in His resurrected glory, He showed the disciples His wounds and said, "Touch me and see" (Luke 24:39.

These were not just signs of weakness to Mara anymore — they were signs of love. He entered the full weight of our humanity so that no one could ever say, "God doesn't understand me."

His Emotions and Relationships

The more Mara read, the more human Jesus became to her:

He wept at Lazarus's tomb(John 11:33-35.

He felt distress in Gethsemane Matthew 26:38.

He grew angry at injustice Matthew 21:12-13.

He showed compassion for the crowds Matthew 9:36.

He loved deeply—calling His disciples friends John 15:15.

These emotions were not flaws; they were expressions of a perfect, sinless humanity. Jesus didn't suppress feeling — He redeemed it.

A Human Mind and Will

Perhaps most moving for Mara was Jesus' prayer in Gethsemane:

"Not as I will, but as thou wilt." Matthew 26:39.

Here, she saw His human will surrender to the Father's divine will. He wrestled. He felt the weight of what was to come. He chose obedience through anguish. That night, Mara realized that even submission and struggle were part of Jesus' human experience.

She was also struck by His words in Mark 13:32, where Jesus said that even He did not know the day of His return — only the Father did. This was not a denial of His divinity but a reflection of His real humanity. He lived within the limits of a human mind.

The Revelation of His Divinity

As her understanding deepened, Mara began to see that the same Jesus who felt hunger and sorrow also carried the full power and glory of God Himself.

Jesus once declared, "I and the Father are one" John 10:30. His opponents knew exactly what He meant — that He was claiming equality with God. Later, when Philip said, "Show us the Father," Jesus gently replied:

"Philip, how is it that you do not know Me, and I have been with you this long? He who has seen Me has seen the Father." John 14:9, paraphrased.

Those words struck Mara deeply. The Father she had always prayed to — unseen and holy — had made Himself known in Jesus. To see Jesus was to see God.

Mara remembered another verse, where Jesus said, "Before Abraham was, I AM" John 8:58. In that statement, He used the very name God revealed to Moses in Exodus 3:14 — "I AM THAT I AM." This wasn't poetic language. It was a direct claim to eternal existence, the declaration of the divine.

The Mystery Made Clear

Through all this, Mara finally understood:

Jesus was fully God and fully man — one person, two natures, perfectly united.

He entered our condition completely — body, mind, and emotion — yet remained perfectly holy and divine.

His deity didn't cancel His humanity; His humanity didn't limit His deity.

In Him, heaven and earth met in perfect harmony. Mara whispered in awe:

The One who understands me completely is also the One who created me.

The Unique Mediator

Now Mara saw what this meant for her personally: Only Jesus, the God-Man, could stand between a holy God and a broken world.

Paul's words in 1 Timothy 2:5 resonated deeply:

"For there is one God, and one mediator between God and men, the man Christ Jesus."

Through His humanity, He identifies completely with our weakness and pain. Through His divinity, He connects us to the Father and offers eternal life.

He was not just a messenger bringing peace; He was the peace. He was not just a teacher pointing the way; He was the way. And as He said in John 14:6.

"I am the way, the truth, and the life: no man cometh unto the Father, but by me."

The Bridge Between Heaven and Earth

Mara imagined a vast chasm — humanity on one side, separated by sin, and God's holiness on the other. No amount of good deeds, religion, or human effort could cross it. But then she saw Jesus — arms stretched wide upon the cross — one hand reaching out to humanity, the other reaching toward the Father. He became the bridge.

Through His humanity, He bore the pain of sin and death. Through His divinity, He overcame them both, opening the way to eternal life.

The Living Mediator

Even now, Mara realized, the One who died for her prays for her:

If any man sin, we have an advocate with the Father, Jesus Christ the righteous." 1 John 2:1.

He continues to intercede, defend, and restore. The cross was the moment where justice and mercy met, where God's holiness and humanity's brokenness were reconciled through the One who held both natures in Himself.

By the end of her journey, Mara understood:

His humanity makes Him compassionate and understanding.

His divinity makes Him powerful and eternal.

His role as Mediator makes Him the only way for humanity to be reconciled with God.

Mara bowed her head and whispered with awe:

He understands me because He became like me.
He saves me because He is God.
And He brings me to the Father because He stands between us — forever my Mediator, my Way, my Truth, and my Life.

The Trinity Revealed: God in Three Persons

Mara's understanding deepened as she learned about the Trinity—the Christian doctrine depicting God as three distinct Persons in one essence: the Father, the Son (Jesus Christ), and the Holy Spirit. Although the Trinity is a profound mystery, it illuminates how God operates in the world and in the lives of believers.

The Father is the Creator and the source of all life, initiating relationship and reconciliation with humanity. He is the One who made all things and sustains them by His power and love.

The Son, Jesus Christ, is the Savior who provides the path to reconciliation with God through His life, death, and resurrection. His sacrifice on the cross exemplified the ultimate act of love and became the cornerstone of Mara's faith. Through His obedience and humility, He revealed both the depth of God's mercy and the perfect example of righteousness.

The Holy Spirit continues to play an active role in the world today, guiding, comforting, and empowering believers to live according to God's will. Mara found reassurance in the promise of the Holy Spirit's presence in her life, as described in John 14:26 "But the Comforter, even the Holy Spirit, whom the Father will send in My name, He shall teach you all things and bring to your remembrance all that I have said unto you." This understanding strengthened Mara's confidence that she was never alone in her struggles; the Holy Spirit was with her, teaching her and reminding her of the truths she was learning.

The Holy Spirit's role is to continue the work of Jesus by indwelling in believers, guiding them, and reminding them of His teachings. This presence transforms lives, providing comfort, wisdom, and strength. As Mara prayed and sought guidance, she began to experience the Holy Spirit's work in her heart and mind, noticing how her faith grew and her hope was renewed.

Through this revelation of the Trinity, Mara understood that God is both personal and relational. The Father initiates and sustains, the Son redeems and reconciles, and the Holy Spirit guides and empowers. Together, they work in perfect harmony to draw humanity closer to the God who loves them completely.

Giving Yourself to Him

Giving yourself to God involves more than being a Christian, attending church, or reading the Bible. True surrender means fully relinquishing your life—your desires, plans, and control—over to Him. It is not just about accepting Jesus as Savior but about embracing a radical transformation in how we live, think, and act.

In Matthew 16:24, Jesus calls us to "pick up your cross and follow Me." The cross symbolizes sacrifice, suffering, and submission. Picking up our cross means laying down our own will to follow God's plan, choosing obedience even when it is difficult. This act of surrender requires us to submit every part of our lives—our ambitions, finances, relationships, and emotions—to God's will.

Paul captures this internal struggle in Romans 7:19: "For the good which I would, I do not; but the evil which I would not, that I practice." True surrender acknowledges this conflict, leaning on God's grace while trusting His transformation in us. Following Jesus is a continuous process of letting go of control and trusting God with the outcome.

This highlights the struggle we face in choosing righteousness over sin, making it evident that surrendering to God's will often feels more challenging than giving in to our sinful nature. But is that what it means to be a child of God? The moment you resist yielding, you risk becoming rebellious—like a child living under their parents' roof while insisting on their own terms.

In Galatians 5:17, we are reminded that "For the flesh lusteth against the Spirit, and the Spirit against the flesh: for these are contrary the one to the other." This internal conflict shows why surrender can feel like a battle; our flesh often desires what is easy and familiar, while the Spirit calls us to a higher standard.

Until you fully and wholeheartedly give yourself to God, His ability to work in your life and free you from the bondage of your past remains limited. True freedom comes when we acknowledge our limitations and trust in His strength to guide us. As stated in Philippians 4:13, "I can do all things in Him that strengtheneth me." When we embrace this surrender, we open the door for God's transformative work in our lives, allowing us to break free from the chains of our past and experience the fullness of life He offers.

As 1 John 1:9 affirms, "If we confess our sins, He is faithful and righteous to forgive us our sins, and to cleanse us from all unrighteousness." Transformation occurs through a process of surrendering your life to God and accepting the grace He freely offers. This means actively confessing your sins and recognizing your need for His forgiveness. When you invite the Holy Spirit into your life, He begins to change you from the inside out, renewing your mind and heart. As Romans 12:2 states, "And be not fashioned according to this world: but be ye transformed by the renewing of your mind, that ye may prove what is the good and acceptable and perfect will of God."

As you grow in your relationship with God, you will begin to reflect His character in your thoughts, actions, and choices. This journey of transformation is ongoing and involves a daily commitment to seeking God, studying His Word, and applying His teachings to your life. The more you rely on His strength and guidance, the more you will see His transformative work manifest in your life.

Consider the thief on the cross next to Jesus. Despite a life of wrongdoing, he surrendered to God moments before his death. In 2 Peter 3:9, we are reminded, "The Lord is not slack concerning His promise, as some count slackness, but is longsuffering toward you, not wishing that any should perish, but that all should come to repentance."

Consider the great biblical figures in the Bible, many of whom were deeply flawed and succumbed to sin. Adam and Eve disobeyed. Moses struggled with anger. David committed adultery. Solomon fell into idolatry. Paul was a persecutor of Christians. Yet, God used each of these sinners to fulfill His divine plans.

This illustrates that God is not preoccupied with the extent of our sins; instead, He is a loving Father eagerly awaiting the return of His prodigal children. He longs for us to recognize our sinful state and turn to Him in genuine repentance. This is why God called David a man after His own heart—despite his failures, David consistently repented and sought to turn away from his sins.

Thankfully, Mara chose to respond to God's call, embracing the healing and transformation that followed. If she had allowed herself to succumb to hopelessness, she would have been unable to fully surrender to God, thus limiting His work in her life. The moment Mara gave everything to God through Christ, her life was altered. She laid down her burdens of pain, fear, and insecurity at His feet. It was only in that release that the Holy Spirit began to work in her heart. She found strength in Jesus to break free from the patterns of self-reliance that had kept her bound for so long. Restoration, healing, and renewal are possible and promised to those who surrender their lives to Him. Mara's story is living proof of this truth. By surrendering to God through Christ, she experienced transformation—not just in her life, but in her relationships and her heart.

God desires the same for each of us. We are called to surrender not out of compulsion, but from a willing heart. God purchased each of us at the costly price of His beloved Son's blood, and He expects us to acknowledge this by submitting to Him. Merely calling oneself a Christian is insufficient. Some may hide behind the label of Christianity while engaging in grievous sins. Genuine repentance and a willingness to submit your life to God is the first step toward cultivating a personal, intimate relationship with Him.

To experience the fullness of God's grace, we must lay aside the sins that ensnare us and fix our eyes on Jesus, the only way to the Father. So, have you surrendered your life to God? Do not withhold certain areas from Him. If He is to be on your ship, let Him be the captain.

Recognize that you are not your own; you belong to God. The only sinless person to walk this earth is Jesus Christ, who came to die for our sins. Regardless of what you have experienced or done, He is ready to save you, help you heal, and use you as a light for others. He will teach you how to grow in grace and become more like Him. What a beautiful promise.

Recognize the Need for Reconciliation
Reconciliation begins with understanding that sin has separated us from God. Sin creates a barrier between

humanity and God because God is holy and cannot be in the presence of sin. Romans 3:23 says, "For all have sinned, and fall short of the glory of God." Recognizing this truth is the first step toward reconciliation. We must acknowledge that we are broken and in need of a Savior.

The Power of Repentance, Baptism, and Surrender

Mara had made mistakes in her life. She had hurt others, told lies, and sometimes acted out of anger. Deep inside, she felt heavy with guilt, unsure how to make things right. One day, Mara decided she could no longer ignore the weight on her heart. She knew she needed repentance—not just saying sorry, but a complete change of heart and mind, turning away from past mistakes and choosing to follow God's commands. As Acts 3:19 says, "Repent therefore, and turn again, that your sins may be blotted out, that times of refreshing may come from the presence of the Lord."

Mara realized that the first step to healing was acknowledging her sins and trusting that God's forgiveness is unconditional. 1 John 1:9 reminded her, "If we confess our sins, He is faithful and just to forgive us our sins and to cleanse us from all unrighteousness." Even though remembering her past actions brought guilt, she held onto Psalm 103:12: "As far as the east is from the west, so far does He remove our transgressions from us."

Determined to change, Mara began to take real steps. She prayed earnestly, pouring out her heart to God, confessing every wrong she had done, and asking for His help to transform her life. She sought forgiveness from those she had hurt, making amends wherever possible. Mara also refused to continue old habits that led her into sin, choosing instead actions that reflected kindness, honesty, and love. She began studying the Bible daily, learning God's ways and committing to live according to His commands. Slowly but surely, her heart and mind began to change, and she felt the peace that comes from truly turning back to God.

After repenting, Mara chose to be baptized, stepping into the waters as a symbol of leaving her old life behind. Peter's words echoed in her heart: "Repent and be baptized every one of you in the name of Jesus Christ for the forgiveness of your sins; and you will receive the gift of the Holy Spirit" Acts 2:38. As she rose from the water, Mara felt a newness in her soul—a heartfelt appeal to God for a pure conscience, just as 1 Peter 3:21 says: "Baptism... saves you, not as a removal of dirt from the body, but as an appeal to God for a good conscience, through the resurrection of Jesus Christ."

Mara's journey did not stop there. She accepted Jesus as her personal Savior, believing His sacrifice on the cross had covered all her sins. 2 Corinthians 5:21 reminded her, "Him who knew no sin he made to be sin on our behalf; that we might become the righteousness of God in him." Through faith, she received God's grace and forgiveness, a free gift, not earned by her actions Ephesians 2:8-9.

The Holy Spirit began to work within her, transforming her heart and mind. As Ephesians 4:22-24 describes: "Put away, as concerning your former manner of life, the old man, that waxeth corrupt... and be renewed in the spirit of your mind, and put on the new man, created after God in righteousness and holiness of truth." Mara noticed her thoughts, actions, and desires aligning more and more with God's ways.

She embraced her identity as a new creation in Christ. 2 Corinthians 5:17 declares, "If any man is in Christ, he is a new creature: the old things are passed away; behold, they are become new." Mara now lived with a fresh start, showing love to others, walking in obedience, and growing closer to God every day.

Part of her transformation included reconciliation with others. As God forgave her, she forgave those who had hurt her. Colossians 3:13 instructed her: "Forgive each other, if any man have a complaint against any; even as the Lord forgave you, so also do ye." This brought healing to her relationships and deep peace to her heart.

Finally, Mara learned the importance of remaining in Christ. John 15:4 reminded her: "Abide in me, and I in you... except ye abide in me, ye can do nothing." By walking with God daily—through prayer, reading Scripture, and following the Holy Spirit—she continued growing in faith, love, and holiness.

Through repentance, baptism, and surrender to Christ, Mara experienced the full joy of reconciliation: a life transformed, a heart renewed, and a future filled with hope, grace, and purpose. Her story became a shining example of the beauty of turning to God, showing that anyone can start anew, no matter their past.

Becoming New in Christ

The true source of strength that brings healing and reconciliation to broken relationships is God. In Christ, we find new beginnings, restoration, and renewal—promises echoed throughout Scripture that offer hope to all who choose to embrace them fully.

Becoming new in Christ is not just about changing our actions; it is about a deep transformation of heart, mind, and soul. True renewal in Christ involves both outward changes and allowing God to reshape your identity, heal your wounds, and align your lives with His purpose

As followers of Christ, we gain eternal life and a new beginning here on earth. Only the Great Physician can offer this kind of healing that reconciles broken relationships and restores wounded hearts.

Before Christ, our desires may have been shaped by the world—seeking approval, fleeting pleasures, or material gain. But as we embrace our new identity in Christ, our desires begin to change. As we align with God's will, our focus shifts from worldly ambitions to heavenly pursuits.

Psalm 37:4.
"Delight thyself also in the Lord; and he shall give thee the desires of thine heart."

As we find joy in the Lord, He begins to reshape our desires to align with His will. Our desires are no longer driven by temporary satisfaction but by a deep longing to live according to God's purpose.

Isaiah 61:1.
"The Spirit of the Lord God is upon me; because the Lord hath anointed me to preach good tidings unto the meek; he hath sent me to bind up the brokenhearted, to proclaim liberty to the captives, and the opening of the prison to them that are bound."

As our hearts are transformed, we notice a shift in how we respond to challenges. Impulsive reactions driven by anger or frustration are replaced by a gentle and calm spirit. We begin to speak with love, grace, and peace, reflecting the love of Christ in all our interactions.

Colossians 3:12 .
"Put on therefore, as the elect of God, holy and beloved, bowels of mercies, kindness, humbleness of mind, meekness, longsuffering."

God's transformation in us produces new attitudes, including gentleness and humility. We no longer rely on our own strength but trust in God to guide and strengthen us through life's difficulties.

The journey will test your faith, and there will be moments when doubt creeps in, causing you to question God's love. Mara faced these same challenges. But she learned to rely on Christ's strength in her moments of weakness.

Hebrews 12:2 reminds us that Jesus is "the author and perfecter of our faith." He is the one who strengthens us when our faith wavers and sustains us when we feel weak. It is in Him, that we find the strength to press on and become the people God created us to be, even in the face of trials and challenges.

As ambassadors of Christ, we are called to be reconciled to God, and, through Him, to be reconciled to one another. As 2 Corinthians 5:20-21 reminds us: "We are ambassadors therefore on behalf of Christ, as though God were entreating by us: we beseech you on behalf of Christ, be ye reconciled to God. Him who knew no sin he made to be sin on our behalf; that we might become the righteousness of God in him."

God's desire for all His children is for them to be made new in Christ.

This is the power of becoming new in Christ—letting go of the past, embracing His grace, and stepping into the new life.

Learning to Love Herself

Mara had always been the kind of person who gave until she had nothing left. She had been taught—subtly, persistently—that her worth was measured by how much she served others. Loving herself, she was told, was selfish. Caring for her own needs was somehow wrong. And yet, after years of bending herself to fit everyone else's expectations, Mara found her heart growing heavy with resentment, frustration, and exhaustion.

It was only slowly that she began to understand something revolutionary: true self-love is not selfish—it is essential. It means caring for herself spiritually, emotionally, mentally, and physically, so that she could live fully and love genuinely.

Jesus' command to love God and love others as you love yourself had always seemed simple on the surface. But Mara had overlooked the last part. How could she love others as she loved herself, if she did not love herself at all? She often responded with grace to the mistakes of friends and colleagues, saying gently, "It is okay. Try again." But her inner voice, the one she reserved for herself, was far harsher: "You failed. You are not enough."

Mara realized that she had never been taught to extend the same compassion to herself. She began to practice seeing herself as she would a dear friend: someone who deserved patience, understanding, and care, especially when life felt unfair.

Jesus had modeled this too. When His disciples were overworked, exhausted, and too busy to eat, He did not demand they push harder. He called them to rest. Mara saw that self-care was not indulgence—it was a vital part of being able to serve others effectively. Without rest, she had nothing left to give.

Learning to love herself meant finding balance. She learned to give without losing herself, to serve from a place of joy rather than obligation. If she was exhausted or overwhelmed, she gave herself permission to step back. She embraced the truth that God loves a cheerful giver, not one who serves with anger or resentment. As Romans 12:8 reminds us, "Whoever contributes, let him do it with sincerity; whoever serves, let him do it with his whole heart."

Mara practiced small acts of self-compassion daily. When she made mistakes, she forgave herself, reflecting on what she could learn instead of beating herself up. She remembered Ephesians 4:32: "And be ye kind one to another, tenderhearted, forgiving each other, even as God also in Christ forgave you." She realized this applied to herself too.

She also learned to balance service and rest. If she volunteered, worked, or helped others, she made sure to carve out moments to recharge. The Sabbath, she discovered, was more than a command—it was a lesson: God designed a rhythm of work and rest, so His children could sustain themselves in body, mind, and spirit.

Seeking support became another vital lesson. Mara found strength in reaching out when she struggled emotionally or mentally. She learned that asking for help was not weakness but an act of courage, a way to bear one another's burdens as Galatians 6:2 calls us to do.

Finally, she learned to say no. Setting boundaries was difficult at first, but Mara discovered that honesty about her limits allowed her to live intentionally and faithfully. Saying no was not rejection; it was protection of her well-being and a commitment to follow God's call for her life.

Through all of this, Mara began to feel herself whole again. Loving herself did not diminish her love for others—it amplified it. The grace, patience, and compassion she extended to herself overflowed into her relationships. She learned that when her jar was full, she could pour out freely without fear of running empty.

Mara's journey to self-love was not easy, but it was transformative. She discovered that caring for herself, setting boundaries, seeking rest, and forgiving herself were not acts of selfishness—they were acts of obedience, trust, and surrender. In learning to love herself, Mara finally understood what it meant to love as Jesus commands: fully, generously, and with a heart grounded in God's grace.

Do not overwork to be rich; because of your own understanding, cease. Proverbs 23:4

> *I WILL GIVE THANKS UNTO THEE; FOR I AM FEARFULLY AND WONDERFULLY MADE: WONDERFUL ARE THY WORKS; AND THAT MY SOUL KNOWETH RIGHT WELL. PSALM 139:14*

God's works are indeed wonderful. And guess what? That includes you! He is your Creator; He gave you your life. Since you are fearfully and wonderfully made in the image of God, you cannot say you do not love yourself. That would be almost like saying you do not love God.

"Anyone who does not love does not know God, for God is love" 1 John 4:8. Once again, this includes yourself. If we are children of God, and God is love, then we have that love within us. Like the genes we have inherited from our biological parents, love is the spiritual gene we have inherited from our heavenly Father.

By Their Fruits Ye Shall Know Them

Mara's life had been marked by pain—deep, personal wounds that few could understand. She had been abandoned by those she trusted, mistreated by people who should have protected her, and targeted in ways that left scars on her heart.

Abuse, both emotional and physical, had shaped much of her early life. And yet, even in the darkest moments, she clung to a phrase that had once been spoken over her: "Ye shall know them by their fruits."

At first, it seemed impossible to see how those words applied to her. How could she bear fruit when so much of her life had been filled with betrayal, mistrust, and pain? But slowly, Mara began to understand that these words were not about others—they were about her own life. Faith had to be more than words; it had to be visible in how she responded to the wounds that threatened to define her.

To bear fruit is not about being perfect. It is about letting God work in the broken places, so that the things we do reflect His Spirit. Love, joy, peace, patience, kindness, goodness, faith, gentleness, and self-control—these weren't abstract ideals for Mara. They were the seeds she needed to plant in the hard soil of her life.

Patience was the first challenge. Anger and resentment rose often, especially when memories of betrayal or abuse resurfaced. Mara had every reason to lash out or withdraw, yet she learned to pause and lean on God. Forgiveness became her first act of courage—choosing love over bitterness, even when the wounds felt fresh. Each small step forward felt like a fragile sprout breaking through hardened ground.

Joy came slowly. Mara had been abandoned and mistrusted, and the weight of those experiences could have left her numb. Yet she began to notice small signs of God's faithfulness: a friend who stayed when others left, a quiet sunrise, a comforting word of Scripture. Joy, she realized, was not the absence of pain—it was the presence of God's peace within it.

Peace was another teacher. Mara learned that true peace did not mean her life was free from chaos or fear. It meant choosing calm and trusting God even when the world had been cruel. Acts of kindness and goodness followed naturally as she grew stronger. She offered compassion to those around her, returned favors without expectation, and resisted the temptation to respond in bitterness. Slowly, the fruit began to appear.

Faithfulness and self-control became quiet victories. Mara learned that choosing what was right, even when it was hard, gave her freedom instead of restriction. She practiced gentleness in moments that demanded anger, self-control when she was tempted to lash out, and humility in the face of mistreatment. Every choice, every act of integrity, was proof that God was at work in her life.

Jesus had said: "Every tree that bringeth not forth good fruit is hewn down, and cast into the fire. Wherefore by their fruits ye shall know them." For Mara, these words became a call, not a warning. Faith had to be visible, lived, and practiced, especially in the face of past hurt.

Watching Mara transform was like witnessing a quiet miracle. She didn't become perfect overnight, nor were her scars erased. But the fruit of God's Spirit—love where there had been bitterness, patience where there had been rage, kindness where there had been mistrust—became visible in her actions. Her life, once targeted and abused, now reflected healing and hope.

By the time she began to stand firmly in her restored self, she realized something profound: the fruits of the Spirit—love, joy, peace, patience, kindness, goodness, faith, gentleness, and self-control—are living proof that even the most wounded heart can bear good fruit when surrendered to God. And in Mara, that transformation was undeniable, beautiful, and ongoing.

Fighting in the Spirit
The Battle Within: Arming for the Fight

THE LORD SHALL FIGHT FOR YOU, AND YE SHALL HOLD YOUR PEACE.

EXODUS 14:14

The Armor of God

Mara's journey required her to put on the full armor of God every single day. She understood that this was necessary because 1 Peter 5:8 reminds us, "Be sober, be watchful: your adversary the devil, as a roaring lion, walketh about, seeking whom he may devour." Mara knew she could not afford to leave herself vulnerable. Each day was a battle, and her spirit and flesh were constantly at war.

Like Peter, Mara's flesh often wanted to revert to old ways when others offended her. Her flesh whispered that others would see her as weak if she did not fight or prove herself. Yet there was also the still, small voice of the Spirit, gently reminding her of God's promise:

Dearly beloved, avenge not yourselves, but rather give place unto wrath: for it is written, Vengeance is mine; I will repay, saith the Lord."
—Romans 12:19.

Mara realized the importance of putting on the full armor of God each day, as described in Ephesians 6:10-18 "Put on the whole armor of God, that ye may be able to stand against the wiles of the devil." This armor includes the belt of truth, the breastplate of righteousness, the shield of faith, the helmet of salvation, the sword of the Spirit, which is the Word of God, and the shoes of readiness that come from the gospel of peace.

Each piece represents a vital defense against the lies, fears, and temptations that attacked Mara daily.

When one fails to put on the full armor of God, vulnerability to spiritual attacks increases. The enemy knows how to exploit weaknesses and target vulnerabilities. Here are some ways the devil attacks when the armor is neglected:

Belt of Truth

Without It: Satan twists facts and plants lies in the mind. Thoughts such as, "I am not good enough," or "God does not care about me," take hold. Without truth to stand on, insecurity and doubt flourish.

With It: The belt of truth allows one to fight Satan's lies with God's Word. Mara reminded herself, "I will give thanks unto thee; for I am fearfully and wonderfully made" Psalm 139:1. Her value came from God, not from anyone else.

Breastplate of Righteousness

Without It: The heart becomes vulnerable to guilt, shame, and condemnation. Satan whispers, "You will never be good enough. God will not forgive you."

With It: The breastplate protects the heart. Mara understood that her righteousness came from Jesus, not her own actions. "Him who knew no sin he made to be sin on our behalf; that we might become the righteousness of God in him" 2 Corinthians 5:21. She could resist the enemy's lies, knowing God's grace covered her.

Shield of Faith

Without It: Doubt and fear overwhelm the spirit. Thoughts such as, "God will not provide for you," or "You are on your own," create hopelessness.

With It: Faith extinguishes Satan's fiery darts. Mara held to promises like, "And my God shall supply every need of yours according to his riches in glory in Christ Jesus" (Philippians 4:19). Trusting God's control kept her hope alive.

Helmet of Salvation

Without It: Doubts about identity and standing with God take root. Satan whispers, "You are not truly saved. You are too flawed for God to love."

With It: The helmet protects the mind. Mara remembered, "For by grace have ye been saved through faith; and that not of yourselves, it is the gift of God; not of works, that no man should glory" Ephesians 2:8-9. She could declare, "I give unto them eternal life; and they shall never perish, and no one shall snatch them out of my hand" (John 10:28).

Sword of the Spirit (God's Word)

Without It: Temptation feels insurmountable. The enemy convinces that resistance is futile.

With It: The Word of God becomes a weapon. Mara followed Jesus' example in the wilderness Matthew 4:1-11, declaring, "I can do all things in him that strengtheneth me" Philippians 4:1).

Shoes of the Gospel of Peace

Without It: Anxiety, fear, and unrest dominate. Conflict seems inevitable, and relationships suffer.

With It: The gospel of peace allows one to walk confidently. Mara held to the promise, "And the peace of God, which passeth all understanding, shall guard your hearts and your thoughts in Christ Jesus" Philippians 4:7. Peace protected her from anxiety and enabled her to bring calm to others.

By putting on the full armor of God, Mara was equipped to stand firm against the enemy's schemes. Each piece of armor, grounded in Scripture, strengthened her to overcome challenges in both spiritual and physical realms. The enemy sought to strike where she was weakest, but the armor protected every vulnerable area. Without it, exposure to lies, accusations, and temptations was certain. With it, she could stand firm, fighting back with truth, faith, righteousness, and the Word of God.

Yet Mara discovered that not all battles were external. Some were fought within. Galatians 5:17 declares, "For the flesh lusteth against the Spirit, and the Spirit against the flesh; for these are contrary the one to the other." The inner conflict between her old nature and her new life in Christ was constant.

The Apostle Paul described this struggle in Romans 7:23: "But I see a different law in my members, warring against the law of my mind, and bringing me into captivity under the law of sin which is in my members." Mara resonated with these words. Many struggles were not the work of the devil, but the tension between sinful desires and the Spirit within her. She took comfort in knowing she was not alone. Every believer faces this spiritual tension and learns daily to walk in the strength and victory found in Christ.

Renewing the Mind for Victory

To truly equip herself for the daily battles between spirit and flesh, Mara understood she needed the Holy Spirit's power to transform her mind.

When Mara neglected to put on her spiritual armor, she found herself overwhelmed by negative thoughts, temptations, and fears. However, when she committed to wearing the full armor of God daily, she was equipped to stand firm, no matter what challenges or attacks came her way.

To handle the internal battle effectively, Mara learned the importance of renewing her mind daily. Romans 12:2 NIV instructs, "Do not conform to the pattern of this world, but be transformed by the renewing of your mind. Then you will be able to test and approve what God's will is—his good, pleasing, and perfect will." For Mara, renewing her mind meant continuously aligning her thoughts with God's truth and letting His Word reshape her perspective and attitude

One of Mara's key strategies was taking every thought captive. Second Corinthians 10:5 NIV teaches, "We demolish arguments and every pretension that sets itself up against the knowledge of God, and we take captive every thought to make it obedient to Christ." This practice involved evaluating her thoughts and ensuring they aligned with God's Word rather than being driven by her fleshly desires or fears.

1. Walk by the Spirit

The Bible instructs believers to "walk by the Spirit, and you shall not fulfill the lust of the flesh" (Galatians 5:16). For Mara, living in step with the Holy Spirit meant seeking His guidance daily. The more she relied on the Spirit's strength, the less power her flesh had over her. Regular prayer, seeking God's will, and asking for the Holy Spirit's help in times of temptation became essential components of her daily life. By following the Spirit, Mara found the strength to overcome her desires.

2. Crucify the Flesh

Mara understood that the Bible teaches we must crucify the desires of the flesh. Galatians 5:24 states, "And they that are of Christ Jesus have crucified the flesh with the passions and the lusts thereof." For Mara, this meant actively putting to death the sinful desires and habits that opposed God's will. She made tough choices to avoid things that led her to sin instead of choosing actions that glorified God. Crucifying the flesh required daily discipline and surrender to God.

3. Set Your Mind on Things Above

Colossians 3:2 urges us to "Set your mind on the things that are above, not on the things that are upon the earth." Mara learned that focusing on eternal values such as God's kingdom, His love, and His purposes helped her stay grounded and less distracted by temporary pleasures and temptations of the flesh. Aligning her mind with heavenly matters brought her peace and strength to resist earthly temptations.

4. Pray without Ceasing

For Mara, prayer became a powerful way to overcome the flesh. Jesus told His disciples in Matthew 26:41, "Watch and pray, that ye enter not into temptation: the spirit indeed is willing, but the flesh is weak." Regular prayer strengthened her spirit and made it easier to resist her desires. Whenever

Mara felt weak or tempted, she would ask God for help, and she experienced His strength and guidance through constant communication.

5. Avoid Temptation

Mara recognized the practical importance of avoiding situations where she knew she would be tempted. Proverbs 4:14-15 says, "Enter not into the path of the wicked, And Walk not in the way of evil men. Avoid it, pass not by it; Turn from it, and pass on." She became mindful of what she exposed herself to, whether it was certain places, people, or media that might trigger sinful desires. If something weakened her spirit, Mara knew it was best to avoid it altogether.

6. Worship

Worship was a vital practice for Mara, allowing her to shift her focus from the desires of the flesh to the presence of God. Worship helped her feel closer to God and diminished the flesh's influence over her. Praising God reminded her of His greatness, love, and power. Psalm 34:1-3 NIV expresses this well: "I will extol the Lord at all times; his praise will always be on my lips." Worshiping in spirit brought Mara's heart and mind into alignment with God's will, making it easier for her to resist the flesh.

By relying on the Holy Spirit and committing to these practices, Mara faced her internal struggles with a renewed mind and a steadfast spirit. The power within her, fueled by God's grace and the Holy Spirit, enabled her to overcome her fleshly desires and live a life pleasing to God. As she continued to grow in her faith, she experienced the profound truth of 2 Corinthians 12:9 NIV: "But he said to me, 'My grace is sufficient for you, for my power is made perfect in weakness."

How the Enemy Attacks

Through Temptation: The enemy knows our weaknesses and tries to lure us into sin. He makes sin appear attractive, downplays its consequences, and tempts us to satisfy our fleshly desires.

Through Division: Satan loves to divide relationships, especially within families and the church. He sows seeds of discord, misunderstanding, and offense to separate people from one another.

Through Distraction: One of the enemy's most effective tactics is to distract us from our relationship with God. He uses busyness, entertainment, and worldly cares to distract our attention from prayer, worship, and the Word.

Through Discouragement: When things do not go as planned, the enemy whispers thoughts of failure, inadequacy, and hopelessness. He wants us to give up on God's promises and doubt His goodness.

The temptation of Jesus in the wilderness is a powerful example of how Satan tries to attack, deceive, and lead us away from God's will. Yet, it also shows us how Jesus used the Word of God as His weapon to resist and defeat the devil. This account is found in Matthew 4:1-11. Let us look at each temptation and how Jesus responded:

After fasting for forty days and nights, Jesus was hungry, and Satan tried to exploit His physical weakness by tempting Him to satisfy His hunger in a way that was outside of God's will.

Satan's Temptation: "If thou art the Son of God, command that these stones become bread" Matthew 4:3. Satan knew Jesus had the power to turn stones into bread, but he wanted Jesus to act independently of plan, prioritizing physical needs over spiritual obedience.

Jesus's Response: Jesus cited Deuteronomy 8:3 in his response: "But he answered and said, 'It is written, Man shall not live by bread alone, but by every word that proceeded out of the mouth of God'" Matthew 4:4.

Lesson: Jesus knew that while physical needs are important, they are not more important than spiritual nourishment. He refused to let His fleshly desires dictate His actions and reminded Satan that obedience to God's Word is the highest priority.

Satan then took Jesus to the pinnacle of the temple in Jerusalem and challenged Him to prove His identity as the Son of God by performing a miraculous feat.

Satan's Temptation: "If thou art the Son of God, cast thyself down: for it is written, 'He will give his angels charge concerning thee: and on their hands they will bear thee up, lest haply thou dash thy foot against a stone'" Matthew 4:6. Satan quoted Psalm 91:11-12, trying to manipulate Jesus into testing God's protection by forcing Him into a dangerous situation.

Jesus's Response: Again, Jesus answered with scripture, this time from Deuteronomy 6:16: "Jesus said unto him, 'Again it is written, Thou shalt not make trial of the Lord thy God'" Matthew 4:7.

Lesson: Jesus refused to use His divine authority in a reckless and prideful way to test God. He recognized that forcing God's hand is an act of pride and disobedience. We must trust God's plan and timing without manipulating situations for our own gain or testing promises for selfish reasons.

The final temptation directly attacked mission to save humanity. Satan offered Jesus worldly power and authority in exchange for worship.

Satan's Temptation: "All these things will I give thee, if thou wilt fall down and worship me" Matthew 4:9. Satan showed Jesus all the kingdoms of the world and their splendor and offered them to Him. The enemy tempted Jesus to take a shortcut to glory and avoid the suffering on the cross and fulfilling His mission.

Jesus's Response: Jesus once again turned to scripture, quoting Deuteronomy 6:13: "Then saith Jesus unto him, 'Get thee hence, Satan: for it is written, Thou shalt worship the Lord thy God, and him only shalt thou serve'" Matthew 4:10.

Lessons: Jesus affirmed that true worship belongs only to God. He refused to bow to the allure of worldly power and shortcuts, demonstrating that our allegiance must be to God alone.

Jesus knew that true power and glory come from God alone and that worship belongs to Him. Satan often tempts us with shortcuts to success or power, but those paths lead to destruction. Jesus resisted by prioritizing His relationship with God and staying focused on His mission, knowing that worship and obedience to God are nonnegotiable.

Understanding Our Real Battle

Mara's Journey: Standing Firm in Faith

Mara had always thought that life's challenges were about the people she clashed with, the circumstances she couldn't control, or the past wounds she carried. But her journey was teaching her a deeper truth: the real battle wasn't visible.

Understanding the Real Battle

Step by step, Mara began to realize that life's struggles were more than they seemed. When frustration, anger, or pressure rose—whether from family, friends, or circumstances—she understood that these emotions were not the real battle.

Ephesians 6:12 clarified the truth: "For our wrestling is not against flesh and blood, but against the principalities, against the powers, against the world-rulers of this darkness, against the spiritual hosts of wickedness in the heavenly places."

The true struggle was not with people or situations, but with unseen spiritual forces trying to deceive, distract, and manipulate her. God gently reminded her: "Mara, it's not them you are fighting. Recognize who your enemy is."

This insight shifted Mara's perspective. She realized that anger, bitterness, and frustration were signals pointing her to the real fight—a spiritual battle that could only be fought with God's strength, prayer, and His Word. Whenever she felt her emotions flare, she paused, remembered God's guidance, and chose to respond with faith, discernment, and reliance on Him rather than reacting in the flesh.

She remembered the story of David and Goliath. David didn't see Goliath as just a giant warrior—he saw him as an opponent of God's purposes. By trusting God's power, David overcame what seemed impossible. Mara understood that her battles would be won the same way: by looking beyond visible struggles and relying on God's strength.

Using the Word of God as Your Weapon

Every time Mara faced lies, doubts, or the temptation to give in to fear, she remembered what she had learned from Jesus' example: Scripture is not just words on a page—it is alive, powerful, and carries God's authority.

When the enemy whispered deception, Jesus responded with truth: "It is written."

That truth became Mara's shield. She realized that God's Word was more than information—it was a weapon that could cut through confusion, fear, and temptation. Like a double-edged sword, it divided truth from falsehood, flesh from Spirit, and darkness from light Hebrews 4:12.

Mara began to meditate on Scripture daily, letting it shape her thoughts, guide her steps, and speak through her. The more she knew God's Word, the more equipped she felt to face life's challenges. She reminded herself: "Your word is a lamp to my feet and a light to my path" Psalm 119:105.

Prioritize Obedience to God Over Fleshly Desires

Mara learned the importance of putting obedience to God above her own desires. Whether it was comfort, pride, or the allure of quick solutions, she saw that yielding to immediate satisfaction weakened her against the enemy. True strength came from relying on God's truth and following His will, even when it was difficult.

She also learned a key lesson about Scripture: it is not a tool to get what she wants, but a guide to help her stand firm in faith. Mara saw that twisting verses to fit personal desires could lead someone away from God's plan. By studying Scripture carefully and applying it with humility, she protected herself from deception and learned to rely on God's plan rather than her own understanding.

Staying Focused on God's Purpose

Life offered distractions—shortcuts, instant gratification, and worldly success—but Mara discovered that these only led away from God's plan. Staying focused required constant reflection, prayer, and the courage to say "no" to what felt tempting but would ultimately pull her off course.

By following Jesus' example—using Scripture, staying obedient, and resisting the lure of pride, power, and self-gratification—Mara discovered that she could stand firm, even when life presented giants that seemed impossible to overcome.

Learning to Recognize the Real Enemy

Mara began to realize something important: the moments when she got angry or frustrated—at family, friends, or people around her—were not the real battles. The true struggle was with unseen forces trying to deceive and distract her.

God's gentle reminder stayed with her: "Mara, it's not them you are fighting. Recognize who your enemy is."

Whenever she felt anger rising, Mara paused to remember that the real opponent was not the person in front of her, but the spiritual forces behind the scenes. She learned to respond with faith, discernment, and reliance on God, rather than reacting in the flesh.

By seeing beyond her emotions and circumstances, Mara began to fight the battles God had called her to fight—and found peace and victory that went deeper than she had ever experienced.

Love Endures All Things

Love may sound beautiful, but true love must endure. God would not describe love as enduring if it were a smooth ride. Enduring love suffers long; it bears pain patiently.

The Bible tells us that love endures all things. This is not some sappy saying that might be found on a Hallmark card—this is God's holy Word. It speaks of a love far deeper than fleeting emotion or surface affection. This is love forged in the fire of faith, the kind that holds steady when the heart trembles.

Mara remembered the nights when darkness became a companion and tears were her only conversation. She cried through the weight of her trials, pouring her pain into the hands of a God she sometimes could not see. She struggled to understand why He said, "Be not weary in well-doing, for in due season ye shall reap if ye faint not" (Galatians 6:9), when her body was tired, her spirit weak, and her heart felt forgotten. Fainting, she realized, was not about falling; it was about surrendering hope.

Even when her heart felt heavy and her prayers echoed into silence, she trusted that His Word could not fail. In the quiet, when the night whispered doubt into her ears, she clung to His promises.

As she read 1 Corinthians 13, her eyes paused on a single, luminous line: "Love endureth all things" 1 Corinthians 13. The words trembled on the page, and Mara longed to believe that love could survive betrayal, silence, and the deep fissures left in her heart by trauma.

She remembered the promise in 1 Corinthians 10:13: "No temptation has overtaken you except what is common to mankind. And God is faithful; he will provide a way of escape, that ye may be able to bear it." She whispered into the darkness, asking how much longer she could endure. Her tears became prayers, and her prayers became a river of strength that flowed quietly through her weary soul.

One still night, Mara understood the truth in a new way. The escape was not to run from her trials. It was to endure, to let God's love carry her when her own strength faltered. Even when love seemed distant, even when she questioned her worth, she remembered Psalm 34:18: "The Lord is nigh unto them that are of a broken heart; and saveth such as be of a contrite spirit."

Love will help you endure the shortcomings of others as you remember that you, too, are a work in progress. As you walk toward perfection, you can extend grace to others, help them rise again, and refuse to be the hand that holds them back. Love teaches endurance not only in pain, but also in patience—with yourself and with those who falter beside you.

Endurance became an act of courage. It was holding on to faith when the heart longed to let go, trusting that tears would one day blossom into testimony. She clung to Jeremiah 29:11: "For I know the thoughts that I think toward you, saith the Lord, thoughts of peace, and not of evil, to give you an expected end."

For Mara, enduring all things was not the absence of pain. It was the decision to trust God amidst it. Even when sorrow whispered lies, she remembered Psalm 50:15: "Call upon me in the day of trouble: I will deliver thee, and thou shalt glorify me." Her endurance became a song of hope, echoing in the chambers of her heart.

Love God, Love Others

As Mara endured, she began to see a new truth take root in her soul. Faith is measured not only by words, but by the love that flows from one heart to another. She realized that to say, "I love God," while harboring bitterness, was like trying to pour water from a sealed jar. Jesus' words rang in her ears, vivid as sunlight breaking through clouds: "Thou shalt love the Lord thy God with all thy heart, and with all thy soul, and with all thy mind. This is the first and great commandment. And the second is like unto it, Thou shalt love thy neighbor as thyself" Matthew 22:37-40. Love was not optional. Love was the measure of faith.

Mara reflected on 1 John 4:20-21: "If a man say, I love God, and hateth his brother, he is a liar: for he that loveth not his brother whom he hath seen, how can he love God whom he hath not seen? And this commandment have we from him, That he who loveth God love his brother also." Her heart trembled at the truth. Love was not simply a feeling. It was a choice. It was active. It was sacrificial.

Love forgave betrayal. It comforted the broken. It lifted those who stumbled. Mara began to understand that love mirrored the heart of God—pure, patient, and enduring. Even when suffering pressed upon her, love did not collapse; it persevered.

She thought of those who had failed to love her back — people she had given her heart to, only to be met with distance, misunderstanding, or silence. Yet even when love was not returned, she felt the quiet urging of the Spirit reminding her that love is not measured by what we receive, but by what we give. She began to see that love was choosing forgiveness when resentment felt easier, and compassion when her heart longed to retreat.

God's Word is clear. When asked what the greatest commandment is, Jesus replied:
"Thou shalt love the Lord thy God with all thy heart, and with all thy soul, and with all thy mind. This is the first and great commandment. And the second is like unto it, Thou shalt love thy neighbor as thyself. On these two commandments hang all the law and the prophets" Matthew 22:37-40.

Mara began to see that love is not optional. It is the measure of true faith. She could follow Christ in name and in ritual, yet if her heart was hardened toward others, her love for God was incomplete.

In her quiet moments of prayer, Mara reflected on:
"If a man say, I love God, and hateth his brother, he is a liar: for he that loveth not his brother whom he hath seen, how can he love God whom he hath not seen? And this commandment have we from him, That he who loveth God love his brother also" 1 John 4:20-21.

Tears filled Mara's eyes as she realized that love is not only what she feels, but what she chooses to do. It is active, tangible, and sacrificial. It is love that forgives betrayal, comforts the hurting, and lifts those who stumble. God's heart is love — pure, patient, and enduring. Love reflects His presence in the world.

Mara remembered the nights she cried out to God, pouring her pain and weariness before Him. She understood that love is what allowed her to endure. Love does not excuse wrong, but it empowers healing. Love does not collapse under suffering, but it perseveres.

"Love is patient, love is kind. It envieth not; love vaunteth not itself, is not puffed up, doth not behave itself unseemly, seeketh not her own, is not easily provoked, thinketh no evil; rejoiceth not in iniquity, but rejoiceth in the truth; beareth all things, believeth all things, hopeth all things, endureth all things. Love never faileth" 1 Corinthians 13:4-8.

Mara realized that love is the lens through which everything else is seen. Prophecies will fail, knowledge will vanish, and human accomplishments will fade; wealth, success, and even relationships are temporary. Only love endures forever. It is the echo of God's own heart.

Her journey was not just about surviving pain or trauma — it was about learning to see others through God's eyes, to act with mercy and grace, and to allow His love to flow through her. Living in God's love meant:

Clinging to His Word even in silence and suffering Psalm 34:17-18.

Extending grace to those who hurt her, just as she had received grace Ephesians 4:32.

Loving those who seemed unlovable, because God's love is not limited by human judgment Romans 5:8.

Mara began to live love deliberately. It was not a feeling that came and went — it was a commitment, a reflection of the heart of God. And in that, she found a profound peace: that no matter how much the world failed her, love would remain. It would endure. It would conquer.

As she looked back on her journey, Mara finally understood that the love which endured in her suffering was the same love that reached out to others in grace. To love God and to love others were not two separate callings — they were one heartbeat, one holy act of faith. Enduring love became active love, and in living that love, Mara found the very presence of God.

"And now abideth faith, hope, love, these three; but the greatest of these is love" 1 Corinthians 13:13.

The Turning Point: The Power of God's Word in Mara's Healing

Mara's journey of healing took a profound turn when she discovered the transformative power of meditating on God's Word. This was not a mere intellectual activity or rote repetition—it was a deeply spiritual and life-altering practice. Meditating on the Word meant more than just reading or memorizing Scripture; it involved allowing the words to penetrate her mind, heart, and spirit. By speaking the words aloud, reflecting on their meaning, and believing in their power, she began to experience their life-changing effects.

The Bible says in John 1:1, "In the beginning was the Word, and the Word was with God, and the Word was God." This truth resonated deeply with Mara. As she read and meditated on the scriptures, she recognized that she was not just reading a book—she was encountering God Himself. The Word of God was not distant or abstract; it was alive and personal, and speaking directly into her situation. Hebrews 4:12 confirmed this for her: "For the word of God is living, and active, and sharper than any two-edged sword, and piercing even to the dividing of soul and spirit, of both joints and marrow, and quick to discern the thoughts and intents of the heart." She clung to the fact that the Word was alive, powerful, and capable of cutting through every lie and stronghold in her mind, bringing healing, truth, and clarity.

Whenever a thought of fear, doubt, or despair crept into her mind, Mara would counter it with the Word of God. She was not at the mercy of her emotions or fears—God's Word gave her the authority to take control of her thoughts and make them obedient to Christ.

The power of meditating on the Word became evident when Mara faced overwhelming fear. She would declare aloud, "For God gave us not a spirit of fearfulness; but of power and love and discipline" (2 Timothy 1:7). Repeating this verse until fear subsided, Mara learned to rely on the strength of God's truth, knowing that His perfect love would cast out all fear 1 John 4:18.

When Mara felt weak or overcome by sadness and depression, the words of 2 Corinthians 12:10 would rise in her heart: "Wherefore I take pleasure in weaknesses, for when I am weak, then am I strong." She would cry out to God in her moments of weakness, asking Him to fill her with His strength, knowing His power was made perfect in her weakness. These verses were no longer just words on a page. They were life-giving truths that she experienced as God's strength sustained her through every difficult day.

Mara also clung to Philippians 1:6, knowing that "He who began a good work in you will perfect it until the day of Jesus Christ." This promise gave her hope that no matter how broken she felt, God was still working in her life, bringing her to wholeness and completion. She often prayed, "Lord, You started this good work in me, and I trust You to finish it. I know You are faithful." This gave her the assurance that her healing journey was not in vain. God was at work, and He would bring her through.

When she felt alone or abandoned, Mara would recall God's promise in Hebrews 13:5, "For he hath said, I will in no wise fail thee, neither will I in any wise forsake thee." She would pray, "God, You said You would never leave or forsake me, and I trust that You are with or forsake me, and I trust that You are with me even now." This truth comforted her during her darkest moments, reminding her she was not alone that no matter what she faced. She was not alone—God was by her side.

As she continued to meditate on God's Word, her mind was renewed, and her spirit grew more resilient. She could face her anxieties with a different perspective. Instead of being overwhelmed, she would pray Psalm 28:7.

The Lord is my strength and my shield; my heart trusted in him, and I am helped: therefore my heart greatly rejoiceth; and with my song will I praise him. Psalm 28:7.

Peace I leave with you, my peace I give unto you: not as the world giveth, give I unto you. Let not your heart be troubled, neither let it be afraid. John 14:27.

Day by day, as Mara meditated on these truths, the strongholds of fear, anxiety, and depression began to break. She saw the transformative power of scripture working in her life, reminding her of God's ever-present help. The Bible had become more than just a source of comfort. It was a weapon of spiritual warfare, as described in Ephesians 6:17, where the Word of God is called "the sword of the Spirit."

Mara was learning to speak life over herself, using God's Word as a shield and a sword to cut through the lies and bring forth healing and victory. Our words have the power to build up or tear down, and the Bible makes it clear that speaking life is an essential part of living a victorious Christian life. Proverbs 18:21 says: "Death and life are in the power of the tongue: and they that love it shall eat the fruit thereof."

It was not just about what she believed in her heart but also about what she declared with her mouth. "The Lord is nigh unto them that are of a broken heart, and saveth such as are of a contrite spirit" Psalm 34:18 . Mara knew that her brokenness did not disqualify her from God's love—it drew Him near.

In this season of her life, Mara experienced the truth of Psalm 23:1-3 this season of her life: "The Lord is my shepherd; I shall not want. He maketh me to lie down in green pastures: he leadeth me beside the still waters. He restoreth my soul."

As she meditated on His Word and trusted in Him, God restored her soul, leading her into a place of peace and strength she had never known before.

The power of reading, meditating on, and declaring God's Word was transforming her from the inside out. The more she allowed the Word to penetrate her heart, the more she walked in all her trials, Mara discovered the life-changing truth that meditating on God's Word daily was the key to her healing. It was not a passive act; it was how the very way she fought her battles, realigned her mind with God's truth, and embraced the newness of life that Christ offered. Through this practice, she found strength, peace, and joy that could only come from God.

Letting Go of Little Mara

Deliverance Meeting

Mara entered the small, quiet room where only two compassionate women awaited her. The leader spoke gently, "Before we begin, we need to prepare our hearts through prayer and repentance. Invite the Holy Spirit to search you, to reveal any areas of pain or bondage, and to bring healing."

Mara bowed her head, feeling the weight of past mistakes and sins. Though she was alone, she did not feel lonely. She understood that prayer and repentance were the first steps toward freedom—an opening of the heart to God's restoration.

Mara sat nervously at the table, her heart racing as she glanced at the clock. Today marked a significant step in her journey toward healing—her first deliverance meeting. After years of carrying the weight of her past, the decision to seek spiritual deliverance felt both daunting and liberating. The heaviness of childhood trauma, the hurtful words of peers and family, and the chaos of her adult relationships had suffocated her spirit.

The primary purpose of the deliverance meeting was to break the chains that had bound her for so long. Mara understood that deliverance was about freedom from demonic oppression and healing from the wounds of her past. It was a chance to confront the fears and insecurities that had taken root in her heart, often manifesting as anxiety and depression. The meeting aimed to bring her closer to Christ, allowing her to reclaim her identity and find peace through His love.

As Mara entered the room, the compassionate woman leading the meeting began by explaining the purpose of the gathering: to acknowledge the areas in their lives where they felt oppressed or trapped and to invite the Holy Spirit to bring healing and restoration.

Mara experienced a powerful sense of vulnerability throughout the meeting as she shared her story. She spoke of the deep-seated beliefs she had internalized over the years—the lies that she was unworthy of love, the belief that her past defined her future, and the thought that she could never truly be free. Each word felt like a release, lifting a weight she had not realized she had been carrying.

The leader guided Mara through prayer and Scripture, and as she followed, a weight began to lift. With each prayer, she felt the tightness in her chest ease, as if invisible chains were being broken. The prayer was not just words—it was a powerful invitation for Mara to release her fears and burdens into God's hands.

During a pivotal moment in the meeting, Mara was invited to pray for personal deliverance. The leader encouraged her to name the specific areas in her life where she sought freedom. With tears streaming down her face, she cried out to God for healing from the trauma of her childhood, the pain of betrayal from loved ones, and the shame that had held her captive. She experienced a profound connection to God in that sacred space, realizing that her past was not her destiny, but His love and grace were.

The deliverance minister gently prompted her to reflect on a painful chapter in her life: the decision to terminate her pregnancy years ago. This choice had haunted her for far too long and filled her with guilt and shame. She had always avoided discussing it, burying the emotions deep within her heart. But today, in this sacred space, she felt the urge to confront the truth of her experience.

"Let go of your unborn child," the minister urged softly. "Name him and release all the guilt and shame associated with the abortion. Give him to the Lord."

Mara closed her eyes tightly, allowing herself to feel the weight of her decision wash over her. "I name you Mark," she whispered, her voice trembling. As she uttered the name, a wave of emotion crashed over her. The sorrow and regret she had buried for years surged to the surface, and she felt the heaviness in her chest begin to lift.

"I release you, Mark," she cried, feeling the guilt and shame dissipate. "I give you to the Lord." In that moment, Mara felt a profound sense of relief, as if the burden of her past was being lifted from her shoulders.

Then, the minister encouraged her to delve deeper. Mara realized she needed to confront the many versions of herself that her past had affected. She sat in the quiet space, closed her eyes, and took a deep breath, allowing herself to feel the weight of her past pressing down on her. In that stillness, she visualized each version of herself—little Mara, teen Mara, and her unhealed self.

As she spoke, tears streamed down her face. "Little Mara, you can let go of the pain and fear. You no longer have to carry those burdens. Go with the Lord."

Her heart ached as she remembered the struggles of her teenage self. "Teen Mara, you do not have to seek approval anymore. You are enough just as you are. Trust in the Lord and find your worth in Him."

Finally, she turned her thoughts to her unhealed self, the woman who had carried guilt and shame for too long. "You are free now," she declared, feeling a warmth envelop her. "Let the Lord take your pain. You are whole in His love."

As Mara surrendered every part of herself to the Lord, she felt a profound release, as if the chains of her past were breaking one by one. The weight of years of pain and struggle lifted. She could feel the Lord's presence enveloping the space, comforting her soul with His peace.

Mara felt a deep calm wash over her as the part of herself that had been hurt the most—the child within—began to heal. She imagined her younger self, the little girl who had been so afraid and broken, smiling for the first time in what seemed like forever. The pain that had weighed her down for years was finally being released.

With her eyes closed, she saw that tiny, frightened child along with other versions of herself who had carried so much pain, walking away and disappearing into the light of God's love. They were finally free, no longer bound by the hurts of the past. In that moment, Mara knew God's healing presence would protect them from further pain.

Tears welled up in her eyes as she spoke softly, "I am here now, and I will take care of us. The Lord has given me the strength and the wisdom to continue." With every word, she felt renewed strength, trusting that God was guiding her into a new chapter of healing and restoration.

"Thank You, Lord," she cried, her voice trembling with gratitude. "Thank You for the healing and the freedom. I trust You with my heart and my journey."

As the final barriers crumbled away, Mara felt lighter, unburdened, and filled with a sense of peace she had never known. She opened her eyes, ready to step into the future, carrying the hope of renewal within her heart.

Now, standing in her place was Esther—the new creation that the Lord had brought forth. Named after the brave and noble queen chosen "for such a time as this," Mara had always felt a connection to Esther. She sensed that God had called her a modern-day Esther to stand in the gap and be a light in the darkness.

"For who knows whether thou art not come to the kingdom for such a time as this?" Esther 4:14. Mara knew she was here for a reason and that God had placed her on this earth to fulfill a purpose. Like Esther, she had been chosen for this time, and she was ready to step into God's calling for her. She was no longer the scared little girl fighting to survive; she was Esther—a warrior, a leader, and a woman after God's heart.

"Being confident of this very thing, that He who began a good work in you will perfect it until the day of Jesus Christ" Philippians 1:6. The Lord had done a mighty work in Mara's life, transforming her from a scared, broken girl into a woman of faith, courage, and grace.

Mara had faced her past, battled her demons, and emerged victorious—not by her own strength, but by the power of God within her. She held tightly to the scripture from Ephesians 3:20, "Now unto Him that is able to do exceeding abundantly above all that we ask or think," trusting that God's power surpasses anything she could imagine, guiding her through her healing and growth.

"Wherefore if any man is in Christ, he is a new creature: the old things are passed away; behold, they are become new" 2 Corinthians 5:17.

But Mara's fight was not over. The struggle driven by fear and anger that once consumed her had now taken on a new form. It was no longer a fight to protect herself from the world; it was a fight for the Lord. She fought not with fists or harsh words but with love, prayer, and the Word of God.

"For our wrestling is not against flesh and blood, but against the principalities, against the powers, against the world rulers of this darkness, against the spiritual hosts of wickedness in the heavenly places" (Ephesians 6:12). Mara understood that her battle was no longer against those who had hurt her but against the forces that sought to keep souls in darkness. Her mission was clear: to win souls for the Lord, bringing others out of the darkness and into the light of Christ.

This was her new fight, her new purpose. She was guided by the scripture from Proverbs 11:30 "The fruit of the righteous is a tree of life; and he that winneth souls is wise," as she sought to lead others to the salvation and hope she had found.

Mara's new purpose was not just about sharing words but about living out the gospel through her actions, pointing others to the same healing and redemption she had received. She dedicated herself to walking in the light of Christ, trusting that her life would reflect His glory and bring others closer to Him.

She knew that the fight ahead would not be easy, but she was no longer afraid. She trusted that the Lord would guide, strengthen, and give her victory.

Mara turned away, leaving the past behind. She was ready to embrace the future, knowing she was not alone. God was with her, guiding her every step of the way.

"Finally, be strong in the Lord, and in the strength of His might. Put on the whole armor of God, that ye may be able to stand against the wiles of the devil"(Ephesians 6:10-11.

Mara had put on the full armor of God, and she was ready. She was prepared to fight—not for herself, but for the Lord, His glory, and the souls He had called her to reach.

From Mara to Esther

In the Bible, Mara initially felt bitter and burdened by her experiences, much like Naomi, whose name means "pleasant." Still, she chose to call herself Mara, meaning "bitter," due to the profound loss and distress she experienced.

Naomi, who faced significant hardship and loss, expressed her bitterness through her name change in Ruth 1:20-21 "And she said unto them, Call me not Naomi, call me Mara for the Almighty hath dealt very bitterly with me. I went out full and the Lord hath brought me home again empty: why then call ye me Naomi, seeing the Lord hath testified against me, and the Almighty hath afflicted me?"

She walked in bitterness, thinking her heart could never heal. But where Naomi's story took a turn toward redemption, so did Mara's. God intervened in her life, transforming her from a place of bitterness into one of grace, strength, and renewal.

Mara's transformation demonstrates what God can do in anyone's life when they surrender their pain to Him. Her heart, once hardened and closed off by suffering, became tender and open through the love of Jesus Christ. Just as God gave Naomi hope, blessing her with restoration in her later years, He did the same for Mara. No longer the broken woman she once was, she embraced her true calling as a modern-day Esther—a woman of bold faith and divine purpose. God chose Mara "for such a time as this" Esther 4:14 to stand in the gap and be a light in the darkness. Her battles no longer defined her, and her identity was not tied to the pain of her past but to the glory of her future in Christ.

As the Bible teaches in Isaiah 43:19, God promises, "Behold, I will do a new thing; now it shall spring forth; shall ye not know it? I will even make a way in the wilderness, and rivers in the desert." Just as God brought life to dry ground, He brought new life to Mara, turning her story around for His glory. Her bitterness was exchanged for joy, her despair for hope, and her brokenness for restoration.

Mara's journey reminds us of the hope we have in Christ. God can rewrite your story no matter how bitter or difficult your circumstances. Like a tree cut down but still sprouts again Job 14:7-9, there is hope for you. Even when life seems bleak, new life can spring forth through the "scent of water"—the presence of God's Spirit. The refining fire that purified Mara's heart is the same fire that can renew yours. What once felt dead can bloom again.

Mara's transformation into a woman of faith and courage stands as a testimony that no story is beyond redemption when God is in charge. Trust Him, for as long as He is the author of your life, your story cannot end in bitterness. There is always hope for new beginnings, and God is faithful to make beauty from the ashes.

A Message of Hope

To every heart that has known the pain of abandonment, rejection, fear, or abuse—
to those who carry the invisible weight of generational trauma—

know this: **your story does not end in brokenness.**
Like Mara, you, too, are being rewritten by the Author of life Himself.

What once felt like a lifetime of suffering
can become the soil where strength, purpose, and peace take root.
Every moment you choose to rise, to forgive, to hope again,
you break another chain from the past.
Your courage to heal becomes a light for others still walking in the dark.

Remember, healing is not forgetting what happened—
it is allowing God to transform your pain into power.
The same God who turned Mara's tears into testimony
is doing the same for you.
You are not what happened to you;
you are what God is doing through you.

So when fear whispers that you're not enough,
or the past tries to pull you back—stand firm.
Declare that your story belongs to the One who redeems all things.
Let love lead. Let grace carry you.
And let faith remind you that nothing is wasted in God's hands.

This book was never just about surviving trauma—
it is about **overcoming it.**
It is about reclaiming your identity, rediscovering your worth, and walking boldly in the freedom that was always meant for you.

The pain of the past may have shaped you,
but it no longer defines you.
You are whole. You are restored. You are redeemed.

So lift your head, child of God.
The worst is behind you.
The best is yet to come.
This is your time to rise—
and this time, you rise **for good**.

Step boldly into your future.
The Lord has begun a good work in you, and He will faithfully complete it.
Your healing, peace, and joy are waiting for you.
Embrace them. Live them.

And never forget: **with God, nothing is impossible.**
This is your time to rise
—from generational trauma, abandonment, rejection, fear, and abuse—
into a life of freedom, love, and divine purpose.

The past may have shaped you,
but it no longer defines you.
You are whole, restored, and redeemed.
Walk forward in grace, knowing that every scar
now shines as proof of God's power to heal
and make all things new.

God bless you!

Connect with NaTonya Scott

For additional information and resources on mental wellness, personal growth, and support, connect with NaTonya Scott through the following platforms:

Instagram freedominhistruth

LinkTree: linktr.ee/FreedomInHisTrruth

Coaching Website: https://freedominhistruth.org/

Mental Health Therapy: https://www.lcacounseling.org/

Books on Amazon: *Mental Health:*

Renewed Strength for Those Battling Depression

Living Anxiety Free While Renewing Your Mind

Course: **Healthy Boundaries and Communication Course:** https://natonya-s-site.thinkific.com/courses/your-first-course

YouTube Channel: @freedominhistruth

Homeless Ministry: https://www.servants247.com/

These resources provide tools, courses, and community support for those looking to heal, grow, and foster mental wellness and emotional strength.

Available Support Resources

Available support resources.
Please visit the websites of the following services and programs—many good resources are available.
o National Alliance on Mental Health (https://www.nami.org/Support-Education/Support-Groups)
o MentalHealth.gov (https://www.mentalhealth.gov/)
Mental Health America (https://mhanational.org/)

Books: https://www.choosingtherapy.com/books-on-depression/

Sondermind -Online or In person Therapy
https://www.sondermind.com/ (**Takes Insurance, Self pay and EAP**)

Rula- Online therapy (Take Insurance and Self pay)
https://www.rula.com/

Better Help- (Takes Self pay and Eap
https://www.betterhelp.com/

A Small Collection of Devotionals Touching on Mental Health
issues can be found at this link:
https://enlightenmentalhealth.org/devotions/

Suicide prevention: **If you are struggling with suicidal**
thoughts or are experiencing a mental health crisis, dial or text the 24/7 National Suicide Prevention hotline at 988, or go
to SuicidePreventionLifeline.org.

References

Bowen, Murray. *Family Therapy in Clinical Practice*. Jason Aronson, 1978.

Brown, Brené Levine, Peter A. *Waking the Tiger: Healing Trauma*. North Atlantic Books, 1997..

Dunn, Judy. "Sibling Relationships in Early Childhood: A Developmental Perspective." *Child Development*, vol. 56, no. 4, 1985, pp. 787–811.

Levine, Peter A. *Waking the Tiger: Healing Trauma*. North Atlantic Books, 1997.

Siegel, D. J., & Bryson, T. P. (2012). *The Whole-Brain Child:* Siegel, D. J., & Bryson, T. P. (2012). *The Whole-Brain Child: 12 Revolutionary Strategies to Nurture Your Child's Developing Mind*. Delacorte Press.

Sulloway, Frank J. *Born to Rebel: Birth Order, Family Dynamics, and Creative Lives*. Vintage, 1997.

www.ingramcontent.com/pod-product-compliance
Lightning Source LLC
LaVergne TN
LVHW051822080426
835512LV00018B/2686